Your Best Poker Friend

Increase Your Mental Edge

ALAN N. SCHOONMAKER, PH.D.

Kensington Publishing Corp.
www.Kensingtonbooks.com

Contents

Acknowledgments

Many people helped me to write this book. Matt Lessinger, Barry Tanenbaum, Jim Brier, and Dave Hench ("Cinch") are very talented writers with whom I have swapped editing for years. They edited these essays before they were published in other places and then again to put them into a coherent book. Matt, author of *The Book of Bluffs,* was exceptionally helpful, making hundreds of suggestions.

Talking to Mason Malmuth and reading his own and his authors' books have greatly improved my thinking. Mason made many suggestions about this book. David Sklansky did not comment directly on the book, but our conversations about many issues have been very helpful. I'd also like to thank all the other poker authors whose work has influenced me. As you will see from the footnotes, I have relied heavily on their published works.

Prof. Arthur Reber and Dr. Daniel Kessler are psychologists and poker players who have given me second opinions on many psychological issues.

Jerry Flannigan is a good friend and fine player who suggested I write about planning and helped me with those essays and many others.

The people who participate in the discussions on the Psychology Forum at twoplustwo.com have provided many subjects for my magazine columns, and some of those columns have been revised and included here. Without their comments I would have run out of ideas a long time ago. Dan Kessler and Dr. Eric Niler are very active on that forum, and they have helped me with several essays.

Jan Siroky and Preston Oade are excellent players who see the game differently from me. Discussions with them have helped me to recognize some holes in my thinking. Jan, a no-limit tournament coach who has helped me with many issues, was my primary source for developing feel and target marketing.

The Wednesday Poker Discussion Group talks about everything related to poker, and our meetings have been extremely valuable. A spin-off of that group discusses only no-limit poker, and these discussions have helped me to make the transition to that game.

The people who play at RoyalVegasPoker.com's "Play the Experts" tournaments provided several useful ideas. I'm grateful to the players, especially Cheryl Connors; to my colleagues, Lou Krieger, Matt Lessinger, Barbara Enright, Max Shapiro, Mike Cappelletti, Rose Richie, and Bob Ciaffone; and to Lou Kelmanson and Mike Emmanual for inviting me to play there.

Donna Lane, my personal assistant, has been helpful in more ways than I can count.

Finally, Sheree Bykofsky, an outstanding agent, introduced me to Richard Ember and helped me to organize and market the book. Richard, in turn, helped me to present my ideas.

Your Best Poker Friend

Introduction

Many poker players are very visibly unhappy. Just look around your poker room. A few people are laughing, joking, and having fun, but far too many are whining, sulking, getting angry, or even going on tilt.

Listen to the way they talk. Are most people saying what a good time they are having or how much money they are winning? No! Most of them are either grimly silent or talking about their bad beats, terrible luck, and undeserved losses.

If I were still consulting as an industrial psychologist and these people were workers, I'd tell management, "You've got a morale problem." In fact, I've seen very few companies with so many grumpy "workers." But they aren't working; they are supposedly playing, and games should be fun. Something is very wrong when a game makes people unhappy.[1]

I believe that *Your Worst Poker Enemy* (*YWPE*), Volume I in this series, was the first extensive analysis of how poker players beat themselves up. In a moment I'll summarize it. Now I'll just say that these two books are an integrated series. *YWPE* mostly analyzed the problems; Volume II, *Your Best Poker Friend* (*YBPF*), mostly proposes solutions.

It is useful, but not essential, to read Volumes I and II in order. If you clearly understand the problem, you have a better chance of solving it. However, in psychology, cause-effect relationships are often cir-

---

1. Surprisingly, there is no clear relationship between satisfaction and results. Some losers are having fun, and some of the unhappiest people are winners, including some full-time pros. A few top players are notorious whiners.

cular: problem A can create or aggravate Problem B, and solving either problem may relieve or aggravate the other one. Therefore:

- Volume I does not just analyze problems; it also recommends solutions.
- Volume II does not just recommend solutions; it also analyzes problems.

Both volumes urge you to be brutally realistic about poker, other
people, and especially yourself. Stop complaining about poker's intrinsically frustrating nature because you can't do anything about it.
You will always have bad beats, losing streaks, annoying opponents,
and so on. Instead, try to understand and learn how to cope with these
frustrations. *Becoming realistic is the first and biggest step from being
your worst poker enemy to becoming your best poker friend.*

Your Worst Poker Enemy (YWPE)[2]

Let's take a quick look at Volume I. Its title came from Stu Ungar,
the greatest poker player of all time. He once said, "At the table, your
worst enemy is yourself."[3] Stu was not referring to his drug addiction,
compulsive sports betting, and other terrible habits. He was talking
only about being your own worst enemy *at the table*. If he was his
own worst enemy, so are we.

We don't have his immense talent, nor do we have his dreadful
habits, but we certainly harm ourselves in many ways. And we can't
get much help from the experts. Virtually all of them tell us how to
beat other people, not how to stop beating ourselves.

Many players are unhappy about their results. Losing players want

2. Much of this material was taken from the introduction to that book. Because I
   am combining quotations, paraphrases, and new text, I omit quotation marks.

3. Quoted by Nolan Dalla and Peter Alson, *One of a Kind: The Rise and Fall of
   Stuey "The Kid" Ungar, the World's Greatest Poker Player* (New York: Atria
   Books), 282.

to become winners. Small winners want to become bigger ones and to move up to larger games to make more money. Big winners want to win even more. It's a natural desire, part of our inherently competitive nature.

Even if they are disappointed by their results, many people do not seriously try to improve them. To do so, they would have to look hard at themselves and change some of their ideas and habits. They prefer to remain in their cocoons of denial, foolishly hoping that they can continue to think and play the same old way but get better results. It will never happen.

Instead of working on their skills and attitudes, many players protect their egos by blaming their results and dissatisfaction on bad luck and other players' mistakes. They think or even say, "I'd be fine if only..."

If you're like that, you may resent my "attitude." I'm a hard-nosed psychologist, and I won't even try to make you feel better. Instead, I will analyze the causes for your problems and emphasize your weaknesses. If your *long-term* results are unsatisfactory:

- You don't know how to play as well as your competition.
- You don't apply your knowledge as well as your competition does.
- You have unrealistic expectations.
- All of the above.

There are no other reasonable possibilities. Don't blame bad luck, because it affects only the short term. If you do blame bad luck, you're just kidding yourself to protect your ego.

I'm a Psychologist, Not a Strategist

For years I was active on the Psychology Forum at twoplustwo.com. My profile there states: "I'm not a poker expert. I'm a psychologist who plays for moderate stakes and writes about poker psychology. I rarely give advice about playing specific cards because many people can do it better." That profile fits both *YWPE* and this book. Both books will help you to become:

- More aware of how psychological factors affect the way you and other people play
- More able to use these factors against other people
- Less vulnerable to the destructive effects of these factors

Most poker writers ignore or minimize these factors. In fact, until Two Plus Two simultaneously published Dr. John Feeney's *Inside the Poker Mind* and my *The Psychology of Poker*, there were no serious books about poker psychology.[4] Nearly all poker books described how people *should* play without analyzing:

- Why most people don't play as well as they know how to play
- Why some people don't even try to learn how to play well

I think that analyzing these psychological forces is essential. People are not computers, and just giving them information will not necessarily change their behavior. Some people will ignore, misunderstand, or misuse even the best-quality information.

If you visit Internet forums, you will see the dramatic effects of psychological factors. Many posters have read excellent books and *Card Player* magazine, but they cannot apply the publications' principles. Their own words clearly show that:

- They rely on instincts or skills they don't have.
- They deny reality about how well they or other people play.
- They blame bad luck for losses caused by their own errors.

4. Mike Caro had published an outstanding book on tells, but it focused on reading other people, not understanding yourself.

- They overreact to anger, pride, guilt, and other emotions.
- They complain bitterly about other people's mistakes that *add* to their expected value.
- They believe in ESP, luck, and many other silly subjects.

Who Should Read These Books?

If you're satisfied with your results and enjoy playing poker, you don't need either volume. One of my favorite sayings is, "If it ain't broke, don't fix it." Since nothing seems broken, why spend time and money trying to fix it?

If you're dissatisfied because you don't know how to play, these books could help you, but you would gain more by studying poker strategy. Read my books *only* if you already understand strategic principles as well as or better than your competition. You need that knowledge more than you need my books. Without it you simply can't play well. Both volumes focus on the psychological factors that prevent you from learning as much as you should learn and getting the full benefits of your knowledge.

Why don't people study strategy? First, some of them are lazy or don't really care that much about their results. They play for fun, not profit. That attitude is reasonable as long as they accept that it costs them money. It's silly if they then complain about their results. However, even people who take the game seriously probably don't study enough for two major reasons:

1. They greatly overestimate their innate abilities. They say, in effect, "Other people need to study, but I'm so talented that I can win without it." That position is correct for a handful of very gifted people, but it's self-defeating nonsense for everyone else.

2. They don't understand how subtle and complicated poker really is. They may want to know the two or three rules

for playing each kind of hand, and there aren't any simple rules.

If you don't understand strategic principles, turn to the Recommended Readings, buy some books, and get to work. Focus more on strategy than on psychology. I made the same point in *The Psychology of Poker*:

> If Freud had played poker and ignored the odds and strategic principles, he would have gone broke. He was the greatest psychologist, but the odds and strategy come way ahead of psychology. To play winning poker, you *must* master and apply the odds and basic strategic concepts.[5]

Understanding theory is necessary, but not sufficient. Lots of people could ace an exam on theory but don't play that well. In fact, more than a few poker authors are broke. In addition, *you* probably don't play as well as you know how to play. You doubt me? Then just answer a few questions. Do you sometimes

- Play hands before the flop or on third street that you *know* you should fold?
- Go too far with hands when you *know* that the pot and implied odds don't justify calling, but you're hoping to get lucky?
- Keep playing when you *know* you're off your game because you're losing and want to get even?
- Let anger, fear, or other emotions affect the way you play your cards, even when you *know* better?
- Take many other actions that you *know* are foolish and expensive?

5. Alan Schoonmaker, *The Psychology of Poker* (Henderson, NV: Two Plus Two, 2000), 5.

If you answered yes to any question, you obviously don't play as well as you know how to play. If you repeatedly answered yes, you are severely harming yourself, and you should stop doing it. That's my goal: to help you to stop making these and other psychologically based mistakes.

The Themes of Both Books

The essays in both books express a few consistent themes that affect almost everything in them.

Theme No. 1: A logical approach works better than an intuitive one (except for a few very gifted people).
This belief is based on my graduate work and faculty experience. The scientific departments of all great universities demand logical, data-based research. If you rely on intuition and anecdotes, you will fail.

They will not accept intuitive positions, because all well-trained psychologists know that people greatly overrate both the value of intuition and the amount of it that they possess. You may make the same mistake. You remember the times you *knew* somebody's cards and how he would play them but forget the times that you were equally certain but absolutely wrong.

Both books frequently quote authorities who emphasize a logical approach and rarely quote (except to disagree with them) the ones who urge people to rely on intuition. Far too many poker books have been written by people who essentially say, "Here is what works for me. Just do what I do." However, many readers can't use their approach because it relies heavily on the authors' personal gifts and experiences, especially their intuition. Learning how to apply logic is immeasurably easier than developing intuition.

A logical emphasis irritates many intuitive players and writers. They naturally dislike it because they have a silly belief: Real players don't use logic; they rely primarily on their intuition. They rarely state this belief directly because doing so would reveal its absurdity. Instead, they make statements like these:

- "Stick to your *first* impression. Have the courage of your convictions."[6]
- "Every poker situation is unique."
- "I never read poker books."
- "You have to develop your own, unique style."

When winning players make these comments, I respect their position. They have proved that they have enough intuition and other gifts to win without relying on logic. But, when losers or break-even players make the same comments, I have extreme doubts about their motives and intelligence. They seem to care more about preserving their illusions than improving their results. They want to rely on their intuition and other gifts even though their results are disappointing.

Theme No. 2: Psychological factors damage your play and distort your perceptions about yourself, other people, and the game itself.

If you understand these factors, you can reduce, but not eliminate, their destructive effects. Because of these factors, you probably

- Know less about the game than you think you know.
- Are less talented than you think you are.
- Let pride, anger, and other emotions adversely affect you.
- Don't seriously try to maximize your profits, despite anything you may say.
- Don't fully accept responsibility for your decisions and their consequences.

6. Doyle Brunson (with many collaborators), *Super System: A Course in Power Poker*, 2nd ed. (Las Vegas: B&G, 1994), 431.

- Expect greater profits than your talents, knowledge, and personality can produce.
- Don't analyze yourself thoroughly and objectively.

After reading this list, some friends told me that I am too hard on my readers. Perhaps I am, but my job is to help you, not make you feel good. Poker is a brutal game. Your opponents will exploit every weakness, so you had better understand and correct them. Otherwise, you cannot reach your potential.

Theme No. 3: You need feedback.

Because you (and I, and nearly everyone else) lack objectivity about yourself, and the huge short-term luck factor makes poker's feedback extremely unreliable, you should get feedback from other people about your knowledge, skill, and self-control. *YBPF* recommends many ways to get and use this feedback.

Theme No. 4: Don't take poker too seriously.

This theme was discussed separately because it was not as directly related to the bottom line: poker is just a game, and games should be played for pleasure. Of course, you should do whatever will improve your play, but don't let poker take over your life.

That recommendation is valid even if you play for a living; don't let poker (or any other job) become an obsession. You would risk much more than your money. You could destroy your work, studies, health, and important relationships. In addition, if you let poker take over your life, you are *much* more likely to go on tilt. If you don't shrug off the inevitable bad beats and losing streaks, your self-concept may be threatened, making you act irrationally.

All of these themes have a common element: the focus is on you, not the other players. Most of the poker literature focuses on how to read situations and other people. That emphasis is certainly reasonable; you must understand your opponents to play winning poker.

But the most important person to understand is yourself. You must ruthlessly analyze yourself, and most players just don't want to do it. So they never reach their potential as players or people. As the previous book discusses, *you* are your worst poker enemy.

How *YWPE* Was Organized[7]

YWPE was based on a simple premise: because poker is a game of incomplete information, *information management is the critical skill.* If you manage information well, you will win. If you manage it badly, you will lose.

Psychological factors cause many information management errors, and you must continually guard against their destructive effects. Egotism is especially damaging. In addition to making you overestimate your abilities, it can cause a huge mistake on an extremely important information management decision: *Will you emphasize intuition or logic?*

"Part One: Intuition Versus Logic" thoroughly discussed the advantages of both and recommended that unless you have clear evidence that you possess the gift of intuition you should rely primarily on logic. It also described ways to prepare, play, and review your game logically. Part One contained the following chapters.

- Introduction
- Which Is Better, Logic or Intuition?
- Should *You* Emphasize Logic or Intuition?
- Labels and Decision Rules
- How Should You Prepare Logically?
- How Should You Play Logically?
- How Should You Review Logically?
- Afterthought

---

7. You may want to skim through this material, especially if you have read *YWPE*.

Because I believe that a logical approach is better for most people, and because I have very little intuition, I did *not* recommend ways to prepare, play, or review intuitively.

When I wrote *YWPE*, I played only limit poker. Now I play mostly no-limit hold'em (NL). Limit poker is mostly a logical, math-based game, but NL *demands* intuition or feel. I have therefore tried hard to develop some feel. I haven't made as much progress as I would like, but I am certainly moving in the right direction. That is, even a rigidly logical, unimaginative guy like me can develop some feel. If you work hard, so can you.

"Reading and Adjusting to Players" on pages 181 of *Your Best Poker Friend* describes a logical way to develop feel. This concept may sound oxymoronic, but it is quite reasonable. Instead of relying on intuitive gifts that you may not have, this section suggests a series of logical steps to develop this ability.

"Part Two: Evaluating Ourselves and the Opposition" in *YWPE* came so early because it has such extreme effects on your results. Many players overestimate not just their intuition, but also their skills, knowledge, and other qualities. The same ego-driven desire to think well of themselves causes them to underestimate the competition.

These mistakes are extremely expensive. If you don't accurately compare yourself to the competition, you will play in the wrong games against the wrong people. Also, because you think you can out-play your opposition, you will play hands you should fold. Part Two contained the following chapters:

- Introduction
- Denial About Ourselves and Our Opponents
- Are You Really "Running Bad?"
- Male and Female Advantages
- We Are All Magoos
- Is It Time to Quit?
- Afterthought

"Part Three: Understanding Unconscious and Emotional Factors" distinguished between how people *should* play and how they *do* play. If you look at what actually happens at poker tables, you will see that "irrational" forces *must* be operating. How else can you explain all the stupid mistakes? Part Three contained the following chapters:

- Introduction
- Psychoanalysis and Poker
- Why Do People Play So Badly?
- Destructive Emotions
- Anger
- Arrogance
- Luck, ESP, and Superstitions
- We Need a Miranda Warning
- Paranoia at the Poker Table
- Machismo
- Preventing and Handling Tilt
- Afterthought

"Part Four: Adjusting to Changes" was essential because our game is continually changing. For example, draw and five-card stud were once the primary games, but hardly anyone plays them today. Even seven-card stud, which was very popular just a few years ago, is being supplanted by hold'em, especially no limit.

Poker has always undergone Darwinian evolution, "the survival of the fittest." If you don't understand and adapt to the way poker is changing, you will slowly get left behind, and you may not survive as a winning player. Part Four contained the following chapters:

- Introduction
- Darwin: The Struggle to Survive
- Darwin: The Poker Explosion
- Darwin: The Technological Revolution

- Darwin: Quantifying "It Depends"
- Darwin: Then and Now
- Darwin: Machismo and Complacency
- Darwin: The Computer as Poker Psychologist
- Darwin: Can Computers Beat Poker Champions?
- Darwin: Afterthought

"Part Five: Handling Stress" stated that you must learn how to handle stress because poker is intrinsically stressful and frustrating. Our interests directly conflict because we want to take each other's money. Someone always loses, and we often lose enough to hurt both our wallets and our egos. Everyone has bad beats, bad nights, and bad weeks. If you can't handle them, these stresses can severely damage your enjoyment, attitudes, and results. Part Five contained the following chapters:

- Introduction
- Losing Streaks
- Why You Lose in Cardrooms
- Vicious Customers
- New Aggravations
- I'm Giving Up on Poker
- Don't Take Poker Too Seriously
- Afterthought

Overview of *Your Best Poker Friend* (*YBPF*)

Because my goal was to recommend solutions to the problems presented in *YWPE*, this book covers all its themes, but it has a broader and longer-term emphasis. For example, Part One focuses on how you can get and use better information and tells you how to become a more efficient learner. Part Four discusses a subject that is almost never covered by poker authors: how to plan your poker improvement.

Part One: Getting and Using Information

The subject of getting and using information comes first because everything depends on it. If you don't acquire, understand, and use information well, you can't play winning poker, nor can you improve yourself. Part One contains the following chapters:

- Introduction
- First Impressions
- Taking Notes
- Playing Online
- Poker Discussion Groups
- Getting Helpful Feedback
- Getting a Coach
- Afterthought

Part Two: Increasing Your Edge

Getting and exploiting edges is your central objective when playing poker. The bigger your edge and the better you exploit it, the more money you will win. Virtually all poker writers tell you how to get and exploit edges, but my emphasis is different. Instead of aiming to improve your strategic decisions, my essays tell you how to increase your *psychological* edge. Part Two contains the following chapters:

- Introduction
- Creating False First Impressions
- Would You Bust Your Own Grandmother?
- Beating the Newbies
- Isolating "Idiots"
- Playing the Rush
- Defending Against the Rush
- Creating Tilt
- Exploiting Tilt
- Afterthought

Part Three: Should You Play No-Limit Hold'em?

One of the best ways to increase your edge is to select games with weak players. Your poker profits ultimately depend on how much better you are than your opponents, and some of the weakest players love NL. This game gives the better player a *much* larger edge, and the combination of weak players and this edge makes NL much more attractive to good players.

Until recently, NL had nearly disappeared. Cardrooms wouldn't spread it because the weak players went broke too quickly. Now the most popular games are capped buy-in NL, and the caps let the fish lose more slowly.

The fish want to play NL because they have seen it so often on television. It's got the glamour, excitement, and big money. It allows players to gamble more wildly than any other game, and it looks so easy. Just push in your stack before or on the flop; then let the dealer turn over the cards.

To take the fishes' money, many people switched from limit to NL, and some of them made a terrible choice. NL is a very different game, and it requires different skills, mental abilities, and psychological traits. If you haven't got them, NL is not the right game for you. Even if you have them, you may still have serious problems switching your mind-set. Part Three contains the following chapters:

- Introduction
- The Essential Mental Abilities
- The Critical Psychological Traits
- Reading and Adjusting to Players
- Which Games Should You Choose?
- Where Should You Sit?
- Where Do You Want the Big Stacks?
- Making the Transition
- Afterthought

Part Four: Developing Yourself

The final part of the book focuses on longer-term decisions that can affect your entire future, such as whether you should move up to bigger games, how you should plan your development, and whether you should quit your day job to become a full-time pro. Part Four contains the following chapters:

- Introduction
- Should You Move Up?
- The Coach's Dilemma
- Your Poker Improvement Plan: Part I. General Principles
- Your Poker Improvement Plan: Part II. Setting Your Goals
- Your Poker Improvement Plan: Part III. Evaluating Your Assets and Liabilities
- Your Poker Improvement Plan: Part IV. Making Your Plans
- Your Poker Improvement Plan: Part V. Monitoring Your Progress
- Should You Quit Your Day Job? Part I
- Should You Quit Your Day Job? Part II
- Afterthought

Summary

Neither book tries to tell you how to play poker. That's what almost every poker book does, and their authors can do it better than I can. Instead, I want to help you to understand yourself, to overcome your weaknesses, and to build on your strengths. Then you will make more money and get more pleasure from this frustrating but wonderful game.

Using This Book

This book is both a textbook and a reference manual. It teaches you principles and suggests ways to get more information. Many of these references are in footnotes.[1] If you want to know why I have taken various positions or would like to have more information, read the footnotes. If you don't care to read further, just ignore them.

If you want certain kinds of help, the traditional poker literature is almost useless. Most poker writers focus on strategic issues, not the ones I discuss in *YWPE* and this book. *YWPE* provided help on problems that are rarely discussed, such as coping with losing streaks, controlling your emotions, and thinking of quitting forever. This book focuses on other rarely discussed problems, such as learning efficiently, changing your mind-set, and planning your self-development.

These problems really bother some people, and they don't know where to get help. If something is severely troubling you, don't read this entire book, at least not immediately. Just look in the table of contents and index for one or two chapters that relate directly to your problem and then focus on them.

You may find exactly what you need. If you don't, go to an Internet forum, especially the ones at cardplayer.com and twoplustwo.com. Many forums have a search function; just type in a subject, and you may find that I or someone else has posted something that solves your problem. If you don't find the answer to your problem e-mail your question to me at alannschoonmaker@hotmail.com. I may answer

---

1. Most poker books have hardly any footnotes, for reasons I discuss on page 24

your question, send you an essay that is not in this book, or refer you to some other writer's work.

Because some essays are designed to help you with specific problems, there is considerable repetition. The same principles apply to a wide variety of problems:

- *Thinking logically* instead of relying on intuition is a central theme of all my writing, and I continually urge you to do so.

- *Studying* helps with almost everything, and I repeatedly recommend it.

- *Learning actively* is the critical step toward developing yourself. Studying is essentially passive. You have to go beyond it by taking positions, challenging yourself and others, getting and using feedback to improve yourself. For example, participating in Internet forums or e-mailing me are forms of active learning.

- *Overestimating yourself and underestimating the opposition* were central themes in *YWPE* but are somewhat peripheral to this book. However, they can never be ignored because they affect almost everything you do. Because you probably overestimate yourself and/or underestimate the competition, you need to get objective information, and this book tells you how to get it.

- *Participating in Internet forums* can provide information and advice you can't get anywhere else. In fact, you can learn more from exchanging ideas with informed people than from any book, including this one.

- *Getting coaching from a professional, a friend, or a discussion group* is probably the best way to improve your skills, perspective, and evaluations of yourself and your competition. You need an outsider's objectivity to reach your potential.

But you should not just passively respond to whatever a coach tells you to do. Instead, become actively involved in the coaching process.

- *Planning your self-development* is discussed in the final section of this book, and the other sections lay the foundation for planning intelligently. It is the epitome of active learning: you thoroughly analyze yourself, set your goals, assess your assets and liabilities, make your plans, and then monitor your progress.

My goal is to help you to think logically about psychological issues that most poker writers have ignored or minimized. These issues have an immense impact on your profits, but making more money is not and should not be your only goal. If you take this book seriously and do all the work, including the unpleasant tasks, you will gain something many poker players never have: a clear sense of who you are, where you are going, and how you will get there. You really will be "your best poker friend."

PART ONE

Getting and Using Information

Introduction

Without good information you are helpless. You need a lot of information to play poker well and to develop yourself as a player. Unfortunately, poker writers have said hardly anything about how to acquire information. They emphasize processing information, not acquiring it.

Most poker books contain only general suggestions about how to get information. They say to study the literature, be alert, count the pot, observe betting patterns, look for tells, and so on, but they rarely tell you *how* to do these things. Most writers seem to assume that you already know how to get information and that you just need help in understanding and using it.

This book considers how to acquire, process, and use information. You need good information about at least three subjects:

1. Poker theory
2. Other players
3. Yourself

Learning Poker Theory

In *Your Worst Poker Enemy*, the chapter titled "How Should You Prepare Logically?"[1] emphasized the importance of studying theory and suggested ways to find good advice. You should read it because many of the books and articles resulting from the poker explosion provide poor information.

1. (New York: Lyle Stuart, 2007), pp. 39–46.

Bad information can be worse than no information. To reduce this problem, use the "Recommended Readings" appendix and read some of the articles listed in the footnotes.[2] Of course, I don't claim that the ones I recommend are the only ones worth reading. I have omitted dozens of good books[3] and hundreds of good articles. Even if you prefer books that I have not recommended, make sure that they fit the criteria listed in "How Should You Prepare Logically?" Otherwise, you can waste a lot of time and money.

The recommended books are solid, and there is a brief comment about each one. I have also indicated whether a book is for beginning, intermediate, or advanced players. Read only the books that fit your level or a lower one. If you try to read too advanced ones, you will probably confuse yourself. Reading lower-level books is okay, because working on the basics is always worthwhile.

My books contain far more footnotes than nearly all other poker texts do. Footnotes help you to get much more information on any subject. Use them. If all you know is what I have told you, you don't know enough. I believe poker writers avoid footnotes for at least two reasons. First, they want to look practical, not academic. Second, they don't want you to realize that they have borrowed ideas from other writers. Some authors act as if something that has been widely known for decades was one of their brilliant insights, discoveries, or even secrets. This is another example of the egotism that plagues poker.

No matter how good the books and articles are, just reading them superficially will not have much impact on your understanding or ability to use poker theory. You should study them, discuss them with other people, try to apply their concepts, and continually seek feed-

2. Many footnotes are for articles at cardplayer.com, an outstanding source of poker information. To find an article, click on magazine & the writer's last name. All articles by a writer are in one place, in order, with the most recent one first.

3. Tim Peters and Nick Christenson have thoroughly reviewed most poker books. Before buying a book, check their reviews at web.mac.com/tbpeters and www.jetcafe.org/~npc/reviews/gambling, repectively.

back on how well you have done so. You need to learn *actively,* the subject of the next chapter.

Reading is not the only or the best way to learn theory. Several essays will show you how to use poker discussion groups, Internet forums, and coaches to improve your understanding and ability to apply theory.

Learning About Yourself and Other People

You cannot learn much about people, especially yourself, from books, articles, DVDs, and so forth. They can teach you the general principles, but you need help from other people. Unfortunately, powerful psychological forces within you and them reduce the flow and your understanding of this critically important information. These forces are as follows:

1. First impressions and stereotypes cause you to miss some signals and misinterpret others.
2. You may not take notes, even though many professions *require* note taking.
3. Defensiveness makes you ignore or misinterpret information that conflicts with your beliefs and biases.
4. Other people do not tell you the truth—especially about yourself—because they are afraid of offending you.
5. Forces 3 and 4 reinforce each other. If you get defensive, you resist hearing the truth and increase others' fear of offending you.

Because of all these forces, you, I, and everyone else, may never learn some critically important information.

Overview of Part One

The chapters in Part One will help you to get and process the information you need about all three subjects: theory, other people, and yourself.

Our first topic of discussion is *learning efficiently*. You have so much to learn and so little time that you should get the full value for the time you spend working on your game. You need to become an efficient learner because the poker literature is extremely weak instructionally. Poker authors generally concentrate on their ideas, not on how to teach them.

Our second topic is *first impressions*. They affect both the information you acquire and the way you process it. Once you label someone, you will become more receptive to information that fits that label, and you will tend to ignore, minimize, or misinterpret conflicting information.

Our third topic is *taking notes*. Although taking notes is essential, nearly all poker players don't take enough of them, and many players take none at all.

Our fourth topic is *playing online*. This activity offers some unique opportunities to work on your weaknesses. Take advantage of these opportunities to improve your game.

Our fifth topic is *poker discussion groups*. These groups are an outstanding source of information on nearly all poker subjects. I have learned more from the Wednesday Poker Discussion Group (WPDG) since its inception and its spin-offs than from any other source except my coaches. In fact, some of them are members of these groups.

Our sixth topic is *getting helpful feedback*. This is essential to developing any skill, and poker feedback is notoriously unreliable. You therefore need to get feedback from other sources such as Internet forums, discussion groups, coaches, and poker buddies. But you won't get much value from them unless you keep your mind open and make it easy for other people to help you.

Our final topic is *getting a coach*. The best source of feedback is a good *coach*. I'm absolutely convinced that every serious player should have one or more. A coach will also help you to understand and apply poker theory and read people. Some of the best coaching comes from poker buddies who meet regularly to help each other.

If you don't develop the habit of critically examining your play, you can't reach your potential. You will repeat the same old mistakes and never get the benefit of all the theory you have studied and all the advice you have received. Unfortunately, most poker players won't look hard enough at themselves.

Regardless of whether you hire someone, swap coaching with another person, or participate in forums and discussion groups, you must understand and adjust to the powerful psychological forces—within yourself and other people—that prevent you from getting critically important information.

So set aside the attitudes that have prevented you from learning the truth about poker, other people, and yourself. Read the good books. Visit the forums, ask questions, post hands, and ask for feedback. Join or start a poker discussion group. Hire a coach or agree to swap coaching with someone. Most important of all, recognize that you don't know enough about the game, other people, and especially yourself. Make learning a top priority, and do everything you can to get as much information as possible.

Learning Efficiently

As a professor, I was often appalled at how badly my students understood materials they claimed to have studied. Poker authors feel the same way. We are delighted that so many books have been sold, but we wonder, "If people are reading our books, why do they play so badly?"

My books have analyzed many psychological factors that prevent you from playing as well as you should. Now let's focus on just one factor: you may not know how to learn efficiently. "Efficiency" is an input-output measure. How much benefit do you get for the time and money you invest? If you don't learn efficiently, you will waste both your time and your money. And, since your time is limited, you won't reach your potential.

Your inefficiency is probably not your fault. The school system often does a poor job of teaching students how to learn. When you were a student, you probably learned how to pass multiple-choice exams, but you may not have learned how to understand what a book really *means* and how to *use* that knowledge.

Many educators test students about the specific facts in a document, and many of the students get acceptable grades. But when educators ask "What were the author's purpose and organization?" and "How can you apply the author's principles?" many students are stumped because they never even thought about these subjects because they rarely appear on exams.

You don't have exams about poker, but you face more demanding tests every time you play. If you don't understand principles or can't apply them well, you lose money. To gain that understanding and ability to apply it, you have to learn *actively:*

A passive approach to books or lectures is much less efficient than an active one in which you ask and answer mental questions, challenge the author, and relate the material to your own experience. . . . Meaningful learning is much faster and more efficient than rote learning. If you understand what an author or lecturer is trying to do, and the way he is attempting to do it, you will learn much faster and retain much longer.[1]

That quotation is from my book *A Student's Survival Manual.* The book states that because most college professors don't know how to teach, students have to become efficient learners, and it describes a simple system for developing their learning skills. You can learn active-learning principles from that book[2] or from countless other sources. When I conducted a Yahoo! search for "active learning," there were more than two million hits. Most of the websites were for teachers, but they also contained material that can improve your learning ability. Here are a few worthwhile websites:

- www4.ncsu.edu/unity/lockers/users/F/felder/public/ Cooperative_Learning.html
- www.acu.edu/cte/activelearning
- www.ntlf.com/html/lib/bib/84-9dig.htm
- www1.umn.edu/ohr/teachlearn/resources/guides/active.html

If you visit these websites, you may be shocked to read how badly you have been taught. Of course, a few subjects are taught actively: math, engineering, medicine, and law teachers usually make students solve problems. But the vast majority of teachers rely primarily on

1. Alan Schoonmaker, *A Student's Survival Manual* (New York: Harper and Row, 1971). Much of this chapter is taken from pages 213–247 of that book. Since I combine quotations and paraphrasing, I often omit quotation marks.

2. Because the book is out of print, it would be hard to purchase, but Amazon.com has a few copies. You can also get it through interlibrary loan.

passive learning. They talk, and the students listen or pretend to do so.

Lectures are a waste of time, but they are the primary instructional method throughout the educational system. Because they grew up with them, many poker teachers rely heavily on lectures, and players pay good money to listen to them. They are all comfortable using a method that became obsolete five hundred years ago. I won't say any more now about lectures. If you'd like more information, read Appendix Two: Don't Waste Your Time in Lectures.

Most of your teachers knew almost nothing about learning. They concentrated on mastering their subjects, but knowledge of chemistry, psychology, or poker does *not* prepare someone to teach students how to understand and apply those subjects.

Most teachers—including poker experts—focus on what *they* will do, not on what the students will do, but they have it backward. Because the learning must take place in you, the important thing is what *you* do, not what the teacher does. Teachers can affect your learning only indirectly, by causing you to take the right actions.

Despite this principle—which is supported by thousands of research studies—most teachers devote virtually all of their preparation to what they will do: the words they will say, the examples they will give, the visual aids they will use, the references they will cite, the jokes they will tell, and so on.

If they looked at what students are doing, they would realize that they are sitting there passively, perhaps listening, perhaps not, which rarely produces much learning. Because most poker writers don't know how to teach, you have to become an active learner. Don't just sit there waiting for an epiphany; take an active role in your own development.

Learning Poker Theory and Strategy

It's not surprising that only a few poker writers understand and apply active-learning principles. Most of them just tell you their ideas, and they may give you an example or two to clarify them. They do *not* give you practice and feedback on applying their principles while playing, and you cannot develop skills without practice and feedback.

The poker literature is not as bad as it used to be. Recent books are much stronger instructionally than older ones. For example, the books of thirty or more years ago contained hardly any quizzes, but more recent books often contain them. Unfortunately, many readers don't work hard (or at all) on those quizzes, even though they may be the most important part of the book. If you can't answer the quiz questions correctly, you obviously don't know how to apply the book's principles. And, if you can't apply its principles, you have no reason to read the book.

Why don't people work hard on the quizzes? Because, after a lifetime of passive learning in classrooms, they don't know how to learn actively, and they may not want to test themselves. They may prefer to skim through the material, pretend that they have learned it, and then go back to playing cards. To learn how to play poker, select books that contain lots of quizzes and study until you get 100 percent on every one of them. A few months later, take them again to ensure that you still understand and can apply the principles. Take the next step by applying these principles to actual hands, then discussing them with other people.

Bob Ciaffone, Jim Brier, Matthew Hilger, Angel Largay, Dan Harrington, Bill Robertie, and several other writers use active-learning techniques. They do it by giving you many problems to solve, providing their answers, and explaining their decisions. In addition to helping you to apply their ideas, they teach you how good players think. I don't say that their theory is better than other authors'. My sole concern is how well they *teach*.

Because I am most familiar with Ciaffone and Brier, I will focus on their book *Middle Limit Hold 'em Poker.* They described the action in hundreds of hands and then asked: "What do you do?" They then answered that question and gave their reasoning.

They stimulated an extraordinary amount of discussion. In addition to lively face-to-face debates, there were thousands of posts on Internet forums and some of the arguments became quite heated: For example:

- "They are absolutely right. The best way to play that hand is . . ."
- "No! No! No! They are utterly wrong. You should . . ."
- "You're both wrong! They were right about what you should do, but their reasoning was wrong because . . ."

Just participating in these debates helped people to understand and apply Ciaffone and Brier's principles. These debates also had an unusual benefit. Occasionally, one of the authors would make an admission that hardly any poker authors have made: "We were wrong." He would describe their original position, repeat what critics had said, and say, "I can see now that the best way to . . ." That is, by taking positions, explaining their reasoning, and listening carefully to critics, both the students and the teachers were actively learning.

That's the learning model I hope you use. Read something. Take a mini-quiz. Try to apply its principles. Take a position and explain your reasoning. Get feedback from other people. Keep your mind open and learn from their reactions. When you're wrong, admit it. This approach works for *all* kinds of learning.

Learning About Other People

Active learning is even more important for learning about other people for two reasons:

1. Much of the information you receive is unreliable. Poker is a game of deception. Your opponents usually don't want you to understand the way they play or the cards they hold, and they will try to confuse you.

2. Forces inside you cause you to miss or distort information. You may see what you expect to see or are afraid of seeing. For example, your own biases and first impressions of anyone can cause you to ignore or minimize contrary information. If you have a certain image of someone, you may miss clear signals that you have misjudged that person.

Because you cannot rely solely on your own perceptions of people, you need help from others. You may find that Joe and Barbara see Harry differently than you do, and that their picture of him is much more accurate than yours. It happens to me all the time, even though I've been a psychologist for decades. I may be embarrassed by my mistake, but that embarrassment is trivial and temporary. The important thing is that talking to others improves my ability to understand people.

"Reading and Adjusting to Players" on pages 181–200 describes an active-learning system for developing these skills. The system is not perfect, but if you use it, you will slowly develop these critically important abilities.

Learning About Yourself

Understanding yourself is the most important subject, and the one that is most dependent on active learning. You cannot learn much about yourself from books, articles, DVDs, lectures, and so on. They can teach you the general principles, but you cannot get much insight without help from other people. Unfortunately, as I noted earlier, powerful psychological forces within you and other people reduce the flow of this vital information and cause you to misinterpret it.

Other people may not want to give you the information you need, and you may not want to get it. Several of this book's chapters, especially "Getting Helpful Feedback," discuss these problems and suggest ways to solve them. I urge you to take them very seriously.

Study the psychological literature.

Even though you cannot learn that much about yourself from books and articles, they are still worth studying. They provide the general principles you need to organize the information you get from other sources.

Naturally, I recommend my own books, but you should certainly read others. Dr. John Feeney's *Inside the Poker Mind* was published the same day as my *The Psychology of Poker*. Our publisher wanted to have a basic book (mine) and an advanced one (John's).

Dr. James McKenna has written three books on poker psychology: *Beyond Tells: Power Poker Psychology, Beyond Bluffs: Master the Mysteries of Poker,* and *Beyond Traps: The Anatomy of Poker Success* (all published by Lyle Stuart). I also recommend *The Poker Mindset* by Ian Taylor and Matthew Hilger. Psychology is one of Mike Caro's major interests, and most of his books contain valuable insights. Barry Greenstein's *Ace on the River* has a marvelous chapter, "Traits of Winning Poker Players." Doyle Brunson's *According to Doyle* and Roy Cooke's *Real Poker* cover some useful poker psychology. There are many other useful books. In fact, because poker is a people game, most experts give useful suggestions about poker psychology.

Don't limit your reading to books about poker psychology, because people don't change the way they think, feel, and act when they play poker. Many other psychology books and articles can be related to poker. So, if you see something that looks interesting, pick it up. You may learn something that dramatically improves your game.

Learn from your own reactions.

Regard everything you read, hear, or experience as opportunities to learn about yourself. If you are playing, reading, or listening to someone, analyze your own reactions to whatever is happening. For example, if you're reading an article, ask yourself a few questions:

- Which points most appealed to me?
- Which points did I dislike or reject?

- Why did I like or dislike those points?
- What do my answers to these questions say about me?

Appendix Five. "Mini-Quiz" contains these and a few other questions to help you to understand both this book and yourself. Take a brief look at it now and write your answers after reading each chapter. If you seriously answer those questions, I guarantee that you will learn much more from this book and anything else you read.

Do the same thing about your own experiences. Every time you have a significant reaction to someone or something, write:

- Your reaction
- Why you think you had it
- How it is similar to and different from your reactions to other people or things, including other books or articles you have read

Take notes about any strong reactions, whether they are positive or negative. If something really pleases or irritates you, remember it and try to understand why you feel that way. For example, if you get irritated when you play against Barbara but enjoy playing against Bill, ask yourself why you feel that way, and how your feelings affect your play.

Every few weeks review your answers to both the mini-quizzes and your reactions to experiences. Look for patterns and draw conclusions about yourself. You may find that you like aggressive recommendations and dislike conservative ones. This pattern suggests that part of your style comes not from a conviction that aggression gets better results, but from a love for action.

Or you may like authors who emphasize intuition, but reject those who recommend a logical, mathematical approach. This pattern suggests that you have neglected the mathematical, logical side of the game and should work on it.

Or perhaps you detest loose-passive games, even though you win more in them than you do in tighter ones. You just hate getting bad beats, even though you end up making more money. This pattern suggests that you are not trying to maximize your profits, that the frustration of having people suck out on you outweighs the money you make from the loose players' bad calls.

Note that I used the word *suggests* in explaining the patterns. I have done so because that's all that these patterns can do. They certainly don't prove anything. You should regard them as hypotheses to be tested by getting additional information.

Sometimes, you can learn the most from a strong negative reaction. Any time something really bothers you, there is a chance that it struck a sensitive nerve. For example, let's say that after reading the chapter titled "Denial About Ourselves and Our Opponents" in *Your Worst Poker Enemy* (*YWPE*) you think the entire chapter is "ridiculous psychobabble" and become angry at me for writing it. Your reaction strongly suggests that you are in denial about something in that chapter, and you resent my pointing it out. How can I draw that conclusion? Because *everybody* denies some things about themselves. The more you insist that you do *not* deny reality, the more confident any psychologist would be that you *are* doing it.

After reviewing your reactions, take the next step: Discuss all this information, especially your inferences about yourself, with someone you trust. Listen carefully to his or her comments. If you both take this exercise seriously, you may learn some surprising things about yourself, and some of the surprises may be unpleasant. Even if you dislike learning it, you need that information to develop yourself.

Take psychological tests.

Because so many people want to learn about themselves, psychological testing is a big business. You have probably taken many IQ tests or variants of them such as the SAT. You may have also taken personality tests such as the Myers-Briggs and the Minnesota Multiphasic Personality Inventory, or MMPI.

I believe that no solid research directly relates IQ and personality test scores to poker success. Nobody really knows what you need to succeed as a poker player. However, there have been dozens of extended discussions on Internet forums about the value and meaning of these tests. People passionately debate questions about IQ scores, Myers-Briggs profiles, and many other tests.

If you take some tests and discuss them with other people, you will certainly learn about yourself. Of course, because there is no solid research relating them to poker, you must not take these tests too seriously, but they can provide valuable insights into your abilities and character.

My other poker books contain some self-tests. They were *not* developed as carefully, nor is there a large research base as you would have with an IQ test, the Myers-Briggs, or the MMPI. Therefore, you should interpret the score more cautiously than you would with a better-known test. If a test score conflicts with more reliable information, it is probably wrong (or you have misinterpreted it).

Despite this limitation, these tests can help you to understand yourself. Use the same general approach with all of them: take the test, write down what you think you have learned about yourself, and then discuss your results and conclusions with someone you trust. My book *The Psychology of Poker* has three tests:

1. "Why Do You Play Poker?" (p. 35)
2. "Rating Yourself" (pp. 96–97)
3. "The Right Stuff Questionnaire" (pp. 289–294)

In the Afterthought of "Evaluating Yourself and the Opposition" in *YWPE* there is a set of self-assessment questions on pages 107–112.

Your Best Poker Friend contains many self-analysis questions. I won't tell you the page numbers because you should not answer them until after you have read the text. In addition, you should take a mini-quiz after reading each chapter.

Understand defense mechanisms.

All of us have things we don't want to learn about ourselves, and we use defense mechanisms to hide those unpleasant truths. They

> serve a very useful purpose. They temporarily reduce our anxiety, make us feel more comfortable, and help us to work on our other problems. Without them we would feel the full impact of all of our anxieties and would become incapacitated. . . . We do pay a high price for this stability. . . . Our defenses are essentially self-defeating; they give us temporary relief, but aggravate our problems. . . . Defensiveness therefore feeds on itself. Underlying problems are not solved; new problems develop; the person becomes more dependent on his defenses; and more and more of his energy is devoted to self-deception."[3]

When I wrote those words about executives, their culture was quite anti-introspective. Executives were expected to concentrate on doing their jobs, not on analyzing themselves. More than thirty-five years have passed, and that culture has changed. Thousands of businesses send executives to seminars and coaches to learn about themselves.

The poker culture is still anti-introspective. Poker players focus on learning strategy and reading other people, not on looking at themselves. I would not be at all surprised if a similar cultural shift occurs in our game. Anyone who observes poker players can't help seeing that we take all sorts of self-destructive actions. We should obviously learn why we do them.

Try free association.

More than a century ago Freud found that his patients' defense mechanisms prevented him from getting certain kinds of information. It was buried so deeply in their unconscious that they could not

---

3. Alan N. Schoonmaker, *Anxiety and the Executive* (New York: American Management Association, 1969), 146–147.

talk about it directly. He developed free association to get this information indirectly. Free association is quite simple: you just say whatever comes into your mind without worrying whether it is rational, senseless, moral, immoral, and so on.

The information comes out in tiny bits, which are often well disguised. Instead of saying exactly what is bothering you, you give indirect hints. Then you and your analyst interpret these hints to help you gain insight into yourself.

You don't need a psychoanalyst to use free association. You may have already used a technique based on it called "brainstorming." It is usually done in groups, and it often lets the group think of new and unexpected ways to solve problems.

You can also talk to a dictation machine. Or you can use a variation of free association called "TACing" (Thinking At the Computer). Just let your thoughts flow and your fingers input whatever crosses your mind.[4]

Free association can give you valuable insights into your character that you never suspected. Then take the next step: discuss these insights with someone you trust.

Final Remarks

You probably have not thought about learning efficiently. You have been too busy coping with other demands—including learning about poker, other people, and yourself—to think about how well you learn.

It's time to learn how to learn. Because there is so much information to absorb, becoming an efficient learner can improve your entire future. If you can learn more efficiently than your opponents, you will have an immense advantage, not only at the poker table, but in business and in most other competitions and relationships.

4. All this material about free association came from "Psychoanalysis and Poker" in *YWPE*. Because I have combined quotations and paraphrasing, I have omitted quotation marks.

The critical first step is to recognize that the passive approach you were taught as a student was fine for taking multiple-choice exams, but it does not create enough understanding and ability to apply the knowledge you need to play well. To make the quick decisions that poker demands, you need to learn actively.

You will not get the full benefit of anything you read without committing yourself to taking action, getting feedback, and relating everything you learn to yourself. Continually ask yourself: What can I *do* to become a better player and a better person?

Let's start this process *now*. Apply active-learning principles by taking a mini-quiz about what you have just read. Turn to Appendix Five and answer those questions about this chapter.

First Impressions

Our first impressions of people and situations affect everything we think or do. Labeling a person, his cards, or anything else affects the information we look for and the way we process it. If later information agrees with that label, we tend to give it too much credibility. If information disagrees with our label, we tend to minimize its importance or to ignore it completely.

The Problems of First Impressions

You may think that you are too intelligent to think this way, but nearly everyone does it, and it creates immense problems. Because winning poker demands objectively assessing players and situations, let's look at some research. Then we'll discuss ways to minimize their effects on you.

A Classic Study

Harold Kelley, my colleague at UCLA, once demonstrated that a *tiny* difference in labels could affect the way people perceived and reacted to everything they saw or heard.[1] After telling his students they would have a guest lecturer, he created a first impression with two nearly identical written introductions. They described his training, degrees, and experience and included one of two sentences:

1. H. H. Kelley, "The Warm-Cold Variable in First Impressions of Persons," *Journal of Personality,* 18 (1950): 431–439.

1. "People who know him well see him as rather warm."
2. "People who know him well see him as rather cold."

Everything else was the same. Throughout the entire class session, the students listened to the same words, heard the same voice, saw the same body language. They had tens of thousands of bits of identical data, but only one tiny difference: "warm" versus "cold."

Observers counted the number of times students interacted with the guest lecturer. Students with the "warm" introduction interacted twice as frequently. They were more comfortable with a "warm" person than a "cold" one, even though it was the same person.

After class, the students assessed the teacher. Students with the "warm" introduction saw him as more knowledgeable, intelligent, informal, considerate, sociable, popular, humane, and humorous. One tiny difference in the introduction made them see and react to him as if he were a very different person.

Medical Training and Research

To minimize the effects of first impressions, medical students are taught to avoid making rapid diagnoses. Their professors know that once they have diagnosed a patient doctors will look for information that supports their diagnosis and minimize or ignore conflicting evidence. Of course, they won't do it deliberately; doctors don't *want* to make mistakes, but they are as human as college students (or poker players).

The law absolutely requires controlling for this effect when conducting research. The Food and Drug Administration will not approve a drug that has not been very carefully tested using *double blind* methods. A drug and a placebo (such as a sugar pill) must be given to carefully matched samples of patients. Both the patients receiving the drug and the doctors assessing its effects must not know who has received the drug or placebo.

If the patients know, the ones receiving the drug would probably respond more positively, even if the drug is worthless. The tendency to improve from worthless drugs is called "the placebo effect," and it is extraordinarily powerful. Placebos have "cured" everything from allergies to cancer.

If the doctors know who gets the drug, they would expect to see more improvement, and they would find it. That effect has been demonstrated hundreds of times. People, even well-trained doctors, see what they expect, want, or are afraid to see.

One study showed that psychiatrists and other mental hospital staff refused to revise their diagnosis even when they had received unequivocally conflicting evidence. Several psychologists went to a mental hospital and complained of hearing voices, a classic symptom of schizophrenia. Despite having no other symptoms, they were diagnosed as having this disease. They then stopped claiming to hear voices and acted normally. The doctors and other hospital staff stuck with the diagnosis long after they should have recognized their mistake.[2]

General Implications for Poker

The effects of first impressions that we have examined are a major obstacle to playing well. We simply cannot win without accurately reading other players and their cards, and anything that distorts our readings is going to hurt our results. We get an enormous amount of information, and later bits often conflict with earlier ones. We must continually look for information and interpret it well to determine

- How people play
- What cards they hold

Ignoring or misinterpreting later information because of our first impressions can cost us lots of money.

The effects of this tendency combine with one of my favorite subjects, the extremely common belief that we are more talented than we

2. D. Rosenham, "On Being Sane in Insane Places," *Science*, 197: 250–258.

really are. Thousands of studies clearly indicate that people overestimate *most* of their abilities.[3] Our first impressions are probably not
that good because we are not as perceptive as we think we are.

Every psychologist has been repeatedly irritated by people who
say, "Do you think I could succeed as a poker player [shoe salesman,
bartender, or whatever] if I wasn't a good psychologist? I'm *good* at
reading people." I have had to fight hard to keep from saying, "Oh, no
you're not. You just think you are."

That same overconfidence makes many people think they read
cards much better than they really do. In *The Psychology of Poker* I
gave an extreme example of this overconfidence. The "Deluded Expert" has "extremely low skill, but extremely high confidence. He can't
read cards for beans, but he thinks he can. He is an amazing combination of ignorance, arrogance, and obnoxiousness."[4] You have probably
met a few. They love to say, "I *know* you've got pocket aces [or what-
ever]," and some of their reads are hilariously wrong; they jump to
conclusions without carefully and objectively analyzing the betting
and players, then insist they are right.

Nearly all of us overestimate our abilities, and this increases the
distorting effects of making quick judgments about people and situations. For example, if a stranger makes an apparently dumb play, we
are quick to categorize him or her as a bad player. But, if we make a
similar play, we may believe we did it for a good reason (we were "advertising" or "mixing up our game" or "playing the player, not the
cards" or . . .). We tend to stereotype or oversimplify our first impressions of others but are much more forgiving (or defensive) about ourselves. After all, we know that we aren't bad players, but we want to
believe that others are. In fact, all of us have underestimated opponents, and we have all paid dearly for it.

3. See "Denial About Ourselves and Our Opponents," pp. 65–74, in *Your Worst
   Poker Enemy.*

4. Alan Schoonmaker, *The Psychology of Poker* (Henderson, NV: Two Plus Two,
   2000), 43.

Because first impressions have such large effects, we have two critically important tasks:

1. Reduce the way first impressions distort our thinking.
2. Create false impressions for our opponents and magnify their effects.

This chapter discusses ways to reduce the first problem, but it is such a natural reaction that it cannot be completely eliminated. Another chapter, "Creating False First Impressions" (pp. 101–104), discusses ways to use them against your opponents. These two chapters should help you to see things clearly while confusing your opposition.

The Dilemma

To reduce the distortions of first impressions, doctors may defer a diagnosis until they have seen blood tests, X-rays, and other information, or they may ask for second opinions. Unfortunately, when playing poker, you can't wait to make judgments, and you certainly can't ask for a second opinion. You have to do something *now*. You must balance the demand for immediate action with the steps that can reduce distortions.

Recommendations

A few simple actions can reduce both the distortions of first impressions and their destructive effects.

Recognize your own limitations.

Poker is a macho game, and self-confidence is essential for success. If you don't have confidence in your judgment, you can't win. Unfortunately, you may have too much confidence. You certainly don't have as much training on analyzing people as psychiatrists, but the research I just mentioned (plus many other studies) clearly proves that even they are misled by first impressions and other psychological factors. If highly trained specialists should be cautious about relying on first impressions, so should you.

Doyle Brunson took the opposite position: "Stick to your **first** impression. Have the courage of your convictions."[5] Since he is an immortal, and his advice supports what many people want to do, they have fallen into the trap of sticking to their first impression and ignoring any contradictory evidence. It makes them feel "macho," and they may even look down at people who don't have the "courage of their convictions."

If I had Doyle's "feel," I would follow his advice, but I don't, and you probably don't either. You may think you do, but research clearly proves that most people overestimate their abilities. Unless you have extremely clear evidence that you've got great feel, don't always trust it. Instead, keep your mind open and be willing to change it. Once you put someone on a hand or decide that he is a certain kind of player, you'll overemphasize supporting evidence and minimize or ignore conflicting data.

Consider many possibilities.

Instead of jumping to conclusions, David Sklansky suggested a different approach to reading hands, and the same general method applies to reading players:

> Do not put undue emphasis on your opinion of your opponent's hand. I know many players who **put someone** on a certain hand and play the rest of the hand assuming he has that hand. This is taking the method of reading hands too far. . . . Instead you must put a player on a few different possible hands with varying degrees of probability for each of these hands.[6]

5. Doyle Brunson (with many collaborators), *Super System: A Course in Power Poker*, 2nd ed. (Las Vegas: B&G, 1994), 431.

6. David Sklansky, *Hold'em Poker* (Henderson, NV: Two Plus Two, 1976), 49.

Keep your mind open.

You may not want to consider other possibilities because doing so implies that your judgment is faulty. An essential step toward improving your reading skill is becoming open-minded enough to reconsider your position.

Do everything possible to make yourself receptive to later information. Regard your first impressions as just starting points and revise them as you get more information. Look especially for contradictory information, for actions that would *not* occur if your first impression was correct.

Test your hypotheses.

The search for contradictory information is absolutely central to scientific research. Virtually all scientists are taught that a good theory is "testable." If you can't create conditions that would *dis*prove a principle, it is not a scientifically acceptable theory. Theories are tested by deriving hypotheses, then creating conditions in which certain events should occur. If they do not occur, then the theory is wrong. You can use the same general method while playing poker.

Make predictions (hypotheses) based on your read. Then check, bet, or raise to see how your opponent reacts. If he does not react the way you expected, your reading could be wrong. Your opponent may have different cards or be a different kind of player than you thought.

Look for patterns.

Of course, one incorrect prediction does not mean much because so many factors can affect someone's reaction. However, if you consistently test your hypotheses, you should see a pattern. Your mistakes will tend to be in certain directions, and those directions could say a lot about you.

For example, when confronted by identical information, optimists usually see what they hope to see, while pessimists see what they fear. One player, Dave, raised this issue in a whimsical, but insightful, post on an Internet forum. "Let's say you raise preflop. Most fish . . . put . . . you on AK. However, they are willing to reevaluate their opinion based on the flop. If the flop is 56T, they continue to assume you have AK. If the flop is 7TK, they . . . change their read to AQ. If the flop is AT6 and they have an ace, they change their read from AK to KK." That is, they change their read to whatever gives them an excuse to keep playing and hoping.

In a reply to Dave, another player, Richie, pointed out that weak-tight players have the opposite reaction. They are so fearful that they put you on whatever hand gives them the best excuse to fold. He wrote, "The Fish *hope* you have a certain hand. The Weak-tight *fear* you have a certain hand."

You must guard against undue optimism, pessimism, and all other distorting emotions. Do whatever it takes to see what is really there, not what you expect, hope, or fear.

Understand your own biases.

Recognizing a pattern is just one step toward reducing these distortions. The critical question is: *Why* were you wrong? You may not be a hopeful fish or a fearful weak-tight player, but you certainly have biases. How can I be so sure? Because everyone has them. A critical step toward reducing their effects is learning what they are.

Get coaching.

Without coaching it is very hard to understand your biases and their effects. They are so central to your thinking that they may seem completely normal. In addition, the poker culture is very anti-introspective; you (and most other players) would rather analyze others than yourself. But you can't analyze other people accurately if you don't understand the way your own biases distort your thinking.

You should therefore discuss hands and players with other people. Tell them how you saw a situation, what you learned, and how you acted. Then ask them to comment on your specific reads and, more important, what those reads say about your thinking.

A coach's comments will be especially valuable if he or she sits behind you while you play. The coach will certainly see things you miss and interpret many signals differently from you. If you carefully compare your readings and your coach's, you will see patterns that reveal your biases. These patterns may also suggest other weaknesses and identify unknown strengths. Nothing can teach you more about yourself (and many other subjects) than an objective coach.

Final Remarks

Everybody's thinking—yours, mine, Freud's, and the world's greatest poker players'—is distorted by first impressions and other biases. These distortions are so central to our nature that nobody can completely escape their effects. To minimize them, we must resist the temptation to jump to conclusions, keep our minds open, and understand and adjust to our own biases.

Apply active-learning principles *now* by taking a mini-quiz about what you have just read. Turn to Appendix Five and answer those questions about this chapter.

Taking Notes

In many professions, nearly everyone takes careful notes. Lawyers are famous for their yellow pads. Doctors know that they cannot treat patients properly without detailed notes and that poor records virtually guarantee losing any malpractice suit. Cops without meticulous records of all the evidence of a crime will get destroyed by defense lawyers. Engineers, accountants, computer scientists, and countless other professionals would not think of working without thorough notes. Yet most poker players—including pros—do not take many notes. This chapter will answer three questions:

1. Why don't more players take notes?
2. How can you take good notes?
3. What should you do with your notes?

Why Don't More Players Take Notes?

Whenever people fail to take obviously valuable actions, there must be strong forces inhibiting them, and some of these forces are probably unconscious. People don't take notes for at least four reasons, and the first two include denial of reality:

1. They want to delude themselves about their results.
2. They think, "Real players don't need notes."
3. They are embarrassed or have misconceptions about note taking.
4. They are just lazy.

I will discuss only the first three. If you're too lazy to take notes, nothing I can say will affect you.

Delusion About Results

Many people want to believe that they win more or lose less than they actually do. If they kept good records, they couldn't deny reality. Barry Shulman wrote:

> If you could divide all the poker players ... into those who keep accurate records and those who do not, you would find ... the record-keeping group would be comprised mainly of winners, and the non record-keeping group would be comprised mainly of losers. ... Record-keeping forces you to acknowledge the truth about your results.[1]

Realistic, thorough players go far beyond just keeping track of their overall results. They record how well they do at limit and no-limit hold'em, stud, Omaha, and other games, and their results at various stakes, at different casinos, and under diverse conditions (such as shorthanded versus full table, afternoon versus late night, and tight-passive versus loose-aggressive games).

Your records may show that you do poorly in ramming, jamming games. If you love them and don't keep detailed records, you may remember the few times you won big but "forget" the more frequent losses. You may dislike tight-passive games but do well in them. You may learn that you win at $5–$10 but lose at $10–$20. The most important decision you make is your choice of games, and without good records you can't make it sensibly.

Believing Real Players Don't Need Notes

The belief that real players don't need notes is just another form of denial. If doctors, lawyers, and so on need notes, how can anyone believe that poker players don't need them? Are we smarter or better

1. Barry Shulman, "Shulman Says," *Card Player,* November 24, 2000.

trained? Is our information so simple that we can mentally record and instantly retrieve it?

We are obviously not smarter and better trained, and our information is extremely complicated. Doctors and lawyers generally deal with one or two people at a time, whereas we have to cope with seven or more, and they keep changing. Unless you have an *extraordinary* memory, you can't remember how every opponent plays. In addition, your opponents' play changes when they get tired, are winning or losing, have had too much to drink, and so on. Pretending you can remember all that information is just a fantasy.

In fact, you probably can't even remember exactly how various key hands were played. I can't, and neither can my friends, including some successful pros. In our discussion group, we often described hands and asked for comments. We were embarrassed when we couldn't answer questions about the size of the pot, the positions and styles of the players, the exact sequence of bets, and so on. We thought we had remembered a particular hand, but we actually had forgotten critically important information.

After being embarrassed a few times, most of us learned to take good notes about any hand we wanted to discuss. And, because we took those notes, we got valuable feedback to improve our game. Were we showing our weakness by taking notes? Or were we just being sensible?

The belief that real players don't take notes is based on denial about our own limitations and ignorance about what real players actually do. Do you think Dan Harrington isn't a real player? He was the most successful player for a decade of the World Series of Poker Championship, with four final tables and a first-place finish. He is also the primary author of three extremely successful books. He knows what the best players do: "In top-class poker you will encounter many players who, after each session, go home and write down everything they've seen at the table. . . . There are players with enormous written notebooks on the habits of hundreds of other players."[2]

2. Dan Harrington, *Harrington on Hold'em, Vol. I* (Henderson, NV: Two Plus Two Publishing, 2004), 179.

Angel Largay, a successful pro and author,[3] once made this report on his own note taking: "At the end of the year I had 857 notes on just 24 players." Unless you are smarter or have a better memory than Dan, Angel, and other successful pros, stop pretending that you don't need notes.

Embarrassment and Misconceptions

You may be embarrassed about taking notes or think that doing so violates some rules. Many people who think that way leave the table or wait until they go home to write their notes so that no one can see them. These are costly overreactions, because

- Most casinos have no rules against taking notes.
- You can't win any money when you're away from the table.
- The longer you wait to write your notes, the less you will remember.

Because I want to keep playing while gathering the most complete information, I *immediately* write notes on three-by-five-inch cards, and I carry hundreds of them in a fanny pack. I also carry a micro–dictating machine for longer notes. If I have played with you a few times, I have notes about how you play. Whenever I join a game, I review my notes on every player.

Many people have asked what I'm writing and why I do it. I usually say, "I'm a psychologist, and I write notes about people." Most people don't object, but I have had a few complaints. One player asked the floor man to stop me. He was told that there was no rule against note taking.

The Downside

Although I have never been stopped, taking notes does have some negative effects. One friend said, "It makes you look like a nerd." So

---

3. In addition to many magazine articles, he wrote *No-limit Texas Hold'em: A Complete Course* (Toronto, Ontario: ECW Press, 2006). This quotation is from page 105, and later pages in that book tell how he uses his notes.

what? I've always been a nerd, and I'm quite comfortable with that image. Besides, doing some smart things can cause negative reactions:

- If you play tightly, some people will think you lack courage, that you aren't a "real gambler."
- If you're deceptive, some people will see you as "sneaky."
- If you're aggressive, some people will resent your "bullying."

If you worry too much about what people think of you, you don't understand what poker is all about. As Roy Cooke once said, "It's not about winning respect. It's about winning chips."[4]

That same friend also mentioned three effects of note taking that are much more important because they could cost me some chips:

1. Some people may become uncomfortable, which can make the game too serious. Instead of relaxing and having a good time, they may concentrate on playing better.
2. A few people may leave and go to a more relaxed table.
3. A few people may focus on me and try harder to beat me.

He's right about making the game too serious, but hardly anyone has left the table because of my note taking. I don't worry about people focusing on me or trying to beat me. Anything they gain by focusing on me will probably be offset by their irrational desire to take my chips. Anyone who sees my chips as especially valuable will probably act foolishly.

Besides, even if a few people play better against me, I gain much more than I lose because I play better against nearly everybody. Virtually everything we do has a price, and the only question is: Is the price too high? Since poker is an information-management game, the answer is an emphatic "No!" I gain much more by taking notes than I lose from these minor negative effects.

4. Roy Cooke, "Perception, Deception, Respect, and Results," *Card Player,* January 23, 1998, p. 13.

Let's put it in terms of *your* bottom line. If you and your opponent are equally skilled but you know more about your opponent than he knows about you, you are going to beat him (and vice versa). So get and retain all the information you can.

Don't Let Silly Reasons Keep You from Taking Notes

I spent many years in a profession that demanded detailed notes, and I place an extremely high value on information. Consequently, I take more notes than anyone I know. If the negative effects we've discussed are important to you, perhaps you should take fewer notes or take them less openly than I do.

However, you should recognize that your memory is extremely fallible and selective. The longer you wait, the less complete and objective information you will have. Your inhibitions will make you miss many opportunities to improve your results and develop your game.

How Can You Take Good Notes?

Let's discuss my own note taking system because it works well. If you don't want to be so thorough or obvious, use a simpler system and take your notes less openly, but remember two points:

1. Write your notes ASAP, because the longer you wait, the more you will forget.
2. Be as detailed as possible. Even if you think a point is trivial, it may be just what you need to make a critically important decision.

To find, update, and use my notes, I write everything on color-coded three-by-five-inch cards; different colors are used for various subjects. I wear shirts with two breast pockets to organize these cards. The ones on the players in the game are in my left pocket, and those on other subjects are in the right one. Notes on other players are kept in a fanny pack with alphabetical markers. I carry a micro–dictating machine for longer notes than I can write quickly. I carry so many notes that a friend called me a "walking filing cabinet."

You may think it's overkill, but complete, accurate notes help both my playing and writing. If I have an idea for an article or a book, or if I think of something complicated about my own or another person's play, I can easily dictate it. Naturally, I leave the table when dictating something.

If I try to remember something, it will interfere with my play. I'll be thinking about it instead of focusing on whatever I have to do now. Once it's recorded, I can shift all my attention to other tasks, such as deciding what to do with the current hand. Your own notes will probably be less voluminous, but they should cover at least four subjects:

1. Your results
2. Your own play
3. Any hand you want to remember or analyze
4. Every opponent you expect to encounter repeatedly

Your Results

Immediately record every chip you buy. If you don't, you will probably mislead yourself. You can easily forget (partly because you want to) some of the chips you bought. Over time those small "forgotten" amounts will add up to real money, distorting your beliefs about your results.

Some people have insisted that they were cheated online primarily because they had never kept accurate records. They believed that they were winning in B&M cardrooms *only* because they "forgot" how many chips they had bought. Because websites keep extremely accurate and undeniable records, they suddenly saw the truth: they were losers. Because they could not accept that truth, they insisted that they had been cheated.

Your Own Play

To reduce the problem of overestimating your skills, you should continually monitor your own play. How well are you playing *now?*

Try to look at yourself and the other players as a detached observer. For example, from observing an opponent's betting patterns and tells, you should infer what cards she holds and predict what she will do. Then compare your inferences and predictions to the cards your opponent shows and the actions she actually takes. Each time you are right or wrong, you learn a little about how well you read players and situations.[5]

Ask yourself: "Why did I make that mistake?" or "Why did I read this situation so well but completely misread that one?" You may find that you can accurately read tight-passive players, but not loose-aggressive ones. Or your reads are better on good players than on bad ones. You can then make better decisions about other players and about your own self-development efforts. If you continually take these steps and keep your mind open, you will slowly develop your entire game.

Pay particular attention to any changes. Every time your play improves or deteriorates, try to learn why it happened. For example, if you find that you've missed a couple of value bets on the river, ask why you did it and write down your conclusions. If your reads have been unusually accurate, ask why and record your answers. Try to understand how conditions affect your play so that you can improve four critical decisions:

1. Should you stay or go?
2. Should you change seats or tables?
3. Should you change your strategy?
4. What should you do differently in the future?

For example, my notes show that my play deteriorates when I can see the television set or I am in slow-moving games with lots of conversation. I get too distracted or annoyed. Seeing this pattern helps me to make better choices of games and seats.

5. A simple system to develop these skills is described in "Reading and Adjusting to Players" on pages 181–200.

My notes also show that I play poorly when I'm hungry, tired, or irritable. You may think that you don't need notes to make such a judgment, but many people ignore these obvious distractions. For example, do you know how well you play when you're tired or angry? Has this information caused you to go home earlier than you had originally planned? If the answer to either question is no, you're costing yourself money, perhaps a lot of it.

Any Hand You Want to Remember or Analyze

General evaluations of your play are helpful, but you should get much more specific. You can't improve any skill without practice and feedback, and poker feedback is notoriously unreliable. Because luck has such huge effects on your short-term results, you must focus your attention on the only thing you can control: your own decisions.

How well did you play various hands? When I play a hand well or badly, I immediately record what happened and rate my play from excellent to idiotic. I record as many details as possible:

- What kind of game was it?
- Who made every bet?
- What kind of players were they?
- Why did I bet, raise, and so on?
- Why do I think my play was excellent, very good, good, questionable, poor, very poor, or idiotic?

I don't like admitting it, but I've made my share of very poor and even idiotic plays, *and so have you.* However, by taking such specific notes, I reduce the chances of repeating certain mistakes. Without similar notes, you may keep making the same mistakes.

With notes on so many hands I have solid data to assess my own strengths and weaknesses and to improve my game. Instead of vaguely wondering, "Maybe I should be tighter or more aggressive or bluff more often," I know what I've done well and badly, how often

I've made various mistakes, how my play has changed over time, and so forth.

In a moment I'll discuss analyzing this information, but you can't make a good analysis of bad data. The computer people have a wonderful expression: "GIGO" (garbage in, garbage out). If your data are garbage, your conclusions must be garbage. One reason that so many players overestimate their abilities is that they have never collected solid data for evaluating their play.

Every Opponent You Expect to Encounter Repeatedly

Because I look for easy games, I play against far more tourists than locals. I play against thousands of tourists every year and take only cursory and temporary notes on them. As soon as the game is over, I throw the notes away (unless the tourists will play a few more sessions before leaving Las Vegas). But I make and keep detailed notes on most locals. I know how they usually play and how their game changes when they are tired, drinking, winning, losing, and so on.

The notes show how their play has changed over time. For example, some locals have slowly shifted from being loose-passive to tight-aggressive. By dating some notes, I can see how they have improved and adjust my strategy. Without notes I might continue to use an obsolete strategy.

Naturally, I use the coding system from my book *The Psychology of Poker.* A loose-passive player would be "7, 3." Someone who is tight before the flop but chases too much would have a tight-loose score of "3-7." A comma separates the tight-loose score from the passive-aggressive one, and a hyphen separates before- and after-the-flop play.

I also record players' tells and telegraphs. Mike Caro wrote a great book about tells, but it contains only general principles. I want to know what it means when a specific player moves his right hand toward his chips, or holds his cards in a certain way. If I take thorough notes, I can slowly learn how to read many people's signals.

If I have written notes about you and you have only a vague impression of how I play, you're at a huge disadvantage. The best way to reduce that disadvantage is to take your own notes.

Use Online Tools

Most poker websites make it extremely easy to take notes, and you would be foolish not to use them. However, because so many people play online, these notes are not that valuable. You may never play again with many opponents, whereas in B&M cardrooms you often play with the same people again and again. People who develop the habit of taking notes online should transfer it to live games. However, there is little evidence of this happening, because hardly anyone openly takes notes.

If you play online frequently, buy Poker Tracker and/or Poker-Spy. They automatically take much more complete notes than you could take, and they summarize and put the information into easily used formats. They record *all* your hands. If you rely on your own notes, you can easily deceive yourself by selecting the ones that support your biases.

For example, a friend insisted that another player was very good, but extremely unlucky. His only evidence was a large number of on-line hand histories that his friend had sent him. They both believed that these histories *proved* that he was unlucky. His opponents had made this runner-runner flush, and that gut-shot draw, and he had lost again and again with top pair, sets, and so on.

My friend was quite offended when I told him that the data were useless because the player had selected the hands. The number of hands selected is irrelevant. Unless they were taken using random sampling techniques, they have no scientific value. For more information about the effects of biased samples, read Appendix D: "Biased Data Samples."

Because the online programs deal only with statistics, you should still take notes about specific hands, your own mental state, the effects of conditions, and so on. Statistics are very valuable, but you should also try to understand *when* and *why* you and others take certain actions.

What Should You Do with Your Notes?

As a student, I learned a painful truth: good notes are worthless if they aren't used well. Some of the most meticulous note takers got mediocre grades because they didn't understand the difference between taking notes, understanding the instructor, and applying the information. They may have done well on multiple-choice tests, but they never really understood the class.

In poker we don't have multiple-choice exams. We have to get good information and then apply it well during the heat of battle. In *Your Worst Poker Enemy*, I covered some ways to use information in "How Should You Prepare Logically?" and "How Should You Review Logically?"[6] I urge you to read those chapters because they relate directly to the issues discussed here.

First, Organization

Unless they are organized, your notes are almost useless. You will not find information when you need it, and you will waste a lot of time looking for it. Once again, I am reminded of my student days. Because some classmates' notes were poorly organized, they could not quickly find whatever they needed.

Poker demands fast decisions. You cannot rummage through a pile of disorganized notes when you are trying to decide where to sit or how to adjust your strategy.

You also cannot carry all the notes you will need. You need a system that allows you to find the group of notes you will need (such as the ones for people who play at a certain casino). Then you must be able to find the notes you need during that session (such as the ones on *this* player).

There are two excellent, user-friendly computer programs for organizing the data about your results: The Card Player Analyst[7] and

6. See pages 39–46 and 51–56 of *Your Worst Poker Enemy*.

7. You can download this program for free at cardplayer.com.

Statking. You just enter each session's data, and the programs will organize it, compute your win rate, standard deviation, and other statistics by game, location, time, and other ways. You can quickly get the data needed for important decisions. For example, you can easily compare your results for

- Various limits
- Different casinos
- Weekdays versus weekends
- Diverse times of the day

This information simplifies some important decisions. Because I do much better in certain casinos early Saturday and Sunday mornings than at other places or during weekday afternoons, I know where and when to play. Notes also help me to make four other critically important decisions:

1. Selecting the right games
2. Choosing the right seats
3. Adjusting my strategy
4. Developing my skills

I'll now discuss only the first three. I'll extensively discuss developing yourself later on. Of course, your self-development depends on the quality of your information.

Selecting the Right Games

Your most important decision is selecting the right games. If you choose a game with better players, you are going to lose. It really is that simple. I change games frequently, and I never do it to "change my luck." I continually evaluate the players in my own and other games. If another game seems better, I'll change, and that decision will be based not on whims or wishes, but on solid information about the players. Without good information, your game choices can be little more than guesses.

Choosing the Right Seats

Your choice of seats is almost as important as your choice of games. Ray Zee, an extremely successful player and writer, listed "Bad Seat Position" as one of the ten most important reasons for losing. According to Ray,

> Find yourself in a seat with the wrong player on your right or left, and you can assure a trip to the withdrawal window of your bank. You have to move to find a spot at the table where you get the best of other player's faults. And at the same time do not suffer from a seat that the good players or aggressive ones pound you to death. Many times great games are not worth staying in because you cannot move position at the table.[8]

I change seats very frequently, and some people have asked, "Why did you change seats when you were catching cards in that one?" They don't understand that cards are random, but people are predictable. My notes tell me to sit to the left, right, or far away from various players.

I want predictable players on my left and unpredictable ones on my right, to reduce surprises. I generally want the Rocks on my left, and the Maniacs on my right. However, some Maniacs are predictable, and having one of them on my immediate left makes me the "semi-permanent button." I can often act last, even if I'm in early position. I can check or call a bet, let the Maniac bet or raise behind me, and trap everyone. Conversely, I can thin the field with vulnerable hands by betting into the Maniac and having him raise.

Maniacs can be predictable because they almost always bet or raise

8. Ray Zee, "The Ten Most Important Reasons for Losing," twoplustwo.com's *Internet Magazine,* May 2005. This quotation will be repeated because seat selection is especially important in no limit.

or because they telegraph their intentions. Because of my notes, I know many people's signals. I don't mean obvious telegraphs such as grabbing chips. Nobody needs notes to identify that one. But many signals are much subtler, and I can understand their significance only by building up a database. What did a player do with his hands, posture, face, cards, and so on, and what action did he take afterward? With enough notes, a pattern may slowly emerge.

For example, one loose-aggressive player did not have any obvious telegraphs, but a lot of notes revealed a pattern:

- If his right hand was close to his cards, he would fold.
- If his right hand was close to his chips, he would call.
- If his right hand was not close to either, he would raise.

After "cracking the code," sitting to his right became a top priority. It gave me a huge edge over him and the rest of the table. A player with great intuition might sense what he was going to do, but, thanks to lots of notes, I *knew* it.

Adjusting My Strategy

Adjusting to different types of people has been the central focus of three of my previous books on selling, negotiating, and poker psychology.[9] The general principles are the same for all three: you have to understand how people "play," and then adjust your strategy to fit particular players.

Some players with great intuition can make these adjustments without even thinking about them. They just know how Harry, Susan, and John play, and they can make extraordinarily insightful moves against them. For example, Layne Flack once said, "I seem to have an intuition in poker that is amazing."[10] Because you and I don't have his

---

9. *Selling: The Psychological Approach, Negotiate to Win,* and *The Psychology of Poker.*

10. Layne Flack, *Card Player,* March 16, 2005.

gift, we should build up databases on people, slowly learn how each one plays, then use that information to make strategic adjustments.

Final Remarks

Many people don't take notes for silly reasons, and the silliest is the belief that real players don't need notes. A few extraordinarily gifted players such as Layne Flack don't need notes. He has even said that he doesn't read books or discuss hands with other people. I have to read and reread the books, talk about theory and hands, and take lots of notes. You should do the same.

You almost certainly overestimate your abilities. Almost everyone does, including me. Our selective memories let us preserve our delusions. We remember the great reads we made on "gut feel" but forget our terrible mistakes. Unless you have an *extraordinary* memory or intuition, you should take notes to build a database about your results, your play, and your opposition and then use it to answer the critical questions:

- Where and when should you play?
- Which game and seats should you select?
- How should you adjust your strategy?
- How can you develop your own skills?

Don't let false pride prevent you from making good decisions. Poker is not about proving how smart you are. It's about winning money, and you will win more if you take good notes and use them wisely.

Apply active-learning principles *now* by taking a mini-quiz about what you have just read. Turn to Appendix Five and answer those questions about this chapter.

Playing Online

Several friends have asked me why a psychologist would play online. They know that I write about poker psychology, enjoy socializing, and focus intently on body language. Online would seem to be exactly the wrong place to play.

First, the Bad News

We lose lots of pleasure and information by playing online, and these losses are very important to me. First, live games let me meet old friends, swap jokes and gossip, and just enjoy being with people. Online games provide none of these pleasures.

Second, because I've been trained to observe people, I rely heavily on the way they dress, sit, talk, relate to each other, hold their chips, and make their bets. My training in body language increases my competitive edge in live games, but not online.

Because I place such a high value on socializing and observing, my friends were surprised when I started to play online. Let's look at why I'm doing it. We'll ignore the standard reasons such as being able to play whenever I like, because in Las Vegas there are always good games somewhere.

Now, the Good News

Online poker offers me unique opportunities to improve my game. Because I live in Las Vegas and write about poker, I frequently talk to excellent players. These conversations have shown me how limited my game is. My results have been excellent, but only because I select games very carefully and play only against weak players. I was so comfortable and successful that my game wasn't developing. To succeed in tougher games, I need new skills, but I naturally don't want to pay too much "tuition."

Online play lets me concentrate on my weaknesses at extremely low cost. Let's use a golf analogy. If your short game is weak, don't pay green fees to play complete rounds of golf. Go to a park or driving range and hit a hundred chip shots.

Reading Betting Patterns

Because I could read body language well, I wasn't paying enough attention to the betting patterns and developing my skill at interpreting them. I'm not bad, but I should be much better. Online poker is perfect because there isn't any body language. If I don't read betting patterns well, I'll lose. That fact literally forced me to develop this critically important skill.

You may think that an intelligent person would not need to be forced to develop essential skills, but most people rely on the skills they have. If those skills produce satisfactory results, they may not bother to develop others.

Playing Shorthanded

I do very well at full games, but my results worsen as the number of players decreases, and heads-up, I'm just a break-even player. When I first published this essay, that sentence read "with less than four opponents I'm a losing player." That is, I no longer lose in two-, three-, and four-handed games. Playing online is the primary cause for this improvement.

B&M cardrooms rarely spread shorthanded games, and you will almost never see a heads-up match. Again, online play is ideal. Many sites have tables for only five or six players, and a few of them offer heads-up play. To keep down my "tuition" bill, I played shorthanded for very low stakes.

Improving My Assessments of Players

You might expect psychologists to excel at reading people quickly, but we are trained to *avoid* snap judgments. Once we label someone, we would naturally ignore, minimize, or distort later information. Withholding judgment is a fine principle for my professional practice, but some poker situations demand making rapid assessments. Many people handle these situations far better than I do.

Since I've been taught to gather lots of information before making judgments, I take copious notes about players. However, I can take even better notes while playing online than I can during live games, for the following reasons:

- Each player's name is on the screen. I often can't learn a live player's name, which prevents me from keeping and retrieving notes about the player.
- I can use the computer, not index cards, making online notes immeasurably superior. I can type faster than I can write, and everything is legible. I can also cut and paste; use CAPITAL LETTERS, **bold**, and *italics* for emphasis; and make corrections.
- Instead of having to search through index cards, I can just click on the player's icon.

Playing Tournaments

I've always enjoyed tournaments but done poorly in them. My disappointing results have been caused partly by my weaknesses in shorthanded games and the fact that I don't read players quickly. Because people continually go broke and get replaced, the intuitive players have a huge edge over me. In addition, the number of players continually changes as players get busted. Tables often become shorthanded before breaking; and the final table always becomes shorthanded.

Many websites offer extremely inexpensive tournaments. The multi-table ones let me work cheaply on all the tournament skills, and Sit N Go tournaments are even better. Instead of spending hours and money trying to get to that final table, I can work on my greatest tournament weakness immediately.

Analyzing My Own Game

We should all monitor our own play and then discuss it with other people. Good notes can help us to identify our strengths and weaknesses and plan our self-development. While playing online, I start a Microsoft Word document to record hands, list questions to ask people, and comment on my own play. I can also dictate extremely complete notes.

This information becomes the basis for discussions with my friends, study of various books, and focused work on my game. Being able to record this information is probably online poker's most valuable benefit.

The Bottom Line

My results have never been as good online as in B&M cardrooms, and I still don't enjoy the games as much. For the first few weeks I actually lost money, and my win-rate was trivially small for the first six months or so. Those poor results were an investment in my education.

That education has paid off and it will continue to do so. I gained experience in situations I once avoided and put new weapons into my arsenal. I still have a long way to go, but I have definitely made progress. For example, I won three tournaments at RoyalVegasPoker.com and cashed many other times. Online poker will never replace live games for me, though. I want to use my observational skills and get the unique pleasures of live play. Nevertheless, online poker is still a great way to develop my game.

Should You Play Online?

The answer is the same as it is for most poker questions: "It depends." Online poker is not for everyone, and you should ask yourself some questions before deciding. How much do you care about the standard issues such as finding a game whenever you want and playing at home in your bathrobe? Also, how do you feel about losing social pleasures and body language? Then consider the developmental issues discussed here:

- What are your strengths and weaknesses?
- How dependent are you on tells?
- How well do you read hands from the betting pattern?
- Are you willing to take notes and discuss them with others?
- Is improving your game important enough to spend some money and time in uncomfortable situations?

This sort of analysis isn't easy or pleasant, but you can't make an intelligent decision without it. If you think playing online might be pleasant, instructional, or profitable, try it. But start small; if you don't like what happens, be ready to change your mind.

Apply active-learning principles *now* by taking a mini-quiz about what you have just read. Turn to Appendix Five and answer those questions about this chapter.

Poker Discussion Groups

During the past eight years I've attended more than three hundred meetings of various poker discussion groups. Some were with two or three people, whereas others were with much larger groups, especially The Wednesday Poker Discussion Group (WPDG) and its spin-offs. Some meetings had a structured agenda, whereas others had free-flowing conversations. I really enjoyed and learned an immense amount from these meetings.

The WPDG

The WPDG has had over two hundred meetings in Las Vegas plus about twenty near Atlantic City. I doubt that any similar group has met so often. In fact, there may not be another group like ours anywhere. The meetings are extremely enjoyable, and they have greatly improved our play and our understanding of what is happening in the poker world. We may gain even more from the friendships we have made. You often hear about networking; we do it every Wednesday.

We don't have dues or a formal membership list, but well over three hundred people have attended various meetings. Some of them are regulars, others live outside the area and join us whenever they visit Las Vegas, and some people just drop in once or twice. We are recreational players, props, semi-pros, and professionals who play from low to very high limits as well as no limit, both live and online. Several members write for *Card Player, Bluff, All In,* PokerPages.com, Two Plus Two, Kensington, and other publications and publishers.

We have been mentioned in more than fifteen articles in many publications, and many visitors have commented about us on Internet forums. We have gotten visitors from all over the United States and more than a dozen countries in Europe, Asia, and Australia, and even a South Pacific island.

We meet almost every Wednesday afternoon for casual socializing, serious discussions about poker strategy, and varied presentations. The WPDG and its spin-offs have had presentations and question-and-answer (Q&A) sessions from (in alphabetical order) Ashley Adams, Jim Brier, Mike Caro, Roy Cooke, Nolan Dalla, Jan Fisher, Barry Greenstein, Mark Gregorich, Russ Hamilton, Linda Johnson, Lee Jones, Rich Korbin, Lou Krieger and Arthur Reber, Angel Largay, Mason Malmuth, Tom McEvoy, Ed Miller, Daniel Negreanu, Puggy Pearson, Blair Rodman, Matt Savage, Al Schoonmaker, Mike Sexton, Barry Tanenbaum, Mark Tenner, and several others.

These presentations have covered no-limit and limit hold'em, seven-card stud, stud/8, Omaha/8, tournament news and rules, selecting the best game, poker as a business, life on the tournament trail, the World Poker Tour, the World Series of Poker, and many other subjects.

Two groups have been spun off from the WPDG. One group meets almost every week to discuss limit hands. We focus on particular types of hands and ways to play them under varied conditions.

The other group meets every week to discuss no-limit strategy. There is a different chairman each week, and he controls the agenda and sends out a pre-meeting reading assignment. We have had several small tournaments and cash games, and we sometimes follow an unusual procedure. After an interesting hand is over, we show our cards and discuss our reasons for each decision. For example,

- "I raised on the flop because . . ."
- "I folded because . . ."
- "I just called because . . ."
- "You should have reraised because . . ."

The lessons we learn are far more important to us than the small amount of money at stake. By showing our cards and discussing our strategy, we all develop our games. This procedure is consistent with our overall objective: *By examining ourselves and commenting on each other, we all become better players.*

The Benefits of Discussion Groups

Discussion Groups can do an immense amount to improve your play, results, and enjoyment. For some problems and opportunities they are the best source of help. A well-organized group can

- Give you constructive criticism about your play, strengths, and weaknesses.
- Improve your understanding of poker theory.
- Help you to find the best games.
- Teach you new games.
- Tell you what is happening in various places.
- Help you to find the right books, articles, and DVDs.
- Provide "scouting reports" on players.
- Expand your circle of friends.

Getting Constructive Criticism About Your Play, Strengths and Weaknesses

Nearly every meeting includes thorough critiques of several hands. Members describe hands that they or someone else played, and the group thoroughly analyzes what was done well or poorly. It can be embarrassing to have your play dissected, but it is always informative and helpful.

Where else can you get face-to-face, constructive criticism from several serious players? And the critics may know your game so well that they can link a hand to your general style, strengths, and weaknesses. The discussion often goes beyond specific hands to general self-development issues.

Not all the discussion occurs during meetings. We also exchange e-mails that discuss hands, strategic issues, and self-development techniques (plus many other subjects).

Because the group has become quite large and has existed for several years, we have repeatedly improved our ways to communicate with each other. First, we added an e-mail exchange program; we just send an e-mail to a Yahoo.com address, and it gets forwarded to everyone. People comment on many e-mails, creating a small, private forum.

Second, Cary Darling, our Internet expert, has created and continually improves our website, wpdglv.com. It now includes forums. They have a huge advantage over most online forums: instead of swapping posts with strangers with anonymous screen names, we exchange ideas with people we know well. Because we have played and talked together again and again, we can comment on each other's habits, motives, strengths, and weaknesses.

For example, after a hand is described, a friend may point out, "You made the same mistake in the game we played last week." Or someone may say, "You seem to have overcorrected an old weakness. You used to be weak-tight, but now you're gambling too much."

We also provide useful criticisms while playing. After watching a hand, one of us may pull another aside and suggest ways that the hand could have been played better. Or we may see that someone is playing badly, drinking too much, or going on tilt. We tell him to watch out or directly say, "Go home." Sometimes the player won't listen, but more than a few people have taken that advice, which may have prevented serious losses.

We don't soft-play each other, comment during a hand, or do anything else that violates poker ethics or etiquette, but we trade a lot of invaluable information. The most valuable information is about ourselves. Because as poker players we often lack objectivity about our own play, and we are particularly bad at understanding our emotional states, this kind of information can greatly improve *your* results.

For example, our no-limit group was polled on the critical skills, psychological traits, and mental abilities for limit versus no limit. Some of us recognized that we had some serious flaws that had to be corrected.

More generally, we have made self-examination and self-development key priorities. We help each other to recognize our strengths and weaknesses and then plan to develop ourselves. *The bottom line is that we give each other serious, well-intentioned coaching for free.*

Improving Your Understanding of Poker Theory

Poker theory is often hard to understand. Much of it is counter-intuitive, and even serious students can get confused. The presentations and Q&A sessions with famous experts have helped us to understand their written works and the way their minds operate.

Our regular meetings are essentially seminars on theory and strategy. We discuss books and articles, apply their principles to specific hands, and debate issues. Again and again, I have recognized that I misunderstood a principle, and other members feel the same way.

Finding the Best Games

Because we play all over, we naturally help each other find good games. We exchange information about the number of games at various stakes, the players, rake, dealers, comps, food, and so on in every room in Las Vegas and a few other places. If someone is going to visit, for example, Los Angeles, Phoenix, or San Francisco, etc., he can learn in advance where to play.

Learning New Games

Many of us want to learn how to play Omaha/8, razz, stud/8, and other games. We have private tournaments and cash games, and they may include games that are new to some of us. Because some people lost significant money at first, we now play for modest stakes. We want to have fun and learn these games, not bust each other.

Finding Out What Is Happening in Various Places

Many of us travel, and we make trip reports about what is happening in Los Angeles, Tunica, Foxwoods, and other poker locations. We also share interesting website links, news about important developments such as pending legislation that will affect poker, the lawsuit over the prize money for the 2006 WSOP Championship, the lawsuit between the players and the World Poker Tour (WPT), and anything else that may interest other members.

For example, Linda Johnson told us how Steve Lipscomb, Mike Sexton, she, and others created the WPT, and Linda and Jan Fisher keep us informed on how it is developing and the fascinating people they meet while working the tournaments.

Linda got our complete attention when she told us about Andy Beale's enormous game. She was seated at the next table at The Bellagio when Andy was playing $100,000–$200,000 against Gus Hansen. Even though she was playing $100–$200, seeing all that money changing hands affected her concentration.

Finding the Right Books, Articles, and DVDs

So many books, articles, and DVDs have appeared lately that nobody can keep up with all of them. Most of them are never reviewed, and the few reviews you can get are often biased. In fact, some of the compliments you read on book covers are from people who have never even read the book. They are just helping a friend.

We don't have that problem. Our members buy lots of books and other materials, and we tell each other about them. If we like or dislike a book, we say so. In addition, because we know how the other members play, we may say that a book is good for Joe, but not for Suzanne.

Getting "Scouting Reports" on Players

The faster you learn about your opponents, the better your results will be. You want to know how strangers play and whether any familiar people are playing differently from usual.

If I see a friend, I will ask for a "scouting report." He may tell me to avoid a certain game or to put myself on the list for another one. If I'm joining my friend's game, he will report on the players. For example, he might say, "Seat 2 is loose-aggressive. Seat 4 is a rock. You know Joe in Seat 5; he's usually a solid player, but he took a bad beat and is on tilt. Seat 6 is drunk."

Some reports are much more complete, and they may even include specific tells or mistakes that someone is making such as raising too many hands, chasing, or playing scared. Of course, if I know something, I share it with my friends. These scouting reports give us a tremendous advantage over outsiders.

Expanding Your Circle of Friends

Because the goal of poker is to take each other's money, many players can't relax at the table, and poker etiquette prevents much socializing. Our game also attracts competitive people, and we often have difficulty relating to each other.

Our group eases this problem. Since we relate so closely with and and are so supportive of each other at our meetings, we also eat together, go to movies, take occasional trips, and do all the other things that friends do. As one high-limit player put it, "I don't come here to talk about poker strategy. I do it all the time. I'm here primarily to socialize."

I feel very privileged to belong to this group and urge you to visit us. You can learn more about us, including the time and place that we meet, at wpdglv.com.

Start Your Own Group

A visit with our group can be enjoyable and educational, but you will gain much more from your own group. Here are some steps to create and preserve a good discussion group. Preserving one is *much* harder than starting it. Many discussion groups have been started, but most of them don't last very long.

Clone Howard Burroughs: For the first four years, Howard was the "glue" that held us together. He chaired the meetings, kept us on track, and brought a few hands and questions to discuss. He e-mailed reports of our meetings to regulars and visitors.

Without Howard we never would have become so tightly connected, nor would we have our own forums. You *must* have a Howard, but we won't let you have ours. You will have to get your own.

Howard could not get to many of the recent meetings, but Ben Orenstein, Jay Wilder, Steve Evans, James Perkins, Shannon Dindia, and some others have taken over his responsibilities. They have done a fine job of building on his foundation.

Start with a core of committed members. The first few meetings are critically important. Most groups don't survive more than three or four sessions. To persist, you need a few people who really want the group to succeed. In addition to attending nearly all meetings, they must prepare for them by recording hands, finding interesting articles, or making notes about topics to discuss.

Dave Adams and I were the only people at the first few meetings of the group that became the WPDG. We had to invite a lot of people to get a third (Matt Lessinger), but we slowly grew. After we moved to Las Vegas, Matt wrote a *Poker Digest* article that helped us to attract more people.

The spin-off groups from the WPDG started the same way. Only a few people wanted to discuss limit hands or no-limit strategy, and we had to invite others to join us. Then all three groups flourished.

Invite many different kinds of people. Once you've got it going, you have to expand to ensure survival. You need at least fifteen players to have a full table at a home game each week. People sometimes have other commitments or just don't feel like attending a session. A discussion group needs at least that many regulars to continue.

To get them, you should invite anyone who might be interested.

Most of them will politely turn you down, some will come to only one meeting, and a few will become regulars and bring their friends.

The critical point for us was the arrival of Linda Johnson and Jan Fisher. Until then, we were a small group of low- and middle-limit players. They know everyone in poker, and they invited most of the notables mentioned earlier.

It's great to have famous players, but they won't come to many meetings. You should probably try for the mix we have: small-, medium-, and high-stakes players; recreational players to experts; men and women; young and old. You may think a more homogeneous group, such as only advanced players, is better, but the mix of ages, skills, and motives actually enriches the discussions.

The experts provide advanced insights, and the recreational players—especially the relatively new ones—ask questions or make points that the more experienced players would not even consider. This combination of naive questions and sophisticated answers makes the meetings more interesting and helps all of us—even the experts—to develop our games.

On the other hand, some groups should be more homogeneous. We have had two spin-offs because some people wanted to work on specific issues. The narrower a group's focus, the more homogeneous that group should be. People who play only limit won't benefit from the No-Limit Discussion Group's (NLDG) meetings, nor would top pros, because we play in smaller games (1-2 to 2-5 blinds).

Balance socializing and serious discussions. If the meetings are too social, some people will see them as a waste of time and stop coming. If they are too serious, they will seem like "work," and others will drift away.

The main group slowly evolved a balanced pattern. For the first hour we eat lunch, socialize, and have small-group discussions. Then the chairman calls the meeting to order, and we spend an hour or two discussing serious issues. During that time we meet as one group. If a few people want to discuss something else, they move away so that they don't disrupt the meeting. If people start a private conversation in the main room, the chairman asks them to stop disrupting the meeting.

To get this balance you need an agenda and a strong chairman. As Matt Lessinger wrote, "Without an agenda the conversation can become too vague and general."[1] The same thing can happen if the chairman is too soft. Many poker players don't listen well or they have their own pet subjects or they want to push their own opinion. The chairman will often have to step in to keep the discussion focused.

Of course, if the chairman is too heavy-handed, people will get offended and stop coming. Howard was an ideal chairman because he balanced firmness and good humor, and your chairman needs both qualities.

The spin-off groups do not socialize much. They often have a fixed agenda and may even have a reading or other preparatory assignment such as the completion of a survey.

The mix of socializing and serious discussions will change from time to time. Some meetings will be more businesslike, and others will be primarily social. You have to find the mix that fits your members and objectives.

Clone Barry Tanenbaum. Barry is our resident guru. We have several outstanding players, but he is our go-to guy for strategic advice. He is a highly regarded coach, attends most meetings, is always willing to answer questions (even "dumb" ones), and helps us to understand how experts think. You need someone like Barry to raise the level of discussion. Without him, our meetings would not be nearly as serious or valuable.

Invite speakers. Speakers add an essential element: new information. After a while, you can tire of hearing the same old people

1. Matt Lessinger, "Wait! Let's Discuss This," *Poker Digest,* May 17, 2001, pp. 18–19.

making the same old points. Because we're based in Las Vegas and some of us know other writers and experts, many distinguished people have spoken to us. It will be harder for you to get top speakers, but you can get some talented local experts or visitors. If you ask often enough, you will find some very good people to talk to your group. Many poker players love to talk about themselves and their ideas.

They may also welcome the opportunity to develop those ideas. The best way to learn a subject is to teach it to someone else. By explaining their positions to other people, they recognize holes and inconsistencies and deepen their own understanding. They may also want the group's constructive criticism.

The demand for presentations, articles, and books has exploded, and some people in your area may be planning to give a talk or write for publication. If so, they could benefit from making a presentation and getting feedback from a smaller, less threatening audience. Many of the people who have talked to us did it for practice before writing for publication or giving talks to other audiences such as Poker School Online, BARGE, various seminars, and The World Poker Players' Conference.

They were following an old show business tradition: practice before performing. Before opening on Broadway, most shows have tryouts in smaller towns. They can see how a show looks and is received by less important audiences. Then they can revise the show.

Prohibit bad-beat stories. Matt Lessinger emphasizes this point: "We occasionally share bad beats, but only if the hand has some legitimate instructional value, and that value cannot be anything such as, 'Don't play against stupid people who are calling preflop with 9-2 because they will catch two small pair to beat your pocket aces.' Maybe you tried to slow-play your aces preflop, you let the big blind see a free flop of 9-5-2. . . . Now you have legitimate discussion material: Don't slow-play aces."

Make self-examination a central objective. As I have repeatedly stated, most poker players don't look hard enough at themselves. A discussion group is the ideal place to improve your self-understanding. Let me quote Matt again: "One of the first things we did . . . was to go around the room and say, 'Here is what I need to work on,' and then we each listed three areas for improvement."

Meet in a quiet restaurant. We have changed locations several times, partly because Las Vegas is a large area, and partly because we had not found the ideal location. For the past several years, we have usually met in a separate and quiet room in Binion's coffee shop. You need a place that lets you eat because it's part of socializing.

However, most restaurants are much too noisy for serious discussions. The ideal place would be a centrally located restaurant with private meeting rooms. It also should have a wide variety of food, because people get bored easily.

Unfortunately, no matter where you meet, some people will complain about the location, food, noise, temperature, prices, service, and so on. Before we settled on Binion's, we had several irritating discussions about where to meet. Even after several years of stability and general satisfaction, those discussions occasionally start again.

The NLDG came up with a simple solution: the chairman picks the location. Usually, we meet at The Tuscany's coffee shop, but if someone is willing to chair a session, we will go wherever he wishes. This system saves a lot of time and aggravation, and it gives people an added incentive to take responsibility for a meeting.

Do It!

It isn't easy to start a group and keep it going, but good things are rarely free or easy. If you put in the time and effort, you will find that you will develop great friendships, have lots of fun, and greatly improve your game. Visit us when you come to Las Vegas, and start your own group.

Apply active-learning principles *now* by taking a mini-quiz about what you have just read. Turn to Appendix E and answer those questions about this chapter.

Getting Helpful Feedback

Some of the best suggestions for columns come from private e-mails. For example, Robert Anderson wrote: "Here at the forum a lot of people ask for advice. We want to know how to play this or that hand or ask for opinions on other subjects. I just thought that the most important thing when you ask for advice is to be open to the answers you're getting."

He's right, but people often want *con*firmation, not *in*formation. Instead of wanting to learn something, they want to be told, "You're right." For example, a poster seemed to be asking the question, "Why are people so cheap?" But he was really just ranting about an extremely generous friend.

Several people told him, "You're wrong," and he rejected their opinion. I told him, "You're not listening to what people are trying to tell you." *Dozens* of additional people tried to help him see the truth, but he never admitted it. In fact, his final post said that we were all idiots.

This poster's position is an extreme example of refusing to accept other people's advice. He really wasn't looking for it; he just wanted to rant. Others whine about bad luck and losing streaks, insist that they are playing well, and reject—sometimes angrily—criticisms of their play or suggestions about how to improve it.

The desire to rant, whine, or appeal for sympathy is a major—and sometimes the only—factor causing many comments we hear or see on our forums. Far too many people just want to express their frustrations and reinforce their delusions.

Of course, it's not an either/or situation. Our minds are not open or closed; they vary between almost completely closed to almost completely open. Note my use of the word *almost,* because hardly anyone is completely open- or closed-minded.

That poster who called us idiots was extremely closed-minded, but he may suddenly realize that he is wrong. A dedicated scientist will try to keep his mind open but cannot help looking at information in a somewhat biased way. Despite his best intentions, the scientist may unconsciously give more weight to information that supports his position than to conflicting data.

Let's represent degrees of open-mindedness by using a continuous scale. Zero represents completely seeking confirmation with a closed mind, and ten is the opposite extreme, seeking information with an open mind.

Closed-minded									*Open-minded*	
0	1	2	3	4	5	6	7	8	9	10

Seeking	Seeking
Confirmation	Information
Rants	Research
Whines	Studying
Bad-beat stories	

Our motives and moods affect where we fit on the scale. When we are angry, depressed, feeling sorry for ourselves, or in some other emotional state, we would probably be toward the closed-minded end. When we are sincerely interested in learning or discovering, our minds open up, and we seek new information. Note that none of the activities are at zero or ten and that there is a bias toward closed-mindedness. It occurs far more frequently than open-mindedness.

Your goal should be to move toward greater openness, to try for the objectivity that characterizes good researchers. Try to conduct informal "research" about an important subject such as how to play a hand, overcome a bad habit, or learn a new skill.

The conflict between the desire to get good information and to reinforce our ego-protecting delusions never ends. We all have both desires. I usually want to learn, but sometimes my other motives get in the way. For example, when friends criticize my play, I should shut up and listen, but I may "explain" my actions: "You don't understand. I raised because . . ."

Sometimes, I really am explaining, but frequently I am just *defending* myself. Why do I do it? Because, being human, I naturally want to deny my mistakes and protect my ego.

You probably do the same sort of thing. In fact, we usually have mixed motives whenever we discuss something serious. We want both information and confirmation, but they directly conflict with each other. Now that the problem has been defined, let's discuss ways to reduce it.

Keeping Your Mind Open

Robert Anderson said it very well: "The most important thing when you ask for advice is to be open to the answers you're getting." Look at the evidence dispassionately. What does it say?

The poster who insisted that we were all idiots was obviously closedminded. If dozens of people say he is wrong and only he thinks he is right, he is almost certainly wrong. The same principle applies to you. For example, if you describe the way you played a hand and most people— especially the better players—say you misplayed it, you probably did.

Looking Critically at Your Own Actions and Motives

Continually ask yourself, "Why did I say or do that?" You will often realize that you are trying to defend your ego, not learn. Whenever you realize that you're being defensive, *stop* doing it.

Refraining from Explaining or Defending Your Position

Don't say why you acted in a certain way. Don't say, "Yes, but . . ." First, it will close your mind and prevent you from hearing what people are saying. Second, it will reduce the flow of information. People may feel that you are defensive and stop commenting or start arguing with you. You will learn much more if you just listen.

A friend once said, "I'm not sure I agree. . . . Isn't the whole point of a discussion to have a back-and-forth interchange? Otherwise, the conversation is completely one-sided. I think it is okay to defend or explain your position as long as you listen openly to the responses."

He has a good point: if you can have an open-minded interchange, you may learn even more. So let's use that old rule "It depends." If, but only if, you can keep your mind open, and if the other person will also remain objective, it's okay to explain your position. If you're not *sure* that both of you will remain objective, just shut up and listen.

Refraining from "Shopping" for Confirming Opinions

Because people have different opinions, you may be tempted to go "shopping" for confirmation. Let's say I ask Mason Malmuth and Barry Tanenbaum about a hand and they say, "Al, you misplayed it." Because they are much better players than I am, their opinions should be enough to convince me. Unfortunately, if I'm defensive, I may ask for some more opinions, especially from people who are likely to agree with me. If I ask enough people, somebody—perhaps a weak player—will tell me exactly what I want to hear: "Al, that's just the way I would have played it."

Aha! I've gotten the confirmation needed to protect my ego, but I have also reinforced my own denial. Even if five experts say I'm wrong and only one weak player supports me, I have support for my denial. You have probably gone confirmation shopping. If the first one or two people you consult say you're wrong, stop shopping, accept reality, and learn from your mistake.

Listening Actively and Visibly

Listening works best in face-to-face conversations, but some of its techniques can be used on Internet forums and elsewhere. Listening is not the same as just sitting there doing nothing. It is an active, visible process that communicates to others, "I am really trying to understand you." Active-listening techniques have been discussed in hundreds of places, and you should learn more about them. The literature on performance appraisals is particularly useful. Now I will just summarize a few of the main points.

1. *Concentrate.* Let your entire manner communicate that you are taking the other person's comments seriously. You are not just waiting for him or her to pause so that you can talk (and perhaps say how wrong the person is).

2. *Take notes.* Doing so supports the impression that you are trying to learn, helps you to remember whatever is said, and makes it easier to see patterns.

3. *Maintain eye contact.* Look people right in the eye, but do it in a nonchallenging way. Let your eyes show that you respect the other person and are trying hard to understand him.

4. *Restate points in your own words.* Show that you are trying hard to understand. Paraphrase remarks and then ask, "Is that what you mean?" One or both of you will sometimes realize that the message you heard is not the one the other person sent. Then he can try again.

5. *Look for patterns.* Try to go beyond the specific comments and relate them to larger issues. For example, a critique of

the way you played one hand may suggest something about your basic style, strengths, and weaknesses. You can then discuss other hands or your general approach to poker to develop your overall game.

6. *Ask for specific examples.* If you are discussing just one hand, there is no need to ask, but if you are talking about more general subjects, you need specifics. For example, if someone tells you that you are too loose, ask which hands you played loosely. If you are told that you don't check-raise often enough, ask when you should have done it and how to recognize future opportunities.

7. *Say "Thanks."* Let people know that you appreciate their help and honesty. If people believe that you really appreciate their help, they will offer more of it. Conversely, if they think you are defensive or unappreciative, they will either turn off or argue with you.

Final Remarks

These principles apply to virtually all attempts to get help. They should be used whenever you post on Internet forums, discuss hands with your buddies, get professional coaching, and so on. The critical element is exactly the one Robert identified: we need to keep our minds open.

If we keep them open and actively seek information, we can reduce denial's destructive effects and grow as players and as people. Conversely, if we close our minds, we will continue to deny reality and to make the same old mistakes.

Apply active-learning principles *now* by taking a mini-quiz about what you have just read. Turn to Appendix E and answer those questions about this chapter.

Getting a Coach

Several people have said that I overemphasize the need for coaching. Because they have succeeded without coaches, maybe they don't need them. But I certainly do, and you probably do too. If you don't want to pay for coaching, you can swap coaching with poker buddies.

Why You Need Coaching

You cannot learn some things without a coach's help, and you will learn others more quickly and easily with that help. You particularly need coaching if you want to play professionally or to move up to larger games. Without an outsider's help you cannot objectively assess yourself, nor can you develop your full potential.

Your coach does *not* have to play as well as you do. In fact, some of the best coaches are not great players. You can see this pattern in sports. Hardly any of the top football, baseball, or basketball coaches were great players. Many great players have so much natural talent that they don't know how to help less gifted people. You can certainly learn from a merely good player if he understands poker well and has certain other qualities.

A coach's most important contributions come from his detachment and objectivity. He can look at you with a more analytic pair of eyes. For example, Tiger Woods has a coach. Does his coach play as well as he does? Of course not—nobody does. Yet Tiger accepts his criticisms to improve his game. Many other professional athletes do the same.

Because professional athletes have coaches and many poker pros have stated that they work on their games with their friends, I think it is extremely foolish for losing and marginal players to do without a coach. And they refuse to get coaching for the same sorts of psychological reasons I have discussed so often, especially egotism.

These players may be too proud to accept help or criticism. Because poker is so macho, they just cannot accept that they need any help. They are going to do it their way regardless of the consequences. You may think you are so strong and talented that you do not need help, but you will do better if you get it.

Several of my friends are professional coaches,[1] and none of them just teaches poker theory or strategy. They all analyze their students' strengths and weaknesses and then provide the *specific* help that each one needs. The lessons they would give to you would be quite different from the ones they would give to me.

This book and *Your Worst Poker Enemy* are a series, and six of the series' major themes are directly related to the coaching issue:

Theme No. 1: You should think logically. A good coach must act logically, not by "feel." An intuitive coach may not analyze exactly where you are strong and weak. A logical coach will take your game apart, tell you what to do differently, and explain *why* you should change. In addition to various other benefits, he will help you to develop your own analytic and logical abilities. You will learn how to take your own game apart.

Theme No. 2: Most people do not objectively evaluate themselves and the competition. One of a coach's most important tasks is to help you to see yourself and the competition more objectively. I will be less biased than you are and probably has more information than you do. This analysis is particularly important if you want to move up. You cannot compare yourself to the players in the larger

---

1. Appendix F: "Recommended Coaches" contains the names and contact information for several coaches whom I wholeheartedly recommend.

game because you have never played there. A coach with the right experience can tell you how your skills compare to theirs and help you to get ready to play against them.

Theme No. 3: Unconscious and emotional forces affect nearly everything we do. These forces are extremely powerful, and because they are hidden you need help in identifying them and resisting their destructive effects. Some coaches lack the training to comment directly on these forces, but others will help you to see how they affect you.

For example, a coach may point out that you don't bluff enough, or are reluctant to check-raise. She may then say that those weaknesses suggest that you are uncomfortable with and inhibited about poker's deceptive and manipulative aspects.

Theme No. 4: You cannot learn much about yourself without good feedback. You certainly know that you can play badly and get good results and vice versa. You therefore need someone who can look objectively at your decisions and tell you what you are doing right and wrong.

Theme No. 5: You have to keep your mind open. To get the most benefit from coaching, apply the principles of "Getting Helpful Feedback," and these principles apply to developing all skills. That article was derived from the vast literature on performance appraisals. Workers have the same defensive reactions to criticisms as poker players.

We see the same reactions among writers. Every professional writer has at least one "coach," and most have several. We call them "editors." We may not like their criticisms, but we accept our need for them. We know that we have the same defensiveness, denial, and other weaknesses as poker players.

Let me use myself as an example. I swap editing with several poker writers, and I am especially good at reducing their wordiness. Despite that skill, my own writing is often much too wordy. Why? Because I fall in love with my own words and don't want to change them. I can't see them as "just words." They are *mine,* and I can't be objective about them. So my friends do for me what I do for them: clarify obscure points, cut out the unnecessary words, smooth the flow, and correct other errors. I swallow my foolish pride and try to keep my mind open when they criticize my work.

Many wannabe writers respond quite differently. They flatly refuse to accept criticism, or they get defensive about it. They essentially insist, "Don't touch my wonderful prose. I know what I want to say and how to say it." As I've told many of them, "If John Grisham and Tom Clancy can accept editing, maybe you should do the same."

If professional writers, athletes, and poker players believe that they need coaching, maybe you do too. I'm fortunate because I have several "coaches," friends who help me with both my playing and my writing. I want to express my gratitude to them. They are (in alphabetical order) Jim Brier, Richard Ember, Jerry Flannigan, Dave ("Cinch") Hench, Matt Lessinger, Mason Malmuth, Jan Siroky, David Sklansky, and Barry Tanenbaum. Without their help my playing and my writing would be a lot weaker.

Theme No. 6: Your coach or poker buddy should be brutally honest with you.

I urge you to find coaches or buddies who will tell you unpleasant truths. They don't have to be great writers or thinkers. They just have to be willing to look hard at your game and be brutally honest with you. They need to care enough about your development that they will tell you things you don't want to hear.

For example, I once told Barry Tanenbaum about a hand I thought I had played very well. He told me that I had made serious mistakes on the turn and river. Of course, I was briefly offended. At first, I wished he had said, "Al, you played it very well," but quickly realized I needed his bluntness.

If he had been more considerate about my feelings, I wouldn't have learned a damned thing. But he knew I needed that information. My other friends have done the same thing countless times, and I'm grateful for their honesty. That's what you need: somebody who will tell you the unpleasant truths you need to hear.

Apply active-learning principles *now* by taking a mini-quiz about what you have just read. Turn to Appendix E and answer those questions about this chapter.

Afterthought

Poker is an information-management game, and you cannot get good results without managing information well. Your critical tasks are as follows:

- Getting as much unbiased information as possible
- Giving away as little information as possible

The chapters in Part One have focused on ways to increase the flow of unbiased information. The second task is discussed in several other places.

Your biggest enemy is your own biases. They affect the information you notice and the way you remember, interpret, and use it. You may think you are unbiased, but *nobody* is, not even the most dedicated and objective scientist.

Because biases have such extremely destructive effects, scientific researchers use a large number of controls to reduce biases. And even then bias affects their results and conclusions. The history of science contains thousands of examples of researchers finding what they wanted to find because they bent some of the research rules.

Some mistakes were caused by deliberate "cheating," but more occurred just from carelessness. Most scientists do not want to deceive themselves, and they are generally more objective than poker players because:

- Most scientists sincerely want to know the truth. That's why they became scientists.

- They are trained to distrust their own desires.
- They are taught to use methods to make their data more objective.
- Their results, methods, and conclusions are intensely reviewed by outsiders before and after publication.

Yet mistakes in science frequently occur.

Most poker players are not remotely as objective as scientists, nor do they have any training to prevent the effects of biases. Unless you have scientific training, you probably don't know how to protect yourself from the effects of your biases.

Even if you are a scientist, you may not think like one about poker. You naturally want to believe that you play well, and luck has such huge short-term effects that you can easily deceive yourself about your abilities (and many other subjects).

These chapters have described some ways to reduce the effects of your biases. If you use active-learning principles, read and discuss the right books, take notes, get feedback from other people, and monitor yourself, you will slowly acquire the information you need about poker theory, other players, and yourself. But the critical step is opening your mind. You *must* continually battle your own biases, continually question your conclusions, and continually ask yourself: *Am I accurately interpreting the evidence or distorting it to make myself feel better?*

PART TWO

Increasing Your Edge

Introduction

Most poker writers try to increase your edge by improving your strategic decisions. Although these decisions are extremely important, I will not focus on them. You can get much better advice from others. These chapters focus on increasing your *psychological* edge by confusing people, exploiting the newbies' bad play, isolating weak players, putting opponents on tilt, and utilizing similar ploys.

We'll start with "Creating False First Impressions" because they can have large, immediate effects. People react not to who and what you are, but to what they *think* you are. If you can create the right false impression, they will make many costly mistakes.

The effects of ruthlessness are discussed in "Would You Bust Your Own Grandmother?" Jack Straus, a Poker Hall of Famer, once said he would bust her, and many players admire and copy him. If you are that ruthless, you have a huge competitive edge against more tenderhearted people. Conversely, if you are softhearted, people like that have a huge edge over you.

We have recently had a massive influx of new and terrible players. They are giving away their money, and "Beating the Newbies" tells you how to get your share of it.

"Isolating 'Idiots'" discusses a common tendency. Many players like to isolate "idiots," but they often mislabel people. Some people are much smarter than they look, perhaps even smarter than you are. If you overplay your cards to isolate them, you may *decrease* your edge or even become an underdog. Conversely, isolating the right players in the right way can greatly increase your profits.

Rushes are one of poker's great experiences, and—partly because they occur so rarely—you may not know how to exploit them. You may also become intimidated or ineffective when other players go on a rush. When someone is on a rush, many players seem to believe that the laws of probability have been suspended. This delusion can create many profitable opportunities. "Playing the Rush" recommends ways to get the most value from your own rushes. "Defending Against the Rush" shows you how to profit from other people's rushes.

"Creating Tilt" and "Exploiting Tilt" are the final subjects, because if you can put someone on tilt and exploit it well you can make a lot of money. Tilted players often throw their money away, and some kinds of tilt are contagious. When someone is playing crazily, other opponents may get off balance and play stupidly. Your biggest problem is keeping your head when other people are losing theirs.

Although these tactics will increase their expected value, relatively few people use them effectively, and some people won't even try them. They may dislike feeling "phony" or regard some ploys as improper or unethical. These inhibitions obviously reduce their ability to gain various psychological edges. Their reluctance to take profitable actions clearly supports the point made earlier that many people don't try to maximize their profits.

Be honest with yourself. To maximize your profits, take the actions recommended here, plus many others. If you are not willing to do some of these things, ask why and accept the costs of your inhibitions. You need to understand and work within all of your limitations, including your skills, motives, and values.

Creating False First Impressions

Your opponents react not to what you are, but to what they *think* you are, and their first impressions have a huge impact on your image and the way they process later information. They will overemphasize information that fits their first impressions and ignore or minimize conflicting data.[1] When playing with strangers, it often pays to create a false first impression.

General Principles

As the dandruff shampoo ads put it, "You never get a second chance to make a first impression." Start with highly visible actions that color everything your opponents will see later. Straddles are very visible, especially the first few times you are under the gun. Raises, especially check-raises, are much more visible than calls, and checks and folds are almost invisible. If you straddle at your first opportunity, reraise with a pair of deuces, isolate someone who raised with ace-king, and win, many people will remember it long after forgetting that you folded most hands.

Although the "wild man" image is easy to create, it may not be the most profitable one. It gets you a lot of action on your big hands but reduces your chances of bluffing. Creating a false tight-passive image takes longer and is much harder to do, but in some games it can be much more profitable. Your bluffs will succeed more often, winning whole pots.

1. The ways that first impressions distort thinking were discussed on pages 41–49.

Creating that image is harder because players don't pay much attention to people who fold. You could call attention to your tightness by saying, "I haven't had a hand worth playing since I sat down." You could even fold hands "angrily" and ask, "When will I get something worth playing?"

Many people—especially in smaller games—pay more attention to how you look and sound than to how you play, and even good players can be affected by these signals. *Create a false image by your looks, clothes, voice, words, and general "attitude."*

If you are young; have green hair, three earrings, and a nose ring; seem drunk; and raise crazily your first few hands, some players may label you "Wild Kid," and the weaker players may never notice that your subsequent play is very solid. If you are an older woman who dresses conservatively, speaks rarely and softly, plays hardly any hands, and almost never raises, some players may label you "Timid Old Lady" and let you win bluff after bluff.

Of course, the first impression has to be *credible.* That "Wild Kid" and "Timid Old Lady" couldn't swap images. *Your appearance and image must have consistency.* Otherwise, players will see right through your act, realize you are deceptive, and watch you closely, which is exactly what you don't want them to do.

You also need consistency between your early and later actions. Despite first impressions, people are not blind or stupid. If the disparity between your early and later play is too great, the observant and dangerous players will see that you were faking it.

Your image also must fit your strategic objectives. Because many experts have analyzed the effects of various images, I won't discuss the details. I'll just make the obvious point that there are always trade-offs. The image that helps you get a lot of action will make it harder to bluff and vice versa. If you don't clearly understand your own objectives and ensure that your image fits them, you may undermine your overall strategy.

Don't Overpay for Your Advertising

Well-run businesses base their advertising budgets on cost-benefit analyses, and you should do the same. If you spend too much, or the benefits are too slight, you will make a bad investment. If you spend fifteen big bets on advertising, you probably can't get it back. If you will play only half an hour, don't spend *anything* on ads, because you won't have time to recover your costs.

Also consider your opposition. Weak players are much easier to deceive than good ones. Since strong ones will study the way you play, don't spend much on advertising against them.

Additionally, consider how rapidly the players turn over. The more rapidly they turn over, the less you will gain, because newcomers won't know what you have done to create a false impression.

Tournaments are a special case. Because the stakes go up, you can get a great cost-benefit ratio *if you will be playing against the same players.* David Sklansky addressed this issue in *Tournament Poker for Advanced Players:* "If it looks like your table will break up soon . . . make no 'advertising' plays, since you will probably not have time to reap the benefits. . . . If you will have to play at a table for a long time, setting up plays for the future [becomes] even more important than in regular side games."[2]

Creating False Impressions Online

Because nobody can see you when you are online, you can pretend to be almost anyone: a huge, aggressive young man with a beard and tattoos can get away with calling himself "Grandma Susie." Some men have gotten great results by using women's names and pictures. They say that other men underestimate their skills or make incorrect assumptions about their styles.

2. David Sklansky, *Tournament Poker for Advanced Players* (Henderson, NV: (Two Plus Two Publishing, 2002), 55.

One wrote: "Many men will give you lots of action just to play in hands with you if you are willing to respond to their almost inevitable flirting. And the non-flirtatious men often go into a knight-in-shining-armor mode and stick up for you. . . . They seem to fall all over themselves to lose to you, help you, offer advice, provide info about themselves and their playing styles, and so on."

Final Remarks

In his ancient classic *The Art of War,* Sun Tzu wrote: "All war is based on deception," and several writers have made the same point about poker. Without deception, poker cannot exist. If we played with our cards faceup, the game would fall apart. Because we don't know each other's cards, and we misunderstand how others play, we make many mistakes.

First impressions are particularly important because they distort the way nearly everyone processes later information. You therefore have two critically important tasks:

1. Understand how you are biased by first impressions and do whatever you can to reduce these biases.
2. Create first impressions that confuse your opponents, and then reinforce these false first impressions to gain an edge over them.

It isn't easy to think or act this way. You may be much more comfortable when yielding to your biases or acting naturally, but *it is natural to lose.* In fact, most cardroom players are long-term losers. If you want to be a winner, you have to do the unnatural things that winners do.

Apply active-learning principles *now* by taking a mini-quiz about what you have just read. Turn to Appendix E and answer those questions about this chapter.

Would You Bust Your Own Grandmother?

Jack Straus, a poker immortal, once said, "I'd bust my own grand-mother if she played poker with me." Vince Lombardi, the great foot-ball coach, expressed a similar attitude: "Winning isn't everything; it's the only thing." Their intense, ruthless competitiveness helped them to enter their respective Halls of Fame, but it created many other prob-lems.

Neither of them was normal, pleasant, or balanced, at least not at a poker or football game. Normal people are not willing to bust their own grandmothers, nor do they regard winning as the only thing. Un-fortunately, very few pleasant, balanced people get into the Halls of Fame—not for poker, football, or anything else.

From a lifestyle or mental health perspective, being balanced is highly desirable, but the ruthless competitors usually win. Many poker winners and most champions have read and agreed with Straus's position. In fact, he is respected, not just for his success, but also for his ruthlessness.

Tournament rules support his position, and the opposite tendency, soft-playing, is clearly forbidden: "The general consensus is, and most rulebooks dictate, that soft-playing in tournaments is *not* allowed, and any occurrences of it are subject to penalties and punishment up to disqualification."[1] This rule is necessary because certain types of soft-playing are a form of collusion that creates an unfair advantage over the other players.

Despite this rule (which is less strictly enforced in cash games),

1. Mike O'Malley, "Soft-Playing," *Card Player,* July 16, 2004.

many people would not bust their grandmother. I am using "bust" in the same sense that I believe Jack Straus meant: It does not mean taking her last chips in a $5 buy-in tournament; it means taking every penny you can get.

Words Versus Actions

Because poker players value machismo, some people will claim that they would bust their grandmother or anyone else, but they don't really mean it. Some players—including outwardly macho ones—take more tenderhearted actions than just refusing to bust their own grandmother.

For example, they may check down the nuts or suggest that a drunk or beginner go home. A friend said that a blackjack player sat down in his $15–$30 game and played very stupidly. A solid player advised him to quit because she didn't feel good taking his money. A couple of other players echoed her sentiment. My friend said, "I really didn't care one way or the other. My attitude was that he's going to lose it at blackjack; he might as well lose it to us." But she insisted it wasn't right, and they gave up a chance for some easy money.

Most professionals would bust that fish, but they occasionally show their "softer side." For example, at the final table of the 1999 Tournament of Champions, Louis Asmo had pocket aces and made a huge pre-flop raise. David Chiu thought for a long time before showing his kings and folding. He was certainly wondering whether he had made the right play, and that distraction could have damaged his concentration.

Louis then showed his hand, relieving David's tensions and doubts. Instead of wondering whether he had made a big mistake, he learned that he had made a great play. It built his confidence and removed the distraction, which helped him to win the tournament. Louis's gesture was a long way from the "win at all costs" mentality that many professionals endorse, and it may have cost him thousands

of dollars. In other words, some people—even excellent professionals—talk a more ruthless game than they play.[2]

Whom Would You Bust?

Many players won't bust a wide variety of people. For example, a
long thread on an Internet forum was titled "Just witnessed the worst
part of poker." The poster reported watching a heads-up match in
which one player beat another for about $90,000. He was appalled be-
cause the winner beat the loser "out of **everything**. . . . You took everything, he has nothing left to live for."

He believed (but others disagreed) that the loser "is a gambling ad-
dict who really didn't know what he was doing." This series of posts
("thread") debated whether it is morally acceptable to take advantage
of other players' psychological weaknesses such as a gambling addiction. Other threads have discussed the morality of busting drunks,
mentally retarded people, close friends, beginners, and so on. Many
people do not regard winning as supremely important.

The Hard-Liners' Position

Some people regard Straus's position as an "ethical imperative" and
condemn the opposite tendency, soft-playing anyone, whether it occurs
in a tournament or cash game. They insist that "there are no friends at the
poker table," that you should play as hard as possible, not just to increase
your profits, but to support poker's "all against all" competitive ethos.

For example, Doyle Brunson wrote:

The correct attitude is that folks play poker because the game ap-
peals to them. They like the blend of luck and strategy and are will-

2. Several members of our discussion group—including two World Series of Poker
    bracelet holders—told us that showing his aces was an extremely stupid mistake.

ing to compete for money. To do this, you need opponents, *real* opponents who are as intent on beating you as you are on destroying them.

By providing good competition, players are celebrating the spirit of poker. Soft play runs contrary to the nature of the game. Those who don't understand the simplicity of that statement should quit playing until they do.[3]

Note his use of "correct attitude" and "destroying" and his insistence that people who don't agree with him should quit playing. He clearly believes that the *only* correct motivation is ruthless competitiveness. Many people share his narrow view of motivation, but many others disagree. In fact, people play poker for a wide variety of reasons, and these other motives may be more important to them than winning.

To committed competitors, it is the act of winning, not its extrinsic rewards, that matters. For example, Dana Smith states, "The monetary rewards are like rivers—they flow through life—whereas winning has a sustaining effect on your being."[4] Nolan Dalla expressed the same sentiment in somewhat different words: "Every enduring poker champion . . . has an insatiable desire to win."[5]

All these quotations show that certain people—especially champions—are not at all normal or balanced while playing. Normal people do not have insatiable needs, nor do they want to destroy people.

The Soft-Liners' Position

Several live and online discussions indicate that many people are willing to lose money by being gentle. They will not bust their grand-

---

3. Doyle Brunson, *According to Doyle,* (New York: Lyle Stuart, 1984), 21–22.

4. Dana Smith, "Mickey Appleman: The Epitome of Intelligent Judgment Combined with Gambling Flair," *Card Player,* December 22, 2000.

5. Nolan Dalla, "Once Upon a Time in America: The John Bonetti Story," *Card Player,* May 1, 1998.

mother and various other people such as family members, close friends, beginners, helpless drunks, gambling addicts, and visually impaired people. Their reasons for sacrificing profits are rarely considered because many poker writers seem to assume that everyone wants (or should want) to maximize their profits.

Family Feelings

Jack Straus used colorful language to emphasize his point: *Everybody* should be attacked ruthlessly. He chose his grandmother as a symbol because grandmothers are so respected, and we are taught from birth to be nice to them. Many people, probably most, are *not* willing to bust their grandmother or other close relatives. They value their families much more than profits or poker's ruthlessly competitive ethos.

Despite recognizing the legitimacy of Straus's position, I believe that openly supporting it is bad for poker's image. Poker is a macho and predatory game, but many, many people do not think that winning is more important than family loyalty. Such ultra-macho statements give ammunition to the extremists who want to outlaw or restrict our game, and they certainly slow down our quest for respectability.

Some poker writers seem oblivious to the importance of gaining respectability. Congress passed and President Bush signed into law a bill that has nearly destroyed online poker in America. Every so often the police raid a poker game and arrest everybody. Some very powerful people *hate* our game, and they will use every weapon we give them to harm it. If we insist that we must be ruthless, we give them a weapon that they will certainly use against us. For example, I can easily visualize people quoting Straus during debates—including ones in congress: "Do you want our children learning that they should bust their own grandmother? We must protect them from this disgusting game."

Poker's negative image affects most of us. Many poker professionals wish their families and friends understood and valued their profession. Some recreational players dislike the way their friends and family regard poker. We want corporations to sponsor tournaments, but most of them won't do it as long as the public sees us so negatively. Executives are nearly obsessed with their corporations' images, and they won't risk damaging them by associating with a game that demands such ruthlessness. We all gain if poker becomes more respectable, but it won't happen as long as some people insist that the *only* way to play poker is to be completely ruthless.

Guilt, Shame, and Ethical Inhibitions

Some people have stated that they would feel guilty or ashamed if they acted too ruthlessly, especially against friends or people who cannot protect themselves. They don't want to be predators who prey on the weak. The fact that poker *is* a predatory game is less important to them than the way they feel.

The strength of these feelings often depends on the closeness of the relationship and the causes for helplessness. The closer people are and the less control they have over their vulnerability, the more inhibited some players feel about busting them.

Many people are concerned about "fairness," which depends on how responsible others are for their weaknesses. For example, they may think it is unfair to exploit someone who clearly does not understand what is happening because of inexperience, mental retardation, or senility.

A beginner could learn to play, but mentally challenged people are almost helpless; so are visually impaired people who cannot see the cards clearly. People with vision or mental problems probably should not play, but some people are still reluctant to take advantage of them.

Hardly anyone feels inhibited about exploiting drunks because they choose to drink too much. Therefore, most people would gladly take a drunk's last chips and hope he bought more, but some of them would soft-play beginners or mentally/visually impaired people or urge them to leave the game.

Attitudes toward compulsive gamblers are somewhere in the middle. People would be harder on them than on beginners and mentally/visually impaired people, but not as tough as they would be on drunks. First, you cannot be sure that someone is a compulsive gambler. Second, many people regard compulsive gamblers as responsible for their addiction.

Dr. Dan Kessler, a clinical psychologist, presented a more nuanced position; "If a compulsive gambler were at my table, I'd take every cent he had and tell him how to get to the ATM machine. But, if he consulted me professionally, I would try to help him with his addiction, and I would certainly recommend that he quit playing poker."

Some people are much more willing to bust college students than older people—especially ones who remind them of their own parents or grandparents. Of course, the opposite pattern also occurs: some people are gentler toward young people than older ones.

Inhibitions also depend on economic perceptions. Some people will gladly bust a wealthy person, but be softer on a working-class one. They don't want to deprive the worker's family but believe that the wealthy person can afford the loss.

Social Motives

Many people play poker to socialize, especially in small games. Playing poker is just a pleasant way to spend a few hours, have a few laughs, and perhaps take some drinks. If they win, great. If they lose but have a good time, they don't really care. Trying to bust others could destroy this social atmosphere.

These players take many negative expected value actions such as refusing to check-raise and not betting on the river. They care more about preserving the "party" atmosphere than winning.

Sex

Many men won't bust a woman, especially a pretty one. Some women take advantage of this attitude by flirting or appearing weak and vulnerable. A few males use female handles online to create that image and reaction. A bearded fifty-year-old man may call himself "Jeanie23" to create a young woman's image, and some men will soft-play him.

Although women are generally less ruthless, they are less likely to change their style to please a man. First, there are so many male players that soft-playing all of them would drastically harm a woman's results. Second, women are less easily manipulated by sex than men.

Lack of Challenge

Many players value the kick of outsmarting good players more than the money they can win from bad ones. They may play their best against tough players, but take it easy on weaker ones. They may also play in tougher games than they can handle. For example, some good players lose a bundle in Las Vegas but come back again and again. They want to test themselves against stronger players, even if it costs them a lot of money.

They want to get their competitive juices flowing, and beating weak players doesn't do it. In fact, if it's too easy to win, the game may be no fun at all. Busting a weak player is like shooting fish in a barrel. Unless you're very hungry, why bother?

Andy Beale is the most spectacular example of someone with this extremely destructive desire to challenge the best. He lost millions of dollars playing against the world's best players. There are conflicting stories about his total losses. Some estimates are as high as $50 million, while others are much lower. He almost certainly lost much more than $20 million. In addition to challenging the world's best players, he gave them two enormous advantages:

1. He let them have the "home court advantage" by playing in Las Vegas.
2. He challenged a *team* of players. They switched players when someone got tired or wasn't playing well, and they compared notes to develop the optimal strategy.

The story of Andy's incredible foolishness can be found on pages 162–163 of *Your Worst Poker Enemy*. If you have a strong desire to challenge superior players, I urge you to read it. You won't lose $20 million, but you can easily lose a lot more than you can afford.

Balanced People Have a Competitive Liability

Unless there are large differences in talent, the more ruthless competitor has a *huge* edge. For example, if we are equally talented and I'm playing tennis for fun but you're playing to win, you're going to beat me. You'll work harder to develop your skills, study my game, and attack my weaknesses. I won't run for some of your shots, but you'll try to return every one of mine, even if you're exhausted.

Exactly the same principle applies to poker. Ruthless competitors work harder, study more, focus better, and do whatever else it takes to gain every possible edge. Balanced people want to win, but it is not an insatiable need. They want to play, not work. They take foolish chances, relax, chat with each other, think about other things, and generally treat poker as a game. When they play against ruthless competitors, they usually lose.

As I wrote in *Your Worst Poker Enemy,* some people think poker is a macho game, but it "is actually a predatory game, and *machismo violates the fundamental law of all predators: Attack the weakest prey.*"[6] When you let other motives inhibit you from attacking the weak, you *must* reduce your long-term profits.

You therefore have to decide how important winning is to you. You simply cannot have balanced motives and be a winner unless you play against only normal people or are *much* more talented than your competition. *If you are not driven to win and play against equally talented but much more ruthless competitors, you are going to lose.*

6. Alan N. Schoonmaker, *Your Worst Poker Enemy.*

You Should Understand *Everyone's* Position

Because nobody has polled a representative sample of poker players, I cannot say how many people agree with each of the positions we have discussed. However, I am sure that a *lot* of people would not bust their grandmother and various other people.

I also believe that poker players and writers should not ignore these noncompetitive motives. No matter what anyone says, *most* people are not totally committed to maximizing their profits. Perhaps they should be, perhaps not, but we must deal with people as they are, not as we think they should be.

To get the largest benefits—both financial and nonfinancial—from poker, you must set aside preconceptions about what people should do. Instead, try to understand

- Your own motives, inhibitions, and attitudes
- The other players' motives, inhibitions, and attitudes

Your own drives can create competitive advantages or disadvantages, and you *must* understand them. Otherwise, you probably cannot reach your real goals.

Other people's drives dramatically affect the way they play and the optimal strategy to use against them. If you foolishly assume that others have the same motives, inhibitions, and attitudes that you have, you will certainly make many avoidable mistakes.

Final Remarks

People can make good arguments for either of the following positions:

- You should bust *anyone*.
- You should not bust certain kinds of people.

Who is right? I don't know, and neither do you, but insisting that there is only one correct way to think and act is arrogant nonsense. The hard-liners' position is right for them because it matches their personal values and beliefs, but they are flat wrong when they insist that it is the only way to play.

I do, however, agree that colluding to soft-play someone is unethical because it creates an unfair advantage. As is so often the case, the critical question is: What are people's intentions? If they are soft-playing to gain an edge against other players, it's clearly wrong. If they do it because they don't want to hurt people, it may or may not be acceptable.

You should act in ways that fit your own values. Don't let anyone tell you: *My way is the only way.* If you sincerely believe that poker should be a take-no-prisoners war, don't let anyone lay a guilt trip on you. Do whatever the rules allow to maximize your profits.

If you value other things more than winning, or if you would feel guilty or ashamed if you were too ruthless toward certain people, don't let others force their views on you. You will encounter this sort of rigidity on many poker issues. Good poker players encourage flexibility about strategy. Their answer to most strategic questions is: "It depends on the situation." But, when it comes to ethical and motivational issues, far too many of them are absolutists. They insist that there is only one legitimate position—theirs.

Nonsense! On this and many other issues, there are at least two legitimate positions. If you are not willing to bust your grandmother, you are not a wimp or a cheater. You just have different motives and values. Those differences will cost you chips, but you may feel that maximizing your profits is not the only legitimate objective.

The important points are to understand clearly *why* you will or will not bust someone and then to make a reasoned decision. When it comes to being ruthless (or anything else), don't be afraid to "march to the beat of your own drummer."

Apply active-learning principles *now* by taking a mini-quiz about what you have just read. Turn to Appendix E and answer those questions about this chapter.

Beating the Newbies

Never before have there been so many new players. Many of them play poker, not because they really like it or have the right skills and personality traits, but because it is so fashionable. It's "in," and they want to jump on the bandwagon.

Even though they are literally giving away their money, many fairly competent players—and more than a few experts—have reacted foolishly to this huge influx. Instead of welcoming the newbies with open arms and adjusting their play, they either get nasty and drive the newbies away or refuse to adjust their play to take full advantage of the newbies' weaknesses.

Most newbies have always played badly, because it takes time to learn how to play well, but today's crop is exceptionally weak. Many of them learned how to play by watching TV, and most of the lessons were wrong. They have seen unknown players (Robert Varkonyi, Chris Moneymaker, Greg Raymer, Joseph Hachem, and Jamie Gold) win five consecutive World Series Championships, and on the final hand two of them had ridiculously bad cards:

- Chris Moneymaker won in 2003 with five-four offsuit.
- Joseph Hachem won in 2005 with seven-three offsuit.

They also saw that Robert Varkonyi won the championship with queen-ten, a mediocre hand, and that he knocked out two other players with the same hand. They have seen many top pros make huge bluffs with utter trash, and others win enormous pots or even championships by catching miracle cards. For example, Chris Ferguson won the World Series Championship in 2001 by catching a three-outer on the river. After seeing or hearing about such moves, newbies naturally conclude that anyone—including them—can win, and they don't have to wait for good cards or play them sensibly. If they just get lucky, they can win with any two cards.

They don't know that the plays they see on TV are carefully selected for their dramatic value. The routine plays—such as folding trash—are essential for long-term success, but they don't get shown. In addition, plays that make sense in shorthanded no-limit final tables with huge blinds are utterly ridiculous when playing limit poker at a full table.

Some TV shows have warnings that amateurs should not try the wild stunts that professionals do on skateboards and motorcycles; the poker shows should have similar warnings about the wild moves they broadcast. The great players can make them when the conditions are right, but amateurs—especially newbies—should not try them.

There have always been clueless players and juicy games, but there have never been so many of them. Although they have made poker more profitable for skilled players, some of these skilled players are extremely frustrated. For example, you have probably heard far too many bad-beat stories because terrible players and extremely loose games naturally produce horrendous beats. There is also continual grumbling that the newbies act out of turn, talk too much, play too slowly, and so on.

Don't Chase Them Away!

Although the newbies have dramatically increased almost every competent player's profits, a lot of good players have viciously criticized them for playing foolishly. For example, a friend was beaten by someone who cold-called a raise on the flop with only a backdoor-flush draw. He went ballistic, calling the other player "unconscious" and storming out of the game. That same week I pulled aside two other semi-pros to tell them to stop berating weak players. One even offered to bet that a terrible player would lose his substantial stack in two hours! His attack was inexcusable.

Countless writers have stated that we should never criticize mistakes because they are our *primary* source of profits. You may believe that brilliant plays are the key to your success, but your opponents' mistakes add much more to your bottom line, and the newbies make lots of mistakes. Every time someone plays trash or calls a raise with a two-outer or makes any negative expected value (EV) play, he increases your EV and long-term profits.

So let this player enjoy the kick he gets when his mistakes win a pot. You're just loaning him the money, and he'll pay it back with usurious interest. I really shouldn't have to repeat these points, but I've never seen so many competent players bitterly assault weak players.

Expect Bigger Profits, but Larger Swings

Loose players (especially aggressive ones) lose lots of money, while increasing your profits and variance. You will win fewer pots, but they will be much bigger. It is simple mathematics: The more players in a pot, the lower your chances of winning it and the better hand you need to win. But, when you do win, the pots can be huge, more than enough to compensate you for your losses and frustration.

With so many loose, clueless players in your game, your win rate should increase, but your standard deviation may increase even more. You may therefore need a much bigger bankroll. If it is just barely large enough for your normal limits, you may have to move down. Of course, you don't want to do it, especially when the games are so soft, but it may be necessary. If you get sent to the rail, you can't make any money.

Change Your Game Plan

Because the games are changing, your strategy also must change. Do not insist on playing the way that works with competent players. Recognize a simple truth: "Your opponents' mistakes create the potential for more profit, but if you play improperly, you may not take advantage of it. *If you do not win in the long run, it is not because your opponents are making too many mistakes; it is because you are.*"[1]

That quotation was from a book about small stakes hold'em, but thousands of newbies are making the same sorts of mistakes in middle- and even big-limit games, and some of the new no-limit players are incredibly bad.

Of course, there always have been terrible players, and Sklansky, Malmuth, Miller, I, and many others have suggested adjustments. Here is a summary of the major adjustments, but you should also read the suggested pages in our books.[2]

Against All Loose Players, Especially Newbies

Most newbies are too loose, but they vary greatly on aggression. Against all loose players, you should make the following changes in your game plan:

- *Make winning the pot your first priority.* In loose games, the pots quickly become so large that winning them must take priority over making them still larger (unless you have a monster hand).

- *Bluff and steal blinds much less frequently.* This point is obvious, yet it is often ignored. Because loose players are going to call you with almost anything, it is silly to bluff and steal blinds. I vividly recall a television interview with Annie Duke, one of the world's most famous women players. When she was knocked out of the World Series Championship, she

---

1. Ed Miller, David Sklansky, and Mason Malmuth, *Small Stakes Hold'em: Winning Big with Expert Play* (Henderson, NV: Two Plus Two, 2004), 18.

2. See pages 151–181 of *Hold'em Poker for Advanced Players: 21st Century Edition* (Henderson, NV: Two Plus Two, 1998), all of *Small Stakes Hold'em: Winning Big with Expert Play* (Henderson, NV: Two Plus Two, 2005), and pages 119–134 and 165–183 of my *The Psychology of Poker* (Henderson, NV: Two Plus Two, 2000).

whined about the terrible player who called her bluff with an extremely weak hand. She blamed him even though *she* had made a huge mistake. She should have known better than to bluff that player. Don't follow in her footsteps. Save your bluffs for the right players.

- *Don't get fancy.* Fancy plays cannot work because newbies are so oblivious that they don't know what you are doing, nor do they react the way you expect. Play solid, straightforward, unimaginative poker.

- *Accept that high cards and big pairs go way down in value and drawing hands go way up.* The more players who enter a pot, the less chance you have to win with top pair, top kicker, and similar hands. Somebody will draw out on you *most* of the time. If you are on the button against seven opponents, jack-ten suited may be a better hand than ace-king offsuit.

Against Loose-Aggressive Players

When many players are both loose and aggressive, the game is the most volatile. You can win or lose more money than in any other type of game, and the emotional swings can be as bad as the financial ones. When you win, you may feel euphoric and invincible. When you lose, you may feel so frustrated that you go on tilt and just give away your money. To beat these games you *must* take several steps:

- *Tighten up.* When you see huge pots won with trash, you may want to jump in with weaker hands than usual, but it is exactly the wrong thing to do. It is going to cost you lots of money to see the flop and play out the hand. Don't start without good cards.

- *Raise and reraise to isolate the wildest players.* Countless pots have been lost by people who did not play aggressively enough. They often insist that "nothing would force out those idiots," and they are right about many players. But *some* of them will fold, and *some* of them would have drawn out on you. If that extra raise wins you only one big pot a night, it is more than justified.

- *Check-raise more often.* This is much less risky than usual because loose-aggressive players (LAPs) will usually bet rather than check behind you. A check-raise increases the size of the pot and can knock out some players, reducing the risk of drawouts.

- *Invite them to bluff.* LAPs love to bluff. In fact, they often get a bigger kick from a successful bluff than from winning with the best hand. If you suspect they are weak, check, let them bluff, and then snap them off.

- *Slow-play very big hands.* LAPs will get much better action than you do, so let them build the pot, and then raise them on the river.

Against Loose-Passive Players

Loose-passive players (LPPs) are almost everyone's ideal opponents, because they give too much action with weak hands, but don't get much action with strong ones. If you can't beat LPPs, don't blame them for drawing out on you; take up chess.

I am *not* kidding. I can't count the number of allegedly competent players who have whined bitterly about people who just call, call, call. They are the weakest players. If you can't beat them, poker is not the right game for you. Make the following adjustments.

- *Play more hands than usual, especially draws.* Because nearly everyone will call and hardly anyone will raise, you can see the flop in hold'em or fourth street in stud quite cheaply. If you hit, you may win a huge pot. If not, all you have lost is one small bet.

- *Frequently bet or raise to increase the size of the pot, not to protect your hand.* The inescapable fact is that you often can't protect it. Lots of LPPs will call two bets almost as often as they will call one. However, because these loose calls have a negative EV, they increase your profits.

- *Bet or raise with strong draws.* Because the odds against making your hand are better than the odds you will get from all the callers, it pays to build the pot.

- *If you bet or raise with a draw on the flop and then get a free card on the turn, take it.* Barry Tanenbaum, my colleague at *Card Player,* often makes this point. Far too many players bet the turn hoping that everyone will fold. Since LPPs will call, why bet? If you raised on the flop with a good draw, you had a positive EV. More people will call than the odds against making your hand. With only one card to come, a called bet usually has a negative EV, so don't make it.

I could go on and on, but the principles are clear. You should recognize that the massive influx of newbies will increase both your variance and your frustration, but it can increase your profits even more. Since poker is a game, not a job, but it is ultimately about winning money, relax, enjoy it, don't criticize, and adjust your game plan.

Apply active-learning principles *now* by taking a mini-quiz about what you have just read. Turn to Appendix E and answer those questions about this chapter.

Isolating "Idiots"

Because some people regard anyone who plays weak cards as an "idiot," they greatly overplay their own cards to isolate them. Sometimes that strategy works, but it can easily backfire. When it does, they may bitterly complain about their luck and never realize that both their assessment of the other player and their strategy were wrong.

They may think, "He must be an idiot to play such junk. Since I am a better player, my cards are probably better than his, and I can outplay him. So I'll raise or three-bet with much weaker hands than normal to get heads-up with him." Isolating weak players is often correct, but the timing—like most other strategic decisions—depends on the situation. The critical question is: What *kind* of idiot is he?

Types of Idiots

Don't assume that someone is an idiot just because he plays a *few* bad hands. It is a natural mistake because those two cards are so easy to evaluate, and we remember them long afterward, especially when the "idiot" draws out on us. Let's say you have

and three-bet an "idiot" who raised with

The flop is

and the turn is

and he check-raises on the turn and bets the river. You may remember it for a long, long time. In fact, it is such a memorable hand that you may not even notice that he plays like that only once or twice a night. If he plays or raises almost every hand, he *is* an idiot, but don't make that judgment on just a few hands.

The number of hands played and the way he acts after the flop are much harder to see and remember than those first two cards. Some of the world's greatest players occasionally play hands that you and I would automatically fold. I have never played with Layne Flack, Daniel Negreanu, or Carlos Mortensen, but I have seen them play or raise with some very weak hands, and they are among the world's best tournament players. Of course, tournaments are different from ring games, but it is easier to make the point with famous names.

Phil Hellmuth wrote that Layne "spots the field by drinking a couple of six-packs of beer while he plays" and that he called a bet and a raise with jack-seven suited.[1] Many of us would look down on anyone who drinks heavily and plays those cards. Is Layne Flack an idiot? If he is, I'd like to be one too.

To get an accurate evaluation of various players you must look beyond a few of their starting hands. The critical issues are

- The *number* of hands played
- How well someone plays after the flop

1. Phil Hellmuth, "The Amazing Layne Flack," *Card Player,* January 1, 2003.

If you are playing with an "idiot" and he plays or raises nearly every hand, is straightforward and easily read, and will call to the river, isolate him and take his money. If he plays only a few bad hands, will fold if his cards have not improved by the turn (as many apparent idiots will do), is deceptive, and will check-raise bluff and make other moves, he may beat you up.

Generally, you should *not* isolate these players, especially if you have to overplay your hand to do it. With them you may want to see how the hand develops before attacking, and you may also want the protection that comes from multi-way action. *Sklansky on Poker* states that with multi-way action "the pot becomes protected on the last round. . . . It is extremely unlikely that anyone will try to steal the pot from three or more opponents."[2]

Even Idiots Get Good Hands

Saying that idiots get good hands should not be necessary, but an enormous amount of money has been lost by people who have ignored this point. They grossly overplay a good, but not great hand such as pocket tens and then bitterly complain, "I'm so unlucky. That idiot raised with

 and

just a little while ago, but, when I finally get against him, he's got pocket jacks." They believe that it isn't their fault that they lost several unnecessary bets. It's just bad luck. Nonsense! They foolishly assumed he was playing trash.

---

2. *Sklansky on Poker* (Henderson, NV: Two Plus Two Publishing, 1994), 55.

Idiots May Have the Information Edge

Because you're a good player, the "idiot" may know much more about your cards than you know about his. You won't play trash, but he'll play almost anything. After the flop, when the real money gets bet, he can have a huge information edge. Let's say he raised; you three-bet with

and everyone folded. The flop was

He *knows* it didn't hit you, but you have no idea whether it helped him. He could have one pair, two pair, a set, or even a straight. If he bets or check-raises on the flop, turn, or river, what do you do? Is he being an "idiot" and betting on nothing? Or is he *outplaying* you?

You may not want to admit that he can outplay you, but it could be true. If he is tricky, the advantage you got from starting with better cards will often become zero or negative. You can't get away from hands cheaply, but he can fold quite easily after the flop when the bigger bets are made.

Better Cards Do *Not* Give That Large an Edge

Countless players have whined about their "terrible luck" because they started with, say,

and lost to someone with

or similar garbage. A few matchups do give you a huge edge, but many of them—such as this one—give you an edge of less than two to one, with all seven cards. This edge will hold up monetarily only if there are no more bets. Because your opponent has the information edge, he will frequently overcome your original advantage.

It is much easier for him to get away from his hand than it is for you. Nobody likes to fold to an "idiot" who may be bluffing. Worse still, he can dump his hand if the flop comes

but what will you do with your

if the flop comes

You probably think you are way ahead, but you are actually way behind. If he folds on the flop or turn when you have got him beaten but forces you to pay off three or more big bets after the flop when he wins, who will get the money? You will win many small pots but lose some big ones. You probably still have an edge, but it is much smaller than you think.

When You Are Playing No-Limit Hold'em

Mistakenly believing that someone is an idiot is particularly common among people who have just switched from limit to no-limit hold'em (NL). When I first published this article, I played only limit poker. When I started to play NL, I made that mistake again and again.

Carefully selecting the hands to play pre-flop is critically important in limit. If someone plays too many weak hands in a limit game, he *is* an idiot because his results depend on *how often* he wins the pot. Playing weak cards gives the opposition a huge head start in a series of short races. No matter how well he plays post-flop, he cannot catch up often enough to beat the game.

But NL results depend primarily on a few large pots. If he wins only one or two of them, he can end up a big winner. Bluffing is also much more important. And someone who plays weak hands well is *much* more likely to bluff or bust you than vice versa.[3]

David Sklansky created the first and most widely used chart of the hands to play pre-flop in limit hold'em, but he flatly rejected that formulaic approach in *No Limit Hold'em: Theory and Practice:* "In deep stack no limit hands derive most of their value from how well they extract money after the flop from your opponents. Comparing hands based on how often they win a showdown or on their 'hand rank' is worse than worthless."[4] If you have aces, and he has dreadful cards such as 3-4, 5-7, or 4-6, you cannot beat him for much, but he can give you a nasty surprise that will cost you all your chips. It has happened countless times, and the losers often insist that the people who took their stacks were idiots.

I learned that lesson the same way I have learned so many others—by losing money. Shortly after starting to play NL (a few months before Sklansky and Miller wrote that book), I was in a game with an extremely obvious "idiot." He had a huge stack, and he was crazily splashing his

3. This subject is discussed in Part Three of this book.

4. David Sklansky, and Ed Miller, *No Limit Hold'em: Theory and Practice* (Henderson, NV: Two Plus Two, 2006), 124.

chips around. He would raise pre-flop to eight or ten big blinds with trash, make large bets with nothing on the flop, bluff outrageously, and so on. But he kept "getting lucky," and his stack kept growing. Everybody was gunning for him, trying to isolate him from the rest of the "good players."

After about three hours I suddenly realized that he was a *much* better NL player than I was. In fact, he was completely out of the class of everybody at the table. He knew exactly what he was doing. He could read us accurately, and we had no idea where he was. I immediately began avoiding him while studying him intently.

I believe that when I left a few hours later nobody else had realized how good he was. The others were still trying to isolate him, overplaying their hands, paying him off, being bluffed out, and so on. And his stack was still growing. It was an expensive lesson, but worth every dollar.[5]

What About the Other Players?

That's enough about "idiots" who really play well. Let's say you're against a genuine jerk. You still have to watch out for the other players because they can beat you both. If you're playing limit and have three-bet with a substandard hand, say

and a very solid player cold-calls or four-bets, you're in big trouble.

He probably has a better hand, and he certainly has position on you. You are between a rock and a hard place. If the flop doesn't hit you, and the idiot bets into you, you don't know what to do about the player behind you. Even if an ace or nine flops and the idiot checks, you can't bet confidently. If the solid player has an ace, it's almost certainly better than yours, or he could beat your pair of nines with pocket tens, jacks, queens, or kings.

---

5. This story is repeated in Part Three, because it had so much of an impact on me.

Recommendations

I won't tell you how to play after the flop against this or that kind of player. Even the experts disagree about this subject. I'm just analyzing the way your thoughts and feelings affect your play. Don't commit strategic errors because you have made incorrect assumptions about the "idiot"; your cards; or, most important, your own abilities. Here are some pointers:

- Don't assume that someone is an "idiot" just because he plays a *few* weak hands. At a minimum see how often he calls or raises and how well he plays on later streets. Some apparent "idiots" are much smarter than you think, maybe even smarter than you are.

- Watch his play after the flop to determine how deceptive and unpredictable he is. The trickier he is, the less you want to isolate him.

- Don't assume you play better than he does after the flop. Overestimating yourself and underestimating your opponents are classic and extremely costly mistakes.

- Make isolation raises with substandard hands only when you're against real idiots and can minimize the risk that other player(s) will cold-call or three-bet you.

All of these pointers are much more important when you're playing NL.

In other words, don't overplay your hands *only* because one or a few players are playing some trash cards. Pick your spots carefully; keep testing your assumptions; and, if you find you're being outplayed, change your strategy or your table.

Apply active-learning principles *now* by taking a mini-quiz about what you have just read. Turn to Appendix E and answer those questions about this chapter.

Playing the Rush

We all get occasional rushes. It seems that the poker gods have smiled at us and then hit us with the deck. It's one of poker's greatest kicks, but—partly because we get them so rarely—we may not know how to take full advantage of these rare and wonderful experiences. And what should we do when someone else is playing his rush? This chapter deals with playing your own rush, while the next one discusses defending against other players' rushes.

Common Overreactions

Some people go on a variation of tilt. A player on an Internet forum wrote: "The feeling of overconfidence takes over and affects my sound play.... Soon I squander the winnings." Another poster agreed: "When I'm running good, I go on positive tilt. I try to run over the table with marginal hands instead of the solid ones that got me there. In addition, I slip into fancy-play-syndrome. Then, before I know it, my stack has dwindled." Someone else said, "Once you've won a few pots and are ahead, you tend to feel like you're on a roll and have winning momentum.... I tend to get a little overconfident and start playing too many hands."

In other words, when they feel they are on a rush, some people become too confident, loose, and aggressive. In fact, that's what people regard as "playing the rush." It's fun and it can build a stack quickly, but the downswings can be brutal.

Doyle Brunson's Advice

Doyle Brunson really plays the rush. In *Super System,* he wrote

If you're going to have a rush, you've got to let yourself have one. You've got to sustain that rush. And to do that, you've got to get in there and play. After I've won a pot in no-limit, I'm in the next pot, *regardless of what two cards I pick up.* I keep playing every pot until I lose one. And, in all those pots, I gamble more than I normally would. . . .

I know that scientists don't believe in rushes, but they make about fifteen hundred a month. I've played poker for almost 25 years now, and I've made millions at it. A big part of my winnings came from playing my rushes.[1]

But You're Not Doyle

I'm one of those scientists, and I *know* rushes have no predictive value. Winning the last hand, or the last five, or even ten hands has absolutely no effect on your future cards. No scientist would disagree with that statement, but many people believe that cards run in streaks, that a rush (or its opposite, a cold streak) can influence later cards.

Why do people believe in rushes? For the same reason they believe in "hot rolls" at the craps table, use lucky charms, and consult astrologers: *they are so frightened by randomness that they deny its essential nature.* I made this point and the next one in "Luck, ESP, and Superstitions" in *Your Worst Poker Enemy*: Your past cards have *no influence* on your future cards.

Does Doyle believe that his past cards affect future ones? I doubt it very much. He "plays the rush" aggressively not because he expects his cards to be better, but because apparent rushes scare people, and

---

1. Doyle Brunson (with many collaborators), *Super System: A Course in Power Poker,* 2nd ed. (Las Vegas: B&G, 1994), 450–451.

he is a master at exploiting that fear. Because Doyle is an immortal—
and his strategy agrees with what many people want to do—they have
followed his advice. A few highly skilled players can do so successfully, but it is *extremely* dangerous for you, me, and other mere mor-
tals. Doyle can get away with his extremely aggressive strategy for
four reasons:

1. He has an uncanny ability to read players and cards.
2. He can be extraordinarily aggressive.
3. He plays no limit (and this advice was in the chapter on no-
   limit hold'em).
4. He has an intimidating reputation, and his entire no-limit
   strategy is based on intimidating people.

Unless *all* of these conditions apply, following his advice can be
disastrous. Because you don't have his gifts and reputation, and may
not be playing no-limit, be *much* more conservative. It's just another
example of poker's primary principle: The answer to nearly every
question, including, "How should you play a rush?" is, "It depends on
the situation."

What Should You Do?

Although a rush will not affect your cards, many players will think
that you are hot, and that belief will affect their play against you. They
may be afraid, and some people will even say, "I'm avoiding you until
you cool down." The more afraid they are, the more easily you can run
over them. However, a few people will have opposite reactions: they
may believe that you are due to run cold, or they may have a macho
desire to "play sheriff." A rush does not change the mathematics of
poker, but it sure changes the psychology.

For a brief time you will have a frightening table image and you
should take advantage of it *but only with the players who fear you and
your rush.* You can play a *few* more hands, be a *bit* more aggressive,

and bluff a *little* more often. As many experts have said, never pass up an opportunity to let them fold a better hand. The danger is—as the previous comments on that Internet forum confirm—you may believe that the rush will continue and play weak or even hopeless hands aggressively.

This danger is particularly great if you are up against someone who is either oblivious or, worse yet, wants to play sheriff. The oblivious players will not be scared, and the sheriff wannabes will deliberately confront you.

Here are a few examples of what you should do. If everyone folds to you on the button and the blinds are tight players (or have expressed their fear of your rush), try to steal the blinds with any two cards. If you are in a shorthanded pot and the flop is all rags without a draw, bluff. If you miss your draw but the board is scary, take a shot at the pot.

But *don't* play marginal hands in early position or total trash in any position (except when you have the right conditions to steal the blinds), or grossly overplay *any* cards. Don't try to bluff calling stations, oblivious players, or "sheriffs." Enjoy the rush, and take advantage of the table image it creates, but don't take foolish chances just because you think you're hot.

Apply active-learning principles *now* by taking a mini-quiz about what you have just read. Turn to Appendix E and answer those questions about this chapter.

Defending Against the Rush

The previous chapter stated that a rush does not affect anyone's cards, but it can greatly change people's beliefs and reactions. Adjust to these changes whenever someone else is on a rush.

The Rusher's Attitude and Style

Many people become too confident, loose, and aggressive when they think they are on a rush. Their attitude can become a self-fulfilling prophecy because the other players react so foolishly. The rush and the confident image let rushers run over the table, which increases their confidence and ability to bully people. You should take advantage of both the rusher's and the other players' foolish reactions.

Other Players' Reactions

When someone is on a rush, the entire table can go on a form of tilt. Both the rusher and his opponents share a delusion—the laws of probability have been suspended—and they may all misplay their hands. The rusher pushes too hard, and the others let him run over them. Sometimes a few people decide to "play sheriff" and overplay their own hands on the foolish idea that "his luck has got to change."

Don't Share their Delusion.

You must always remember that *past hands have absolutely no predictive value*. The odds of any player's having the best cards with next hand are always exactly $1/n$, with "n" equal to the number of players at the table. It doesn't matter whether someone has won the last ten pots or hasn't won one all night; the odds against his having the best cards next hand *never* change.

Play solid poker.

Suggesting that you play solid poker may seem unnecessary, but it's not. Far too many normally intelligent people play foolishly because of their fear of the rush or the macho desire to play sheriff. In a moment I'll suggest adjustments, but they are relatively minor variations on solid poker strategy. You may think that brilliant plays are the key to success, but they have hardly any impact on your bottom line. Most of your profits come from making those mundane decisions correctly. In fact, if you don't play solid poker, making brilliant adjustments to a player's rush—or to anything else—won't have much impact; you'll probably lose.

Assessing Everyone's State of Mind

Although a rush does not change the mathematics, it certainly changes the psychology. Because so many people *think* the odds change and act accordingly, you must remain cool and assess how they are reacting.

First, look at the rusher. Is the rusher overplaying his hands? His play, body language, and words may tell you that he thinks he cannot lose. If he is playing or raising nearly every hand, he is probably overplaying his cards. The odds against his having so many good cards are just too high. Watch the way he looks at his cards: a few people become so confident that they straddle, call, or even raise without looking at their cards, or they have chips in their hands before looking, glance quickly, then bet or raise without thinking.

If someone is clearly overplaying his cards, you should often attack, because he probably has a weaker hand than his betting would suggest. Before the flop or on third street, if you have a pair or big cards that can win without improving, raise or reraise to isolate him. You can bet weaker hands for value but you should rarely bluff, because he will call with trash. You must call on the river with much weaker hands than usual, because he will bluff frequently.

Sometimes, it's better to take the opposite approach: become quite passive; let him bet his trash until the river, and then raise him. Dan Harrington calls it "The Rope-a-Dope,"[1] a term that Muhammed Ali coined for his strategy of letting an opponent wear himself out by throwing too many fairly harmless punches. The choice between an aggressive and a passive approach depends, of course, on the situation, especially whether the rusher is on your right or left, the number of players behind you, and their reaction to the rush.

In general, the aggressive approach works best when you are on the rusher's left and there are no sheriffs behind you, and the passive approach is best when you are on his right. However, the choice between an aggressive and a passive approach also depends on the other players' positions and attitudes.

Then look at the other players. Of course, some players don't react to a rush. They are oblivious and focus only on themselves; in fact, a few of them may not even realize that someone has won several pots in a row, or that everyone's style has changed. For them, no adjustments are necessary; just play straightforward, solid poker.

The frightened players: You may see open fear on some players' faces; their entire manner may become timid and hesitant, and they play hardly any hands. Because they are afraid of the rush, you can expect them to fold their marginal hands and to underplay their good ones. Give their bets and raises much more respect than usual, but exploit their timidity. For example, be prepared to fold when they at-

1. Don Harrington, *Harrington on Hold'em, Vol. 1,* 47–51.

tack, but bluff them much more frequently. If they are behind you, you can easily isolate the rusher. Because they are already afraid of her, they will not want to get caught between you.

The sheriff wannabes: Some people really want to play sheriff. It's a macho thing; they want to show that "*Nobody* is going to push *me* around!" They will gamble more by overplaying marginal hands, reraising to isolate, bluffing frequently, and trying to snap off bluffs.

Against them make exactly the opposite adjustments. Give much less respect to their bets and raises. When a sheriff is behind you, don't try to isolate the rusher unless you have a better hand than usual; the sheriff will call with marginal hands. Slow-play your better hands; let sheriffs show their machismo by jacking it up. Don't try to bluff them, and bet your marginal hands for value. Their machismo will make them call your bluffs and value bets, even with very weak hands.

Final Remarks

Many people get frightened when someone appears to be on a rush, but you should regard it as an opportunity. Because the rusher and most other players are acting foolishly, your expected value should *increase.* Just remember that the odds remain the same, play solid poker, assess the way the others are overreacting, and then make appropriate adjustments. If you do, you will find that other people's rushes actually put chips into *your* stack.

Apply active-learning principles *now* by taking a mini-quiz about what you have just read. Turn to Appendix E and answer those questions about this chapter.

Creating Tilt

When an opponent goes on tilt, your expected value (EV) could sky-rocket. First, he will play so badly that he will just give his money away. Second, the wildly aggressive form of tilt[1] is contagious: when the others see crazy plays and terrible hands winning huge pots, they will often play badly. Sometimes, almost everyone is on tilt, creating a wonderful "party." You will usually gain by creating tilt *if you can maintain your own emotional balance.*

However, the risks and costs are quite large. Although your EV will go up, you may lose a lot of money, because the game becomes so wild that anything can happen:

- You can easily go on tilt; it's hard to keep your head when everyone else has lost his, especially since bad beats will become much bigger and more common.
- If the game gets too wild, you may not have a large enough financial or psychological bankroll;[2] you may play scared and get run over.
- Tensions may rise, making the game much less pleasant.

---

1. Many people think that there is only one kind of tilt, being wildly aggressive. In "Preventing and Handling Tilt" in *Your Worst Poker Enemy* (pp. 193–204), I used this definition: " 'Tilt' means that you are making bad plays—ones you wouldn't usually make—for emotional or unknown reasons." That chapter also suggested ways to preserve your own balance.

2. Your psychological bankroll is the amount of money you can lose without having your play deteriorate. It is almost always *much* less than your financial bankroll.

- Some ways to put people on tilt may violate your principles or your cardroom's rules.

The Ethical Question: How Far Can You Go?

All ethical questions are highly subjective. You might balk at some actions I regard as acceptable and vice versa. There are two ethical issues:

1. Is it acceptable to try to put someone on tilt?
2. If so, how far can you go?

You will have to find your own answers. Some people slow-roll, criticize others' play and intelligence, or call them nasty names. A few even throw chips or cards at other people. I flatly refuse to be nasty or to tolerate nasty people. Poker is a game, and the media are calling it a sport. We should play primarily for pleasure, and we should always practice sportsmanship. We should not try to win at any price, nor should we commit or tolerate rude, humiliating, or threatening actions.

But I draw my personal line at actions, not intentions: If I can be a gentleman and preserve the "let's have fun" atmosphere but put someone on tilt, I will occasionally do it (especially if I don't like him). I may also encourage vulnerable people to keep playing. If someone is losing self-control and is thinking of leaving, I may say, "It's a great game, and I'm going to play another half hour. Why don't you stick around?"

Two types of plays can put people on tilt. First, you can bluff successfully and show it. Some people get mad; plan for "revenge"; think about "woulda, coulda, shoulda"; or just lose their concentration. Being bluffed can even upset top players. For example, at the final table of the 1997 World Series of Poker Championship, Ron Stanley was second to Stu Ungar and slowly acquiring chips. Stu bluffed him out of a huge pot and showed it. If Ron had called, he would have become about even with Stu. After seeing the bluff, Ron's play quickly deteriorated.

Second, if you think someone will go on tilt, you can make plays with slightly negative pot odds but very high "implied odds." That term usually means that you will make money on later streets if you catch your card. For example, the pot odds may not justify calling with a gutshot draw, but, if you make it and collect some large bets on the turn and river, the call has a positive EV.

Let's broaden "implied odds" to include profits in later pots if someone goes on tilt. For example, if someone is close to the brink, you may cold-call a pre-flop raise with a pair of deuces. If you miss your hand and fold, you take a small loss. But, if you flop a set to crack her aces, or your tiny pair holds up against his ace-king suited, he may go ballistic and lose lots of money. Your small "mistake" can pay huge dividends.

Are They Close to the Brink?

Whenever considering implied odds, estimate your chances of being paid off if you make your hand. If nobody will pay you off, don't play without the right pot odds. The same logic applies here: unless you are confident that a bad beat will put someone on tilt, *don't* make dubious plays, hoping to give him a bad beat. Some people have a brink, a sharp edge separating solid ground and a fall into a nearly bottomless pit. They are safe on one side of the brink, but push them a bit farther, and they are gone. Estimate how close *this person* is to that brink.

Although some forms of tilt are quite visible, most poker players try to deceive you about how they think and feel. You may see that somebody has played differently from usual, but you don't know why. You have to infer his emotional state from the way he plays—his words, his facial expressions, his hand gestures, and so forth. It helps to understand which emotions are affecting someone, but it is not completely necessary. The important thing is to understand that he is not acting solely or even primarily from a rational analysis of risks and potential gains, that some irrational factors are affecting him.

Look for *his* triggers. Go beyond what you see now and consider what has happened recently. Learn your opponent's triggers, the factors that will upset him. "Preventing and Handling Tilt" in *Your Worst Poker Enemy* said: Triggers "are individualistic. You may not even notice things which really bother me and vice versa." Try to learn which triggers will put *this* person on tilt. Taking three drinks or losing three racks may put you on tilt, but not seriously bother this person.

Then keep track of his triggers. Does alcohol seriously affect him? How much does it take, and how much has he had tonight? Does he get severely upset after losing a certain amount, and how much has he lost tonight? Do bad beats upset him, or does he shrug them off?

Look for emotional signals. Many players clearly signal that they are close to the brink. They slam down their chips, curse, whine about bad beats, or tell everyone how much they have lost. You have probably heard people go on and on about their bad luck or even say, "One more bad beat, and I'll blow up." When people are showing signs of losing control, a little push can put them on tilt.

When in doubt, ask questions. Many people don't give clear signals that they are on the brink. One minute they are playing their usual, solid game; then after a bad beat or missed draw, they start throwing their money away. Since you don't know what is in their minds, make statements or ask innocuous questions in a sympathetic way so they don't reveal your purpose. If people think you are trying to take advantage of them, they will clam up. But many people want to talk about themselves, especially when they are upset. For example, you could say, "You look a little disgusted." Your opponent might ignore you, but he might be one of those people who just have to express their feelings: "You bet I'm disgusted. That's the sort of crap that's been happening to me all day!"

Or you could say, "You seem to be having a tough time tonight." Your opponent might respond: "Tonight? This is the fifth night in a row I've gotten killed. I'm down three racks tonight and over $3,000 this week. I'm fed up!"

If you know someone fairly well and have the nerve, you can even comment on how much the person seems to be drinking: "Tom, you don't usually drink that much." He might say, "It's my fifth or sixth, and I'm going to have a lot more."

You may think that people will not give away such valuable information, but many people are so eager to talk about their troubles and feelings that they don't think about how their words can be used against them.[3] Once you know how people feel, it is often easy to put them on tilt. Then you will want to exploit their foolishness, which is the subject of the next chapter.

Apply active-learning principles *now* by taking a mini-quiz about what you have just read. Turn to Appendix E and answer those questions about this chapter.

3. This subject was discussed in "We Need a Miranda Warning" in *Your Worst Poker Enemy*, 177–179.

Exploiting Tilt

By definition, people on tilt are playing more poorly than usual because of emotional or unknown reasons. Their mistakes should put money into your pocket. Let's look at ways to get the biggest profits from their emotional imbalance.

Which Type of Tilt?

"Preventing and Handling Tilt" in *Your Worst Poker Enemy* described two main types of tilt. (1) becoming wildly loose-aggressive and (2) playing scared. Because scared players are less profitable and risky, I will spend only a few words discussing ways to exploit them:

- *Respect their bets and especially their raises.* They won't bet without a good hand or raise without an excellent one.

- *Bluff and semi-bluff much more frequently.* They will frequently fold when they should call.

- *Steal their blinds or antes.* They will rarely call and almost never play back at you. If they reraise, you know they have very good cards. If they just call your raise, they probably won't bet or check-raise later, giving you free cards to draw out. If you do draw out on them, their fears may be reinforced, and they can easily become even more timid.

- *Don't make thin value bets, especially ones based on position.* Checking does not necessarily mean they are weak. They will often check very good hands.

- *Don't try to check-raise.* If you check, they will probably check behind you unless they have you beaten.

Now let's look at the more visible, profitable, and dangerous form of tilt, wild aggression.

Monitor Yourself and Everyone Else

Since others often become infected by the "let's gamble" virus, continually look for signs that anyone—especially yourself—is on tilt or getting close to it. When trash hands win huge pots, "idiots" build huge stacks, and your aces get cracked by 7-3 offsuit, you can easily lose your balance. You may even think, "Since I can't win with good cards, I'll play bad ones." Or you may not make a conscious decision but suddenly find yourself taking crazy chances. If you see this happening, take a break or go home.

Look for changes in *everyone*. Solid players will become wild, and others will start playing scared. A few will make intelligent adjustments. You must recognize, understand, and adjust to the changes many players make. *Don't assume that people are playing their normal game.*

Keep the Party Going

Don't say or do anything that will cause the tilted player(s) to regain control or leave the game. Do everything you can to spread the "let's gamble" virus. You want the party to last as long and to be as wild as possible. It is extremely foolish to criticize tilted players, but it happens all the time. People get so frustrated when trash and stupidity beat their good hands that they call them names, or even insist, "If you keep playing like that, you'll go broke." They may embarrass the tilted people into playing rationally or quitting.

Because tilt is contagious, some of the apparently rational players may be getting close to losing control. It may be easy to push them over the brink. Don't be nasty or do anything that would destroy the "wild party" atmosphere, but encourage them to keep playing. For example, you could point out that Harry just won with a two-outer, and Barb won earlier with 7-2 offsuit. But say it with a smile: "It sure is exciting to see hands like that win big pots." Encourage everybody to gamble foolishly while you play solid poker.

Pick the Best Seat

When people are on tilt, position becomes *much* more important. To minimize the unpleasant surprises, you always want unpredictable players on your right, predictable ones on your left. Because tilted players are so erratic, you usually want them to your right. Let the action and surprises occur ahead of you.

However, some tilted players, especially drunks, become quite predictable. Either they bet or raise almost every hand, or they telegraph their moves by picking up chips, getting ready to throw away their cards, or even acting out of turn. If you *know* what someone will do, sit to his immediate *right.* You will be in a nearly perfect position, almost the "permanent button." You can fold your marginal hands and slow-play or check-raise your good ones.

Adjust Your Strategy

My book *The Psychology of Poker* focused on ways to adjust to various kinds of players. Read pages 125–134 and make the adjustments suggested there. Also read "Defending Against the Rush" in this book (pages 135–138). All loose-aggressive games require similar strategic changes. However, because people are acting emotionally, make the following additional adjustments.

Adjustment No. 1: Make sure you have enough chips. Don't play in a wild game with a short stack. You could play scared and get run over.

Adjustment No. 2: Avoid fancy plays. Emotional people are too oblivious and volatile for them to work. Play straightforward, solid poker.

Adjustment No. 3: Tighten up, especially before the flop or on third street in stud. Because you will see trash hands win huge pots, you may want to loosen up. Don't do it.

- Since the first round of betting will often be quite expensive, you need good cards.

- Once you get involved, the pot odds may become so large that you will be tempted to chase and may even be justified to do it. Much of your edge in these games comes from your selection of starting hands. Your superior discipline and judgment are almost worthless if the pot odds justify chasing with almost anything.

- You need to always resist that "let's gamble" virus. If you loosen up just a few times, you can easily find yourself on tilt.

Adjustment No. 4: Check-raise more often. You can do it without much risk of giving a free card. Someone will usually bet, and many people will play for two bets.

Adjustment No. 5: Slow-play big hands more often. Let the tilter do the betting and raising. He will get lots more action than you would. And, if the game has become really wild, others may also jack it up. You may even flop the nuts and have others cap the pot for you.

Adjustment No. 6: Bet into the tilter to thin the field. If the tilter is on your left, the field is large, and your hand is vulnerable (such as top pair, poor kicker), bet into him so that his raise forces out dangerous hands. Let's say you have

in the big blind, and the flop is

If you bet, get raised by someone with a weaker hand, and another player with

folds, two great things happen. First, you win a pot you would not have won. Second, the player with

may go ballistic and start playing crazily.

Adjustment No. 7: Minimize bluffs and semi-bluffs. Somebody will almost always call you.

Adjustment No. 8: Invite them to bluff. Many tilters love to bluff. They may want excitement, and it's much more exciting to bluff than to win with the best hand. So check your marginal hands, and snap off their bluffs.

Adjustment No. 9: Don't fold on the river. Some tilters will bet weak hands for value because they are too off balance to evaluate their chances accurately. Others may call with even less. You will often have to make apparently foolish calls and overcalls. So what? A bad one costs you only one bet. A bad fold can cause you to lose a whole pot, perhaps a huge one. Even worse, you may become upset and go on tilt.

Final Remarks

You may feel that I have overstated the danger that you will go on tilt, but it is very real, and it is almost always there, even if you rarely do go on tilt. Countless players—including many who are normally well controlled—have gone on tilt when games got too wild. Some of them never realized it; they just let their emotions take over while thinking they were still playing well.

Keeping your own balance is, in fact, your key task. If you keep your head while the others are losing theirs, you will dramatically increase your edge.

Apply active-learning principles *now* by taking a mini-quiz about what you have just read. Turn to Appendix E and answer those questions about this chapter.

Afterthought

These chapters discussed subjects that poker writers have generally neglected. You can find a few words here and there on, say, playing the rush or creating tilt, but hardly any serious publications have focused on them. Yet these ploys can give you an immense psychological edge. If, for example, you can put someone on tilt without violating your own or the cardroom's standards, you can gain much more than you would from a brilliant play. People on tilt often throw away huge amounts of money, and they can cause others to do the same.

The profits from the other ploys that we have discussed are smaller and less dramatic, but still significant. Unfortunately, some of these ploys are not easy to use, nor are they risk free. While trying to create or exploit tilt, you risk going on tilt yourself. Trying to run over a table when you are on a rush can cost you many chips. Taking a stand against a rushing player can give you a bloody nose.

But these ploys add an element to your game that many people just don't have. They are so busy computing the odds and making sure they make the technically correct play that they neither see nor exploit the opportunities to get a psychological edge.

Add a new dimension to your game by occasionally "thinking outside the box." Watch people. Learn how they are distorting reality or letting their emotions affect their judgment. Look for creative ways to gain a psychological edge. It's fun, and it can be very profitable.

PART THREE

Should You Play No-Limit Hold'em?

Introduction

No-limit hold'em (NL) is certainly the hottest game around, and many players have made the switch from seven-card stud, Omaha, limit hold'em, and a few other games. Some are winning much more money than ever, whereas others are unwilling to try NL, or they have played a few times and given up. In addition, a lot of people have played only or mostly NL. Until recently, hardly any American poker players[1] started by playing NL; they usually "graduated" to it after years of playing limit.

These chapters are primarily for people who have been winners at other poker games. They will also address a few issues that are important for new poker players. The tiny NL games have so many weak players that almost any reasonably talented and disciplined player can beat them.

The situation is not as inviting in larger games. Most NL games require many of the same talents needed to beat stud, limit hold'em, and so on, but greater amounts of them. They also require some additional qualities that you may or may not have. If you don't have them, playing in all but the smallest NL games could be a mistake.

I will *not* try to teach you how to play NL. For strategic advice, consult Appendix G, "Recommended Readings." My objectives are:

- To help you to decide whether to switch from limit to NL
- To help you with this very difficult transition, should you decide to switch

1. NL and pot limit are much more common than limit in Europe.

To reach these objectives I will focus on the *differences* between NL and other poker games. The poker literature has not clearly explained how NL is different, and how you must change your mind-set to play it well.

Most poker writers tell you how they see the game from their lofty pedestals. They know (or pretend to know) what you should do. They seem to assume that their readers want to maximize their profits and to play the best possible way. They may believe that people can react like computers. Just click a button, change to a different program, and you will quickly and easily change your perspective. Nonsense! Your capacity to change is *very* limited. If you have been playing limit, your reactions don't fit NL's demands. Virtually nothing has been written about the psychological forces that will interfere with your switching to thinking, feeling, and acting like an NL player.

Earlier versions of these chapters were published in *Card Player* a few months after I began playing NL. Jim Brier began playing and writing about NL at about the same time. He had already beaten $100- to $200-limit games and had written extensively about limit hold'em.[2] Despite his knowledge and skills, he had the same sorts of problems that I did.

We wrote our articles while we were struggling, and we made some costly mistakes. We wrote partly to help ourselves and our friends to make this difficult transition. Jim wrote about strategy, while I wrote about psychological problems. I have expanded the *Card Player* articles, and I wrote not as an expert, but as someone who was trying to solve the same problems that you face.

Jim, I, and several other people formed an NL Discussion Group (NLDG). All of us had won at limit, and our biggest problem was reacting like limit players. That's what these chapters are all about: *Changing your mind-set.*

---

2. He has had many articles in *Card Player* and is the coauthor of *How Good Is Your Limit Hold'em?* and *Middle Limit Hold'em Poker.*

Overview

There are eight chapters besides this introduction:

1. The Essential Mental Abilities
2. The Critical Psychological Traits
3. Reading and Adjusting to Players
4. Which Games Should You Choose?
5. Where Should You Sit?
6. Where Do You Want the Big Stacks?
7. Making the Transition
8. Afterthought

Why Even Consider Switching?

Stud and Omaha players are switching because those games seem to be dying. It is often hard to find a game, and the ones they can find are often tough. Hardly any new players want to play stud and Omaha, and the more experienced players are hard to beat.

A similar, but much less severe, shift has occurred in limit hold'em. Some limit games are being spread much less frequently, and many of them have gotten tougher because the weakest players have switched to NL. They like to gamble, and NL is certainly a lot more exciting.

However, the limit hold'em situation is still quite good. So many new people have taken up hold'em—including limit—that some limit players are winning more than ever. They naturally see little reason to change games. If you feel that way, you may be missing a chance to win even more.

Your profits can grow for two reasons:

1. Many of the weakest players *love* NL. Some loose-aggressive gamblers just throw away their money. Some new players have played hardly anything except NL. They saw it on TV,

and they love its apparent simplicity. Just get two cards and push in your stack before or on the flop.

2. Skill differences give you a much larger edge than in limit. In fact, until recently cardrooms would not spread NL, because the weak players went broke too fast. Capping the buy-ins lets the weak players lose more slowly, but they will still lose faster than in limit.

The combination of that larger edge and all those weaker players can give you greater profits with lower risk. In his book on capped NL games, Angel Largay wrote: "Not only are the financial rewards superior to any game requiring a bankroll of comparable size, but the fluctuations are also the lowest."[3]

Of course, you will get greater profits *only if you can play NL as well as you play limit poker.* Unfortunately, you may not be able to play it as well. Several chapters will discuss the factors that prevent good limit players from beating NL.

After I had published several *Card Player* articles, Dave ("Cinch") Hench[4] asked, "Why are you still asking people whether they should switch? Many people have already decided: *They are going to play no limit, period.*"

He was absolutely right, but some made a mistake, and they may not have seriously thought about it before deciding. Some weak-willed individuals play NL just because it is so fashionable. They are the sort of people who will not wear last year's clothes or drive a two-year-old car. Instead of making reasoned decisions, they just do what is "in."

Most poker writers never even consider such irrational motives, but—because they drive the clothing, automobile, consumer electron-

3. Angel Largay, *No-Limit Texas Hold'em: A Complete Course* (Toronto, Ontario: ECW Press, 2006), 13.

4. Cinch has edited many of my articles, and he is a great humor writer. You can read his work at pokerpages.com.

ics, and many other industries—such motives obviously have an immense impact on people's behavior.

Other people make more rational decisions. They say to themselves, "Since the weakest players are in the NL games, that's where I should be." Some of them flourish: they increase both their profits and their enjoyment. Others lose heavily because they don't realize that NL is wrong for them. They overestimate their talents (an extremely common problem), or they don't understand what it takes to beat NL.

Others win money, perhaps a lot of it, but they don't enjoy playing such a stressful game. They switch from having an enjoyable, profitable hobby, "second job," or even full-time occupation to becoming angry, depressed, and frustrated. These feelings may harm the more important parts of their lives such as their personal relationships. You probably would not take an unpleasant job even if it paid well. Why play a game you dislike?

My goal is to help you to avoid *all* of these errors. If you are not going to win enough money, or if you will dramatically reduce the pleasure you get from poker, *don't play NL.*

NL's Psychological Demands

Most poker writers ignore or minimize psychological demands. They want to maximize their profits, and they have the discipline to do whatever needs to be done. Because they assume that their readers have the same motive and discipline, they focus on teaching strategy, while ignoring the psychological factors that prevent readers from implementing their recommendations.

In fact, some famous professionals act extremely emotionally while playing NL. You have seen them rant, rave, whine, and scream on television. If top professionals cannot control their emotions, why do poker authors ignore them?

They ignore them because they focus on how people *should* think and act, not on what they really do. Because NL is much more stressful than limit, it arouses far more intense feelings, and they have enormous—and poorly understood—effects. NL has always been unpredictable, frightening, and frustrating, because you can play well all night and play a hand perfectly but instantly lose everything.

Because of recent changes, NL has become much more nerve-racking. The weakest players often make ridiculous plays, causing extremely painful bad beats. With so many players calling before the flop and chasing after it, horrendous beats occur very frequently.

NL lets you protect your hand much better than any other game. You will have fewer bad beats, but the ones you get will be much more costly and painful. Having your aces cracked by trash, or your top set beaten by a runner-runner flush has always been upsetting, but when you lose your whole stack the pain can be excruciating.

Emotional reactions are particularly strong when you first start playing NL, even if money is not that important. Jim Brier had written extensively about limit hold'em and beaten $100–$200 limit games before playing NL. Yet losing his $100 stack really bothered him. "I felt humiliated. I was forced to buy chips, and I *never* had to do that. I always had plenty of chips in front of me."

Ed Miller had written two books on limit hold'em and had beaten $40–$80 games before starting to play NL. He said, "Whether it's $2,000 or $20, losing your whole stack on one hand is like being hit by a truck." If Jim and Ed feel that way, you and many of your opponents probably have similar feelings.

Of course, in NL you can also double or triple your stack in one hand, but it doesn't have the same psychological impact. Research has found that "the pain of a loss is about twice as much as the joy of a gain."[5] That is, although poker writers often assume that a dollar is a dollar is a dollar, most people do not feel that way.

The *psychological* value of dollars depends on whether you are

5. Barry Tanenbaum, "Understanding Poker Errors Through Prospect Theory—Part 1," with coauthor Rachel Crosen, *Card Player,* October 25, 2005. That two-to-one ratio is the average found in prospect theory research. Some people have higher ratios, and others have lower ones.

winning or losing them, how much you are ahead or behind tonight, how much you have in front of you, and many other factors that are "irrational" from a profit-maximizing perspective. If you understand your own and other people's feelings, you control your own reactions and exploit other people's feelings.

Some people just can't handle their emotions. For example, several friends have stormed out of extremely juicy games from sheer frustration. They moan, "Don't play with those people. They call with *anything!*" One friend left a game because of two outrageous beats. He had gone all in pre-flop with pocket aces and pocket kings and lost to jack-eight suited and six-nine offsuit. He should love a game like that, but he wasn't interested in his positive expected value. He just whined, "I can't take it!"

Some famous professionals have had similar reactions. Even though they are making more money than anyone ever expected, they bitterly complain about the weak tournament players. A few have even said that they may boycott the Main Event of The World Series of Poker because "it has become a crapshoot." Those weak players have created an enormous amount of dead money, but some pros cannot handle the frustration.

Later I will discuss frustration and several other reasons against and for playing NL. Now I will just summarize the essence of my position: *NL is not for everyone. It demands different knowledge, skills, psychological traits, and mental abilities.*

Not much has been written about anything except knowledge and skills. Most poker writers have the necessary mental abilities and psychological traits, so they focus almost entirely on knowledge and skills. But, if you don't have the right mental abilities and psychological traits, increasing your knowledge and skills will *not* make you a winner, not at NL or any other poker game.

In addition to ignoring psychological qualities, most writers have not said much about the differences between the skills needed for limit and NL. They just tell you what this or that game requires and leave it to you to make the comparison. Since these differences are not at all obvious, most players do not know how they have to change when they shift from one game to the other.

Barry Tanenbaum and Jim Brier were among the first to compare directly the skills each game requires. You should read their articles at cardplayer.com. Barry's series began on April 4, 2006, and Jim's on July 15, 2006.

I will discuss a few skill differences but emphasize psychological traits and mental abilities. Before committing yourself to playing NL, ask yourself three questions:

1. Do I have or can I develop the right skills?
2. Do I have the right mental abilities?
3. Do I have or can I develop the right psychological traits?

If one answer is no, you probably should not switch. If two or three answers are no, you *definitely* should not play NL.

You should also remember a central principle: *Most people overestimate both their talents and their ability to change themselves.*[6] No matter how well you think you play any form of poker, don't assume that you will quickly or easily become a good NL player.

Some skills are hard to improve, many psychological traits are difficult or even impossible to develop, and your mental abilities are essentially fixed. You're stuck with what you've already got. If you're not the right kind of person, NL is the wrong game for you.

Don't make the extremely common error of thinking you can change your basic personality or intelligence. Many psychological traits and nearly all mental abilities are almost as fixed as certain physical attributes. You must therefore learn to do your best with what you already have. For example, you cannot play center on any good basketball team unless you are very tall. You would not think, "I will just grow an-

6. Overestimating your abilities was frequently discussed in *Your Worst Poker Enemy.* See especially, "Denial About Ourselves and Our Opponents" on pages 65–74.

other foot taller and then play center." You know you cannot do it, and your chances of becoming much smarter, more courageous, and so on are about the same as your chances of growing taller.

The Right Skills

Because Barry and Jim have already described the skill differences, I won't repeat them. However, their short columns could not tell you how to execute or develop those skills. And, because NL is more complicated and subtler, it takes longer to become a good player. The learning curve is flattened further by the lack of good written instruction *for today's NL games*.

Most have a cap on the buy-in. In addition to dramatically changing the strategies you should use, capping the buy-in changes the opposition you will face. When buy-ins were not capped, the weakest players quickly went broke, so most games had only a few weak players (or none of them). Today's games are full of beginners and other bad players.

Many of them just want to gamble, and the capped buy-ins let them do it without going broke too quickly. They often play NL just like it *seems* on TV, without understanding and adjusting to two critical facts:

1. Most televised hands are in shorthanded games with large blinds. The strategies that work in such games are utterly wrong for full games with small blinds.
2. The shows are edited to emphasize dramatic impact. When trash beats aces, or someone makes a great bluff, it's dramatic. So the bad beats and great bluffs are shown, not the typical hands.

Because they don't understand these differences, the weakest players play too many hands, go too far with them, and make absurd moves.

Unfortunately, because most major poker writers have little or no experience in capped games, the literature is almost entirely based on "real no-limit games" (ones without a cap). In those games you almost never have

- Eight limpers seeing the flop
- Three or more players going all-in before the flop
- Standard opening raises of eight to fifteen times the big blind
- People calling all-in bets and raises with weak draws, top pair, weak kicker, or even worse hands

In many capped buy-in games—especially the smaller ones—these things are routine. The game has changed enormously, but the instructional material has not kept up with the times. Doyle Brunson, the author of the most famous chapter on NL, openly admitted, "I have trouble winning in a game where there's not much money on the table," which means everybody has only "$5,000 or $6,000."[7] His book and most others tell you how to beat games that you will probably *never* play.

Doyle would certainly adjust his strategy if he played in a small game. If Doyle cannot win by using his system in small games, how can you use it profitably? The conditions for which he wrote it do not apply, and you do not have his talent, experience, or ability to intimidate.

Where Are All the Books?

Angel Largay has been a big winner in the smaller NL games, and his newest book, *No-Limit Texas Hold'em: A Complete Course,* focuses on them:

While the proliferation of new poker books has been unprecedented in the last couple of years, the poker canon fails to address

7. Doyle Brunson, *Super System 2* (New York: Cardoza Publishing, 2005), 600.

the game which is, in great part, fueling the poker explosion. The game is Low-limit No-limit, and it refers to a very special form of no-limit in which there is a maximum amount that you can buy-in. Casinos typically refer to this game simply as no-limit, but, in fact, this is a very special form of no-limit which needs to be addressed differently than a traditional no-limit game. The game plays so much differently than a traditional no-limit game that I treat it as a unique structure.

One of the reasons that there is so little material written on this particular form of poker, despite its explosive popularity, is that there are few professionals who have taken to the game. The reason is two-fold:

First, the game simply appears too small and quite frankly, many an expert players' ego demands that they play in a larger game. . . .

Second, those experts who have decided to give this game a shot have discovered that their expert no-limit skills are not completely portable to a low-limit no-limit game. Many expert players simply come to a low-limit no-limit table armed with their regular no-limit skills and, making no adjustments, walk away disillusioned.[8]

His book was published in September 2006. Since then some books have appeared, but the ones on smaller NL games were not written by the top players. When Jim Brier and I were hungry for help, we could not find any books on NL that were remotely as good as the ones we had read (and he had written) about limit hold'em. We needed good advice to play a more difficult game, but we could not find it. The situation has improved dramatically since then, but the NL books are still not as helpful as the ones on limit.

For example, many limit hold'em books give very clear instructions about what to do in many situations. No books on NL give such clear advice, partly because NL is more of an art than a science. De-

8. *No-Limit Texas Hold'em*, 80.

spite their limitations, I recommend several books in the chapter titled "Making the Transition."

The Importance of Starting Hand Selection

One example of the weakness of books on NL is their emphasis on starting hand selection. Some books devote many pages to this issue, and a few of them allocate more pages to it than to any other subject. Some even have matrixes stating how to play various hands in different positions. However, that subject is much less important—and much less formulaic—in NL than it is in limit.

David Sklansky created the first popular ranking system for limit hold'em hands, but his new book on NL completely rejected using hand rankings. "For deep stack no limit, preflop hands derive most of their value from their ability to extract money after the flop from your opponents. Comparing hands based on how often they win a showdown or their poker 'hand rank' is worse than useless."

For example, the highest category this book listed was "bread and butter hands." They are "the hands you would most like to see when you first look at your cards." They include "no gap suited connectors . . . down to five-four suited."[9] Most good limit hold'em players rarely play five-four suited, and they certainly would not include it in any list of "hands they would most like to see."

To win at limit you have to take down a lot of pots, but your no-limit results are driven primarily by a few big ones. And those big pots are often won by deceiving the most vulnerable players. You can double or triple up most easily with small and medium pocket pairs or even tiny suited connectors, especially against people who cannot get away from hands like overpairs and top pair top kicker.

When players' cards were just starting to be shown on television, Russ Hamilton, former World Series of Poker Main Event champion,

9. David Sklansky and Ed Miller, *No Limit Hold'em: Theory and Practice* (Henderson, NV: Two Plus Two, 2006), 124. It was published shortly after I began writing about NL in *Card Player*.

told The Wednesday Poker Discussion Group that he disliked those cameras. He did not want people to know how often he played trash hands like nine-seven offsuit.

Why would be play such trash? Because if the flop is ace, nine, seven, some players will lose their stack with ace-king. If it is five-six-eight, he will bust the same people when they hold pocket kings. Of course, he would play such hands only against the right people in the right situations. Sklansky and Miller would play five-four suited for the same reasons and in the same general way.

I cannot count the number of times I have seen players limp or make a small raise with pocket aces or kings, then go busted to somebody with trash. They whine and complain but frequently have no one to blame but themselves. They let people draw too cheaply, or they did not get away from the hand when they were clearly beaten. Instead of accepting responsibility for misplaying the hand, they may attack the other player: "How can you play that #$%$#?"

The Sklansky-Miller-Hamilton position was supported by a poll of my NLDG. I asked the group members about the relative importance of various skills, psychological traits, and mental abilities in NL and limit. They clearly stated that the most important limit skills were related to having the best hand, while the most important NL skills were related to deceiving opponents.

You do *not* deceive them by waiting for big hands and then playing them in a straightforward manner. Let's say you have aces and make a standard, three big blind raise. The player who calls your raise with trash is far more likely to bust you than you are to bust him.

In today's games, with so many people seeing the flop, aces and kings get cracked all the time. Most NL books do not tell you how to adjust either your play or your attitudes. Later chapters will address both of these adjustments.

The Essential Mental Abilities

Earlier I stated that some people should not switch to NL because "it demands different . . . mental abilities . . . and your mental abilities are essentially fixed. You're stuck with what you've already got."

Many people believe that hard work and discipline can overcome mental limitations, but they are too optimistic. Studying and various exercises can increase your knowledge and skills, but you cannot greatly improve most mental abilities. That conclusion is supported by thousands of research studies. Your brain is not like a muscle; exercise, food supplements, and so on will not have much impact on its capacity.

You also cannot directly measure most mental abilities. You must infer them from your performance at poker or other activities. These inferences are often biased because you want to believe that you are smart, have good intuition, and so on. This problem is aggravated by the poor definition of most mental abilities.

Take, for example, general intelligence, the most important and thoroughly studied ability. Hundreds of millions of people have taken IQ tests, and thousands of research papers have been written about them. But nobody knows exactly what they measure, and there are heated arguments about the precise meaning of "intelligence."

IQ tests measure primarily mathematical, logical, and linguistic abilities, but there are many other types of intelligence. Because of other gifts, some *great* NL players may not have high IQs.

Because NL is so hot, some players have switched to it even though they lack essential mental abilities. Overestimating any personal quality is destructive, but, because you cannot do much about them, overestimating your mental abilities can be catastrophic. If you do not have the "horsepower" to play NL, you are going to lose, and you may lose a lot more than you can afford.

Let's compare your brain to a computer. All poker decisions are situational, but you must consider more factors in NL. To process this increased information well you need more RAM and a faster, more powerful processor. If you haven't got the necessary mental abilities, you can probably beat only soft NL games.

Unfortunately, nobody knows exactly which mental abilities you need to succeed at poker. The SAT, GRE, LSAT, and MCAT predict how well students will do in college and various postgraduate schools, but there are no such tests for poker players. In fact, we are unsure of what makes a good NL player. Some greats have almost no formal education, whereas a few of them are highly educated. Some greats think logically, whereas others are intuitive.

It is easier to define and measure the abilities needed to succeed at limit than at NL. Limit poker is primarily a mathematical and logical game and those abilities can be measured fairly accurately. NL is more of an art, and artistic abilities are extremely hard to define and measure.

In addition, you may not need large amounts of all the mental abilities. A great deal of one may compensate for limited amounts of others. For example, if you have great intuition about people, you can win despite limited ability to understand theory. Let's look at a few of the more important abilities and see how they can compensate for each other.

Mathematical Competence

Poker is a mathematical game. Without above average mathematical abilities, you are unlikely to win at any form of poker. But mathematical competence is especially important for NL, and NL math is different from limit math. Most of the math in limit games is so straightforward that you can do it right at the table. Because there are far more variables, NL math is much more difficult. To play well, you must

- Make all the limit calculations.
- Include the size of your opponents' bets when estimating their hands.
- Estimate the probability of being called or raised if you bet or raise various amounts.
- Estimate the effects of various-sized bets and raises on implied odds. Estimating implied odds is hard enough in limit,[1] but it is *much* more important and difficult in NL.

The math in Sklansky and Miller's *No Limit Hold'em: Theory and Practice* is so complicated that even the authors don't try to do it at the table. They wrote: "We ... don't play poker by solving equations ourselves. We provide the equations because they show you how to estimate and combine probabilities."[2]

Estimating and combining probabilities for so many factors requires far more math abilities than most people have. However, some people have math abilities that cannot be easily defined or tested, and they may have other abilities that offset their mathematical limitations.

Memory

You need a good memory to play any form of poker well. You must remember how people played other hands and then draw inferences from patterns. What cards do they hold? How will they react if you check, bet, call, or raise? How will their reactions change if you in-

1. See Barry Tanenbaum, "A Practical Example of Implied Odds," *Card Player*, August 22, 2006.

2. David Sklansky and Ed Miller, *No Limit Hold'em: Theory and Practice* (Henderson, NV: Two Plus Two, 2006), 8.

crease or decrease your bet or raise? You need a better memory for NL because the patterns are more complicated.

Because all limit bets and raises are fixed, you have usually seen what your opponents did in similar situations. You can therefore make fairly confident inferences about which cards they hold and how they will react to your plays. Your results are driven primarily by how often you are right or wrong.

Your NL results are driven primarily by a few big pots, perhaps only one or two a night, and the patterns are *not* repetitious. Sometimes you will have no precedents at all, but you will have to make an immediate decision. You may have to risk your entire stack without ever having seen *this* player in *this* kind of situation.

For example, many players bet more with stronger hands, but others bet less with them because they want a call. If you haven't got much experience with this player, you may not know which pattern he favors, and if he is a good player, he will deliberately vary the pattern to keep you guessing.

Feel

When making inferences in unfamiliar situations, some great NL players (e.g., Stu Ungar, Doyle Brunson, and Layne Flack) rely on "feel," a combination of observational skills, memory, and intuition. They observe intensely, remember many situations, recognize common patterns, and base their decisions on feelings that they cannot clearly define.

Feel works differently from logical thinking. Instead of taking a series of clearly defined steps, it is nearly instantaneous, and, as many intuitive geniuses have admitted, it cannot be clearly described. Somehow they recognize and understand a pattern that someone without their gift may not see.[3] It is similar to the reactions of great athletes. For example, a tennis player may sense that an opponent is going to

3. *Your Worst Poker Enemy* contains several chapters on intuition versus logic.

hit to his backhand and react almost immediately. If you asked him, "How did you do it?" he couldn't say—he just *did*.

If you have that feel, you are very fortunate, because it gives you an edge over the "scientists" who rely primarily on theory, math, and logic. It would be even better to have both, but hardly anyone is that gifted. Nearly everyone relies primarily on one or the other.

Unfortunately, many people overestimate their feel, partly because it cannot be defined or measured precisely. They remember the great moves they made because they just *knew* what the other people had or would do but forget the times they felt equally certain but were completely wrong. The chapter titled "Reading and Adjusting to Players" will suggest ways to develop feel, but the essential first step is to recognize whether you have it.

Logical Thinking

Unless you have great feel, you need the ability to draw logical conclusions from the way that other people bet and act. For example, if a weak-tight player has raised UTG, he probably has a certain range of hands. If the flop is 4,5,6 rainbow, and the turn is a 2, a large bluff will probably succeed. Since a weak-tight player would never raise UTG with seven-eight or a three in his hand, he cannot have a straight, and he may be afraid to call a large bet. You are reaching the same conclusion as an intuitive player, but by a more clearly defined process.

If you were playing limit logically, you would take the same steps but could not consider the effects of different-sized bets. That weak-tight player is much more likely to call a one-bet bluff than a larger one. But what is the probability that he would call a bluff of one-third, one-half, or all your stack? Which bet has the highest expected value (EV)?

Sklansky and Miller tell you how to calculate EV, but the equations are so complicated and so dependent on probability estimates that you probably cannot do them while playing. So you will often need more than math and logic. That is, you need that elusive, hard-to-define ability called "feel."

Concentration

Whether you make decisions intuitively or logically, you must concentrate to get and process information. All poker requires concentration, but NL is especially demanding.

Limit is a series of similar decisions, and you can beat weaker games almost "on autopilot." Just apply the formulas again and again. You will be right often enough to win. Because you must consider more factors, NL decisions are more complex, and you cannot just apply formulas. Also, if you are right nearly all the time but make one big mistake, you are busted. Obviously, you must concentrate more intensely, not just when you are in the pot, but all the time.

NL also requires concentrating on different subjects. Limit players should focus primarily on pot odds and other mathematical subjects, but NL players must concentrate more on psychology. I will discuss this difference in the chapter titled "Reading and Adjusting to Players."

Planning

In both limit and NL you need to see the big picture and plan future steps. Where are you going with this hand? And what should you do on each street? "If the flop is small cards, I will . . . If the river is a third heart, and he checks, I will . . ." Planning in NL is more complicated because you have more options.

In addition, your plans for both limit and NL should include the future effects of this hand. Longer-term planning is more important in NL, because trapping and avoiding traps are crucial. For example, Sklansky and Miller recommend that you "make obvious errors to induce costly errors."[4]

---

4. *No Limit Hold'em: Theory and Practice,* 233.

Multiple-Level Thinking

To play all types of poker well, you should think of your cards, their cards, what they think you have, and what they think you think they have. Because a decision can double up or bust you, you must often think at more levels in NL. Multiple-level thinking is also much more difficult in NL, because you have more options and must consider more factors.[5]

Final Remarks

NL is such a demanding game that relatively few people can play it well. To assess your potential, you need to look very hard at yourself. You may or may not have the right mental abilities, and the sooner you find out, the better. You must also avoid an extremely common error, overestimating your abilities.

At the moment, the smaller NL games are so soft that you do not have to play that well to win, but this wonderful party will not last forever. Sooner or later, the weaker players will quit or learn how to play. Then you may need a lot more talent than you possess.

After reading this chapter, a friend said I should focus more on poker's current state, rather than discuss what you will need when the games get tougher. He has a legitimate point, but this book, especially its final section, focuses on longer-term development. Too many poker players and writers have an extremely short-term focus.

Switching to NL will take time, and it will probably reduce your winnings at first. Base your decision on your long-term potential; this depends on how well NL fits your skills, traits, and mental abilities.

Apply active-learning principles *now* by taking a mini-quiz about what you have just read. Turn to Appendix E and answer those questions about this chapter.

5. The best discussion I have read on this subject is on pages 168–175 of Sklansky and Miller's *No Limit Hold'em: Theory and Practice.*

The Critical Psychological Traits

NL has been called "hours of boredom with moments of terror," and you need certain traits to cope with both the boredom and the terror. In limit, if your boredom causes a careless mistake, you lose some bets, but in NL you can lose your entire stack. In limit you will rarely be terrified, but the risk of losing your stack can be frightening. NL therefore demands much more emotional control.

In addition to the traits needed to handle boredom and terror, you need to be deceptive and ruthless. All forms of poker require deceiving opponents, but it is especially important in NL, because setting and avoiding traps is so much more important. Ruthlessness is valuable in all forms of poker, but—because most of your profits come from winning a few big pots—it is essential for NL. If you feel inhibited about busting people, you have a severe competitive liability.

All forms of poker require discipline, but limit may require more discipline than NL. Your limit profits depend on repeatedly making the right decision, while your NL profits depend on a few big pots, which are often won by creative moves, and creative people tend to be undisciplined. For example, Stu Ungar and some other notoriously undisciplined people did spectacularly well in NL, but not that well at limit. They need the freedom to improvise that only NL provides.

Risk Tolerance

Without risk tolerance you can't handle NL's greater risks. Jan Siroky, a successful NL tournament coach,[1] put it bluntly: "The absolutely indispensable quality for NL players is *courage*." Doyle Brunson agrees: "Having courage is one of the most important qualities of a good no-limit player. If you don't have it, you'll have to restrict your play to limit poker. You need courage in limit too, but not as much as in no-limit."[2]

Dr. Daniel Kessler, a clinical psychologist, went further in a private email "You need a nearly complete disregard for the value of money." I wouldn't go so far. You need a balance between the extremes of regarding your stack as "just chips" and worrying too much about what they can buy. If you think, "Oh, my God, I'm betting my rent or car payment," you will play scared. It is deadly in all poker games, but especially in NL. If you overreact to NL's greater risks, you will make many costly errors.

Playing Timidly

Fear can make you fold winners, check when you should bet, call when you should raise, or make too small a bet or raise. You may be so afraid of being raised or committing yourself that you give cheap or free cards that beat you, or you may invite opponents to bluff.

Overprotecting Your Good Hands

Fear can also make you bet too much. Tommy Angelo, a poker coach and writer,[3] often talks about a novice with pocket aces. He made a huge all-in pre-flop raise. Everyone folded around to the oldest, wisest player. He asked, "What are you so afraid of?" Then he flashed and mucked pocket kings.

1   Jan's website is sirokypoker.com.

2.   Doyle Brunson, *Super System 2*, 551.

3.   Check out his unusual website, tiltless.com.

Once the pot gets fairly large, fear can become even more destructive. For example, fearful people may push in their stack with top set on the flop, halfway hoping that nobody will call and draw out on them. But, because you get such good hands very rarely, you should get full value from them. Bet enough so that calling is a mistake, but not so much that everyone folds.

After a horrible beat one of Matt Lessinger's students was whining that he should have pushed all-in to protect his hand when he was more than a nine-to-one favorite. Matt disagreed, saying, "It would be worth taking the 10 percent chance of going broke if it meant a 90 percent chance that he would get his opponent's entire stack."[4]

If you're a huge favorite, you should want a call. Don't bet so much that you don't get it. If the fear of being busted will make you misplay your hands, play limit poker or in NL games that are small enough to keep your fears under control.

Trapping Badly

NL is a trapping game, and you need courage to set and spring some traps. You must often sacrifice some immediate expected value (EV) and risk losing your stack to set a trap, and it may backfire. Fear can reduce your ability to set and spring two types of traps:

1. *Slow-playing big, but not enormous, hands:* This is quite risky. In addition to giving up some immediate EV, you take a chance that someone will draw out and bust you. For example, if you slow-play top set with a weak draw on the board, you can lose a lot of money and feel very foolish.

2. *Playing weak hands:* This risks less money but can be quite risky psychologically. If you are deep-stacked and cold-call a standard, pre-flop raise with, say, five-four suited, you will usually lose the small amount you invest. However, once in a while you will bust someone.

4. Matt Lessinger, "Counter-productive Analysis," *Card Player,* April 4, 2006.

Fear of Looking or Feeling Foolish

Both trapping examples can arouse this fear. If you win with that five-four suited, some people will think you are a fool. If you slow-play a hand and lose the pot, you may feel like an idiot. Some people cannot handle embarrassment, nor can they cope with losing a pot by choosing a risky alternative.

Barry Tanenbaum received two critical messages about his article "I Manipulated My Opponent into Winning."[5] He passed up opportunities to win the pot to increase his EV. He did increase it, but EV is not the same as immediate dollars; his opponent drew out to win the hand. Both critics argued that if the choice was between winning 100 percent of the time one way and losing some of the time the other way, then the 100 percent way must be better. They clearly don't understand that EV is the *only* source of long-term profits, and many people share this misunderstanding.

All poker is risky, and NL is the riskiest, both financially and psychologically. If you lack courage, you *must* recognize and accept your limitations. Don't kid yourself and think you can develop it, because you have almost no chance of doing so. *If you can't handle either its financial or psychological risks, NL is not right for you.*

Ambiguity Tolerance

NL is much more ambiguous than limit, because you have many more options and must consider more variables. If you bet or raise, you must decide how much to commit, and all your decisions depend on the pot's size and your own and the other players' stacks. With exactly the same cards, players, and action, you should call with certain-sized stacks but raise or fold with different-sized ones. If you need simple formulas, NL is wrong for you.

5. Barry Tanenbaum, *Card Player*, May 3, 2005.

Pressure Tolerance

If you are playing for stakes that matter to you, all forms of poker demand this quality. You must continue to think and act rationally instead of responding to your emotinos. People crack under pressure in both limit and NL, but, because you can double up or lose your stack, the pressure is much greater in NL. If you cannot remain cool, analytic, and decisive under pressure, NL is definitely not for you.

Self-Confidence

You need enough self-confidence to make risky decisions with incomplete information. Because the risks in NL are greater and the situations are more ambiguous, you need a *lot* of self-confidence. Without it you will be tentative and timid, and you cannot beat NL playing that way.

Frustration Tolerance

All forms of poker are frustrating because our goal is to take each other's money, and we will often lose more than we can handle (either financially or psychologically). Worse yet, the best hand or the best player will often lose. NL is especially frustrating because you can lose so much so quickly.

If you cannot handle frustration, your play will often suffer. Instead of focusing on the current situation, you may be distracted, thinking about past mistakes or bad beats, or wondering, "Why am I so unlucky?"

Going on tilt is the most destructive reaction to frustration, and your chances of doing it depend on your personality. Because NL lets you protect your hands much better, bad beats occur far less often. However, when they do happen, they are much more expensive and frustrating. Your chances of going on tilt therefore depend on which is more upsetting to you: infrequent, but larger losses or more frequent, but smaller ones.

Going on tilt is much more destructive in NL, because you can lose so much so quickly. I have seen people lose seven buy-ins in less than an hour. In uncapped NL games you can quickly blow your entire bankroll. If an occasional large loss can put you on tilt, don't play NL.

Patience

Patience is essential for all poker games, but NL demands a different kind of it. You can grind out a profit at limit just by being disciplined and patient. Simply wait for good cards and focus on pot odds because the implied odds and bluffing potential are rarely high enough to justify playing bad ones.

To exploit NL's much greater implied odds and bluffing opportunities you must combine patience, deceptiveness, and timing. Instead of waiting for cards such as big pairs and then playing them straightforwardly, you should set and avoid traps—with or without big cards. You need the patience to wait for the right *situations,* not just the right cards.

You cannot commit too soon or too late. If you overcommit before the flop, say, by open-raising all-in with pocket kings or queens, you may win the blinds or get called only by better hands. If you overcommit after the flop, you may win a small pot or lose your entire stack.

If the post-flop action is too heavy, you may have to fold your overpair or bigger hand. If you cannot fold good hands when they appear beaten, don't play NL. Many players—especially ones who are very tight pre-flop—cannot do it. They say, in effect, "I've waited hours for these cards, and I'm playing them to the bitter end." It's a prescription for disaster.

Deceptiveness

You can beat many limit games by playing ABC poker, but you need deceptiveness to beat NL. When I polled my NL discussion group, the members said the three most important NL skills are:

1. Avoiding traps
2. Manipulating opponents into making mistakes
3. Deceiving opponents

They said the three most important limit skills are:

1. Selecting hands
2. Folding early
3. Selecting good games

Although "deceiving opponents" was ranked only third among the most important NL skills, those ranked first and second also require deceptiveness. Because they are too predictable, straightforward players are easy to trap. If you know what they will do, just set the trap, and let them step into it. Deceptiveness also helps you to manipulate people into making mistakes. If they know what you are trying to do, they can easily thwart your plans. If you are beating limit games by playing ABC poker, you may have problems with NL's demands for greater deceptiveness.

Ruthlessness

Poker is a ruthless game. Our goal is to take each other's money, and we keep score by counting our chips. There are no points for style, knowledge, and so on. The only thing that counts is how much money you win.

Jack Straus once said, "I'd bust my own grandmother if she played poker with me." He is a member of the Poker Hall of Fame, partly for his skills, partly because many players regard his extreme ruthlessness as the only way to play. The advantages of ruthlessness were discussed in "Would You Bust Your Own Grandmother?" on pages 105–115.

Ruthlessness is much more important in NL than limit. NL is ultimately about beating people out of large pots. If your opponents are eager to bust you but you are reluctant to bust them, you have an enormous competitive liability. In fact, if you don't have a ruthless "killer instinct," don't play NL.

Final Remarks

It is difficult or impossible to change most psychological traits, so take a hard look at yourself before switching to NL. If you don't have the right kind of personality, NL is probably not the right game for you.

Apply active-learning principles *now* by taking a mini-quiz about what you have just read. Turn to Appendix E and answer those questions about this chapter.

Reading and Adjusting to Players

They are important skills for all kinds of poker, but they are *much* more important and harder to develop for NL than for limit. You can beat some limit games by playing a technically correct game, but you cannot beat NL without reading and adjusting well. Reading and adjusting well in limit games does not necessarily mean that you will do them well when playing NL, because NL requires different talents.

Frequency Versus Importance

Your limit results depend primarily on *how often* you make the right decision, while your NL results are driven by *when* you are right. In limit poker, a few brilliant decisions will not overcome the negative effects of many bad or mediocre ones.

In NL your results depend primarily on the few decisions you make when many chips, perhaps all your stack, are at risk. If you are right then but wrong when the pots are small, you will win. Conversely, if you are wrong then, you could win many pots but take a huge overall loss.

In both limit and NL you should identify and adjust to a player's general style such as loose-aggressive or tight-passive. My book *The Psychology of Poker* focused primarily on these tasks, but it dealt only with limit players. Their general style helps you to understand how they play most hands.

Thinking like a limit player can make you rely too heavily on a player's general style. Let's say someone aggressively overplays weak cards pre-flop and makes very aggressive bets, raises, and bluffs in small pots. Perhaps he is a Maniac, perhaps not. You cannot tell without seeing how he plays in big pots. An apparent Maniac may never make such aggressive plays when the pots and bets become huge.

I learned that lesson the same way I have learned so many others—by losing money. Shortly after starting NL, I played against an apparent Maniac.[1] He had a huge stack, and he seemed to be crazily splashing his chips around. He would raise pre-flop with very weak hands, bet with little or nothing on the flop, bluff outrageously, over-bet his good hands, and so on. But he kept "getting lucky," and his stack kept growing. Everybody was overplaying hands, trying to isolate him from the rest of the "good players."

After about three hours I suddenly realized that he was the best player at the table. He knew exactly what he was doing. He could read us accurately, and we didn't know where he was. He was losing small pots but winning large ones. I immediately began avoiding him while studying him intently.

When I left a few hours later, I believed that nobody else had realized how good he was. The others were still trying to isolate him, over-playing their hands, paying him off, being bluffed out, and so on. And his stack was still growing. It was an expensive lesson, but worth every dollar.

The critical point is quite simple conceptually, but very hard to apply: The way that someone plays small pots may not tell you how he plays large ones, and you *must* learn how he plays them. Until you do, avoid playing large pots against her without a huge hand.

Much Less Data

Learning how someone plays large pots is difficult, because they occur so infrequently. In limit you usually see how people have acted in many similar situations before deciding what they are doing in this one. You can get a fairly good idea of how some people play just by

---

1. This experience was also discussed in "Isolating Idiots" on pages 123–130.

counting how often they call or raise pre-flop, and everyone plays that street on every hand. In addition, in limit more people play on every street, and far more hands go to showdown.

After you have seen people play some hands in various situations, you will know whether they are willing or unwilling to raise pre-flop with, say, suited connectors or small pairs in multi-way pots; how they play draws and make hands on the flop and turn; and what they have when they bet or call on the river. With all these data you can quickly learn how to put most people on a fairly narrow range of hands.

Alas, when you have to put someone on a hand with your NL stack at risk, you may have *no* data about how he plays in similar situations. They occur only a few times a night, and he may not have made any very large bets, raises, or calls. Even if he made a few, the hands may not have been shown down. You can be forced to make a critical decision without knowing when and how he will risk his stack.

Another problem is that NL starting hands are much less formulaic. In limit you can often make confident inferences from the way someone plays pre-flop. For example, if a solid player raised in early position, he probably has a big ace or medium to large pocket pair. In deep-stack NL he could have far more hands.

More Complex Decisions

When making NL decisions, you must consider many more factors. You have the same options as in a limit game, plus you must decide how much you will call, bet, or raise, and you must always consider the implications of everyone's stack sizes. If you are out of position, you must think about the effects of checking versus making a small blocking bet. Some people will regard a small bet as a sign of weakness, but it will slow down other players. If you have a large stack and are the last to act, you must be careful about betting with less than the nuts; you could get check-raised for an amount you won't call.

The Complicating Effects of Television

Because so many new players have been influenced by TV, they can be extremely hard to read. How can you put someone on a hand when he does not know what he is doing?

These new players often copy the moves they have seen without recognizing the differences between full-table games with tiny blinds and shorthanded action with huge blinds and antes. They also don't understand that some of the moves they have seen on TV were based on the pros' extraordinary ability to read cards and players. They may push in their stacks at exactly the wrong time.

Lack of Good Instructional Material

In earlier chapters, I said that most books on NL do not deal with today's game. The problem is even worse for the literature on reading players. Doyle Brunson, Phil Hellmuth, and virtually all the famous players who have written about NL don't play in the small games. Does a signal mean the same thing in a huge game full of experts as it does in a $100 buy-in game full of beginners and weak players? I suspect it does not, but I cannot be sure; neither can anyone else.

Regardless of the size of the games they play, nearly all NL writers say that reading players is critically important but don't tell you how to do it. They may give some general categories or descriptions: weak-tight, loose-aggressive, and so on. However, they provide almost no help on *how* to categorize players, especially how to predict their reactions to critical situations.

For example, Doyle Brunson devoted only one page to "Categorizing Players," and he listed only two types: "low-grade" and "high-grade."[2] Are there only two types of players? Of course not, but he doesn't discuss any others. Sklansky and Miller don't discuss most types of players nor do they say much about reading players. They

2. Doyle Brunson, *Super System 2*, 544.

have chapters on adjusting to weak-tight and loose players, and they do give a warning about tough and weak-loose players:

> Until you have experience telling these two player types apart, be extra careful before you start licking your chops over a potential live one. Watch closely and make sure the "mistakes" your opponent is making are for big bets, not little ones. **Don't play your loose opponents for live ones until you see them make at least one major error for a large bet.** If you are somewhat inexperienced, you might want to wait for two major mistakes.[3]

That advice doesn't help much when you have to make a decision *before* seeing a major mistake, which often occurs. So what do you do—fold everything but the nuts? They don't say anything except "be extra careful."

They tell you how to compute the expected value of various-sized bets based on your estimates of the probabilities that various-sized bets will be called. The math is impeccable, but the probability estimates are essentially guesses. They do *not* tell you how to make them.

Their examples suggest that they assume that the probability of a bet's being called goes down as the size of the bet increases. That principle is generally true, but occasionally a small bet may appear more dangerous than a large one. It seems to shout, "Call me," and some players will fold more readily than they would to a much larger bet. Who will react that way? I don't know, and I haven't read anything— in their book or anywhere else—that will help me.

Intuition Versus Logic

Most of the better-selling NL books have been written by intuitive players, and they provide only very general guidelines about reading players, such as "be alert and observant" or "see how someone has

3. David Sklansky and Ed Miller, *No Limit Hold'em: Theory and Practice*, 185

played similar hands" (even though you may not have seen such hands).

They almost never offer much evidence or theoretical support. They essentially say, "Trust your instincts!" For example, Doyle Brunson recommended:

> Once you decide what a man's most likely to have—especially in no-limit—you should never change your mind. You'll probably be right the first time, so don't try to second guess yourself. Have the courage and conviction to trust your instincts.[4]

Of course, he does not tell you how to develop those instincts. He just assumes that you have them.

Nonsense! *Most* people do not have them. I certainly don't, and you probably don't either.[5] I admitted that weakness many years ago in *The Psychology of Poker:*

> After studying and teaching psychology for many years, I am still amazed by some people's intuition. . . . I once worked with someone for months. After meeting him for two minutes, my wife said: "He's a crook; don't trust him." I later learned that I should have listened to her, but she never could tell me how she knew; she just did.[6]

That book was written when I (and nearly everyone else) played only limit. I have since learned that some of its principles apply fairly well to NL, that others do not, and that I am unsure about many of them.

For example, loose-aggressive players (LAPs) are going to bluff frequently, but will *this* LAP (who has frequently made small bluffs) bluff for one hundred big blinds? We all know that you shouldn't bluff most

---

4. *Super System 2,* 551.

5. The differences between intuition and logic were extensively discussed in *Your Worst Poker Enemy,* 19–58.

6. Alan Schoonmaker, *The Psychology of Poker,* 7.

loose-passive players (LPPs), because they will call you down with weak hands, but will *this* LPP call a huge bluff with a marginal hand?

Because NL results depend primarily on a few pots for which we may have hardly any information, the intuitive players have a large edge. They cannot say exactly why they think somebody is bluffing or has the nuts, but their good instincts often let them make the right decisions.

David Sklansky, the leader of the logical, math-based school of poker, made a related point in his NL book: "I have been reluctant all these years to write a no limit book . . . because I know that theoreticians without other talents will still be underdogs to talented non-theoreticians. . . . I'm talking about skills such as . . . reading hands [and] making others play badly."[7]

He did not define their talent, but I believe he meant the "feel" that Doyle described. If theoreticians without feel are underdogs to these people, you and I clearly have to work very hard to develop our own feel.

Developing Your Feel

Arthur Reber has stated that "feel" or "intuition" is really *implicit learning,* "the capacity to pick up information about complex [situations] largely without awareness of either the process or the products of learning."[8]

I asked Arthur to comment on David Sklansky's position. He said that "intuitive" people do *not* have inherently greater capacity to process information, but they pay

> more and closer attention which allows them to pick up the deeper patterns that are out there. . . .
>
>   The gift that you think is "natural" (or innate) is not a gift to acquire knowledge intuitively, it is a capacity for attentional focus—

7. David Sklansky, "About This Book" in David Sklansky and Ed Miller, *No Limit Hold'em: Theory and Practice,* 5.

8. "Implicit Learning," in *Encyclopedia of Cognitive Science* (Macmillan, 2000).

and it is almost certainly driven strongly by motivational factors. Those who really care will focus attention more sharply and put in more time than those who don't. . . . Watching highly skilled practitioners . . . can give you the sense that some people just have skills that seem natural, almost magical. . . . You get that sense that you will never compete with them. . . .

Also, David is making a distinction that feels right to him, but misses the point. If he feels that he, being compellingly analytical, could not compete with the "feel" kinds of players it is because, when he plays, he tends to focus his attention on other elements of the game. That is, rather than attending to the subtle patterns of betting, physical movements, facial changes, vocal stress, hand position . . . he focuses on how much they bet and what the pot and implied odds are. He is not a good intuitive player because of the manner in which his attentional resources are being distributed, not because he lacks some genetic capacity."[9]

It is not an either/or issue. You certainly should not minimize math and strategy, as some intuitive people do, nor should you minimize the behavioral cues, as some mathematical-logical people do. It is far better to do both (if you can handle all that information).

Let's assume that you have relatively little feel because you have not been paying much attention to those subtle patterns Arthur described. If so, the critical question is: *How can you shift your attention to develop "feel"?* People with natural feel have been focusing on these subtle cues for much of their lives, while you have been focusing on other information. To catch up to them, deliberately take two steps that intuitive people take automatically:

1. Gather different kinds of information.
2. Get practice and feedback on understanding its meaning.[10]

9. Private e-mail while I was writing this book.

10. Jan Siroky worked closely with me on this system for developing feel.

Step No. 1: Gather different kinds of information. From the moment you sit down, try to learn what kinds of people your opponents are. *Don't* focus only on the way they play their cards. Learn as much as you can about:

- Their basic personality (e.g., aggressive, conservative, sociable)
- Why they play poker (e.g., to make money, to get the kick of gambling, to test themselves against challenges)
- Their current mental and emotional state (e.g., confident, flustered, angry)

All of this information can help you to understand what they are doing and how you can manipulate them into making mistakes. People generally play poker the way they do other things. Their playing style, clothes, voice, gestures, attitudes, and vocabulary all reveal and express their underlying personality. The more information you have, the more you will understand about your opponents and the better you can adjust to them. You should continually observe, listen, and question.

Observe everything possible. People continually give away information about themselves, but you have to look for it and try to understand its poker implications. For example, someone who bullies waitresses or dealers is probably going to play a bullying style. An older, quiet, well-dressed woman is probably more conservative than a loud, young man with spiked hair and tattoos. Someone who watches the TV while playing is obviously not that serious or too aware of what is happening.

Listen to *everything*, even apparently irrelevant remarks about work, play, family, homes, and so on. Anything you hear can give you insights. If someone whines about how much money he has lost in the pits, he is clearly a gambler, perhaps a foolish one. If he brags about himself, he is probably an egotistical player.

Question anything that can help you to understand people. Some apparently innocuous questions can provide valuable insights into opponents' character:

- Do you mow your own lawn? People who do it own their own property, and they tend to be conservative, perhaps even cheap.
- What's your favorite game besides poker? Craps players tend to be gamblers, even wild ones. Most chess players are unemotional thinkers.
- What poker books and authors do you like? (People generally play the way their favorite authors recommend.)
- Who are the best players? (Someone who admires Dan Harrington will play very differently from a fan of Dan Negreanu.)

Step No. 2: Get practice and feedback on understanding its meaning.
Just gathering information will not have much impact on your ability to read and adjust to players. They are skills, and you need practice and feedback to develop any skill. To learn how to type you must hit the keys and see when you are right or wrong. If you couldn't see the results of hitting the wrong key, you wouldn't learn how to type.

Use the same general process to develop your feel. Continually try to read and adjust to players and make sure you get accurate feedback about how well you have done. Unfortunately, the feedback is less reliable and harder to interpret. If you hit the wrong key, you can immediately see your mistake. If you misread someone or make the wrong adjustment, you may never know it.

For example, if you fold because you think someone has you beaten, you may have been bluffed. If you bluff and your opponent folds, you may think you made a great move even though he had missed his draw.

The general principles for developing these skills were discussed on pages 41–62 of *The Psychology of Poker*. In addition to those general principles, take five steps:

1. Put people on a range of hands.
2. Make predictions about what they will do.

3. Record your results.
4. Analyze the causes for your good and bad decisions.
5. Discuss steps 1–4 with other people.

You need to take these active-learning steps because passive experience will not have much impact on your skills or feel. Some people have played for decades but have hardly any ability to read and adjust to players; but if you take these steps you can develop your abilities fairly quickly.

Because these steps can be very tiring, focus on only a few players at first. Don't completely ignore the others, but concentrate on the one or two players you should avoid or target for doubling up or bluffing. Later, when you have more experience, you can slowly increase the number of players you study.

1. Put people on a range of hands. As I wrote in *The Psychology of Poker* (pp. 61–62),

> A common weakness is jumping to conclusions, then ignoring any contrary evidence. Virtually everyone does it, not just when playing cards, but all the time. It's just a natural human weakness.... I put someone on a high pair or a flush draw, then discount or even ignore other possibilities. This sort of thinking has cost me lots of money.

David Sklansky warned against this tendency:

> Do not put undue emphasis on your opinion of your opponent's hand. I know many players who put someone on a certain hand and play the rest of the hand assuming he has that hand. This is taking the method of reading hands too far.... Instead you must put a player on a few different possible hands with varying degrees of probability for each of these hands.[11]

11. David Sklansky, *Hold'em Poker*, 49.

Note that his position is exactly the opposite of Doyle Brunson's. It's the essential difference between intuitive and logical thinkers. You may sometimes think, "I am *sure* that I know what he has," but you must fight that tendency. Doyle and a few other intuitive geniuses can put someone on a hand with extreme accuracy, but you are not one of these geniuses. If you were, you wouldn't be reading these pages. So accept and work within your limitations.

Study the action all the time. Otherwise, you will miss most of your learning opportunities. You play only a few hands, but you can learn from every hand. When you are involved in a pot, you hope for various cards, and you naturally concentrate on winning the pot. When you are just observing other people, you can be much more detached and analytical about them and yourself.

2. Make predictions about what they will do. The feedback cycle is much faster and more reliable for predictions than for putting people on hands. Because only a few hands go to showdown, you usually will not know whether your reads are correct. But you will get immediate feedback about your predictions. If you expect someone to check but he bets, you should immediately recognize your mistake. If you bet expecting him to fold but he raises, you obviously misunderstood the situation.

3. Record your results. "Taking Notes" stated that most poker players don't take notes, but that some top players take lots of them. Obviously, it is better to copy the good players than the bad ones. The more notes you take, the more you will learn. You will learn the most from your mistakes, the times that people had different cards or acted differently from your predictions.

Every time you make a serious mistake, write it down. "I thought he had a big pocket pair, but he had ace-jack suited"; "I thought he would raise, but he folded"; "I thought he was bluffing, but he had the nuts."

4. Analyze the causes for your good and bad decisions. If you take enough notes, you will see patterns. You can accurately read Joe but cannot read Suzie. You are good at bluffing people, but not at snapping off bluffs. You can bluff certain types of players, but not others. The critical question is: *Why are you making good and bad reads and decisions?* Ask yourself these questions:

- Why did you think he had those hands?
- Which signals affected your assessment or prediction?
- How did you interpret those signals?
- Why was your interpretation correct or incorrect?

To answer these questions, you must ruthlessly analyze yourself. What personal strengths and weaknesses help and hurt you? How can you build on your strengths and overcome your weaknesses? Self-examination is unpleasant, but it is an essential step toward becoming a better player.

5. Discuss steps 1–4 with other people. You will learn fastest by working as a team. If you and another competent player frequently discuss these steps, you will both gain immensely. He will see things that you miss and vice versa, helping both of you to realize why you make certain kinds of mistakes. You may think that someone would not play a hand a certain way, but he will say that the person had played an earlier hand that way. Or you may spot a tell that he misses.

Working with someone will make your thinking clearer and more visible. When you have to explain *why* you put someone on a hand, you will often realize that you were not thinking well. By repeatedly explaining how you reached conclusions, you will recognize the holes and inconsistencies in your thinking.

It is even better to work with a coach. He will probably be more skilled than you are, and he will focus more intensely on developing your skill. Have him either sit behind you or play in the same game. Then take frequent breaks to discuss hands.

Target Marketing

Jan Siroky is a salesman and NL coach, and his "Target Marketing" concept applies to both selling and NL. Good salespeople and NL players apply similar principles. They both

- Avoid tough "customers" and concentrate on the most profitable ones.
- Carefully select the products to sell to *this* customer. Good NL players target some people for bluffs, others for doubling up.
- Vary their strategy to fit *this* opponent and *this* objective.
- Plan their strategy in advance. They know what they will do before they do it, and they carefully set up their bluffs and traps before executing them.
- Base their plans on solid information and do whatever it takes to get it.

Of course, limit players avoid the better players, try to isolate the weaker ones, and don't bluff calling stations, but—because both the risks and potential profits are greater—targeting is much more important in NL. Let's focus on the central target marketing issue: Which players should you avoid, bluff, or select as doubling-up targets?

Players to Avoid

Known pros are obviously dangerous, and they are much more dangerous in NL. The skill differential has greater effects in NL, and they can bust you. Nearly everyone knows that they should avoid them, but some people deliberately confront them. They see them as a challenge or they want to learn from them or they let their desire to test themselves overwhelm their common sense. They usually pay a high price to satisfy these other motives. Unless these other motives are extremely important to you, avoid known pros (unless you have a great hand).

However, you definitely should study them. You can learn a lot, and you may spot some weaknesses that you can exploit. Do the same with the other players you should avoid.

Tricky players are always dangerous, and they can be deadly in NL. They make lots of moves to confuse you, and confusion often determines who busts whom. Since they can read you better than you can read them, don't risk a lot of chips without a great hand.

Make many of your decisions before the flop. Fold marginal hands because you need better cards to compensate for their trickiness. After the flop play everything but the nuts cautiously, especially when you're out of position. Of course, there is a danger here: by acting this way, you may become easier for them to read and manipulate.

You may view them as a challenge and want to outplay them, but it's your egotism talking, not your rational self. Accept that they are trickier than you are, and that you probably can't outplay them. Don't try to beat them at their own game.

If possible, sit to the left of the people you want to avoid. You want to know what they are doing before committing yourself. You probably can't get to the left of all of them, so try to get position on the most dangerous ones. Usually, but not always, the most dangerous players are known pros.

Bluffing Targets

Although big pots are critically important, don't ignore the small ones, especially in games with small capped buy-ins. You need to win some small pots to build your stack to the size needed to win the big ones.

Small bluffs can build your stack without taking large risks. Keep the pot small so that

- You risk fewer chips when you bluff.
- The pots are easier to steal because nobody cares that much about them. My friend Cinch calls them "for sale pots," and you should buy more than your share of them.

Don't try to bluff extremely loose players, whether they are passive or aggressive. They will call you with weak hands. Don't try to bluff tricky players. You don't know what they have or what they will do.

Don't try to bluff confused players. As Matt Lessinger stated in *The Book of Bluffs*, "Confusion leads to curiosity, and curious people will spend money to find out what you have."[12]

Focus on *cowards*, the tight, timid players. Look for signals that say, "I am not going to lose much money today." For example, if there is a minimum and maximum buy-in (such as $100–$300), they buy the minimum. They play few hands. They fold frequently when pressured.

Do *not* try to win big pots from them. If you bet and raise aggressively with less than the nuts, and they stay with you, you are probably beaten. You can often bluff or semi-bluff them by betting or raising an amount that says, "I want you to call." Do *not* make large bluffs, because a small one will usually do the job, and your risk is much smaller. If you make large bluffs, you may trap yourself by running into a powerhouse.

Also bluff *straightforward players* who raise with ace-king and ace-queen but don't make continuation bets when the flop misses them. If they raise ahead of you, you can call with some marginal hands (if you are confident that nobody will call behind you). Because they will miss the flop two-thirds of the time, you can steal a lot of pots from them.

Don't worry about straightforward players having a big pair. If they check the flop, you know they don't have one, and you can take the pot away from them. If they bet and you can't beat a big pair, just

12. Matt Lessinger, *The Book of Bluffs* (New York: Warner Books, 2005), 5.

fold. If you get lucky and can beat an overpair, you have a shot at their stack.

Doubling-Up Targets

Since your NL results come primarily from the big pots, play them against the right people. Certain players are the best targets, and there are some obvious overlaps between them, especially their underlying motivation. They may not play to maximize their profits, even if they believe or claim they do. They are driven primarily by motives such as a need to gamble, dominate, or impress people.

Extremely loose-aggressive players (Maniacs) are the most obvious targets. They are "action junkies" and overplay nearly all their hands. Sometimes you can let them do most of the betting. They would much rather bet and raise than call.

Dan Harrington called this strategy "The Rope-a-Dope." When you have a strong hand, "you can just call a super-aggressive player rather than making what would be normal raises against another player. . . . You encourage him to keep trying to push you out of the pot. . . . You make only one raise at the very end of the hand."[13]

Against Maniacs play large pots only when you have big hands at the time *you* choose:

- *Before the flop with aces or kings:* Make very large raises—preferably all-in—before the flop. Do *not* slow-play them pre-flop hoping to outplay them afterward. You probably can't do it because they know more about your hand than you do about theirs.

- *After the flop with two pair or better:* Wait until you have a big hand and let them bet off their chips. Don't get busted post-flop with weaker hands, especially draws (unless you have a lot of outs). Let them have the small pots while you wait for the hands you want to play for the large ones.

13. *Harrington on Hold'em, Vol. I,* 47.

Bullies are not the same as Maniacs, and they can be easy to recognize, even before they play a hand. They want to intimidate people, and their entire manner says, "I'm the boss, and don't you forget it." Some of them are openly critical or hostile toward players, waitresses, and dealers. They buy lots of chips. They may try to become the "table captain," telling everyone what to do. They show off by overplaying their hands, making large bets and raises, bluffing frequently, perhaps even bragging about their skill and toughness.

Let them think that you are afraid of them. Get them committed to winning the pot. They may even become emotionally committed before becoming pot committed. Let them think, "This pot is *mine!*" Then spring the trap.

Egotistical players are hungry for respect and recognition. They brag about their skills and tell others how to play. They may show their bluffs and folds to prove how smart they are. Although they can be extremely annoying, do *not* tune out or ask them to shut up when they lecture. Instead, encourage them to talk and listen carefully, because they will tell you how to beat them.[14]

Compliment them on their skill: "Well played"; "Great read"; "Nice move." Let them think they are in control, and then trap them for their stacks. Don't check-raise them frequently, because they may take it as an insult. Instead, make small, apparently blocking bets and let them raise you. When you take down a big one, seem relieved: "Whew! I was awfully afraid you had me."

Paradoxically, egotistical players can be good targets for both doubling up and bluffing. They *love* to prove how smart they are by making and showing big laydowns. Although you may be tempted to outsmart them, you should usually—but not always—resist that temptation.

Recognize that you may want to bluff an egotistical player to wipe that smug smile off his face. This understandable desire can cause

---

14. "We Need a Miranda Warning" in *Your Worst Poker Enemy* discusses the way people give away information and how to use it against them.

foolish mistakes. Trying to force a big laydown is obviously risky. It can't be made without a big hand, and you may be unable to get him to fold it. Unless you are convinced that you have created an exceptionally attractive opportunity for him to show off, don't try to bluff an egotistical player.

Straightforward tight-aggressive players (TAPS) are tough in limit games, but excellent doubling-up targets in NL. Because they wait for premium cards, they are easy to read. If, for example, a TAP has raised in early position and you are both deep-stacked, you can call in late position with a wide range of hands. If the flop misses you, fold. If it hits you a little and the flop bet is not too large, you can take off a card. If the flop or turn makes you a big hand but could not have helped him, you have a good shot at his stack.

A small set is ideal. So is 76 with a flop of 458. After waiting for hours to get a big pair, TAPs will bet it aggressively and may refuse to fold when you make your move. They waited this long, and they are not going to get pushed off their premium cards.

In addition to taking their stack, you may make them underestimate you, and you can even put them on tilt. They may get so angry that they will lose several more buy-ins. They may regard you as a lucky fool and try to get revenge for your "sucking out with such trash."

Warning: The same factors that make them targets for doubling up also make them nearly unbluffable with big pairs. Just wait until you have the right hand and situation and go for their stack.

The critical task is to decide exactly when to avoid, bluff, or attempt to bust. You will certainly make serious mistakes. For example, you will try to bluff or double up against the wrong people, or you will attack someone you should avoid. You must therefore be ruthlessly self-critical: continually examine your own performance to identify and correct your own mistakes.

Because it requires a fundamentally new mind-set, target marketing is difficult and tiring. So start with just one or two players. Then slowly expand the number of players you target. In just a few weeks you may be targeting most of the table.

Final Remarks

Reading and adjusting to players are important skills for all forms of poker, but they are absolutely essential for NL. If you cannot do them well, you are doomed to mediocrity or worse.

A few intuitive people have an enormous natural advantage in NL. They just know how to read and adjust to players. If you don't have their gift, you have two choices. First, you can stick to limit, because you can win by just playing a technically correct game. Of course, you would win more if you read and adjusted well to players. Second, you can work hard on *all* these tasks:

- Gathering information by observing, listening, and asking questions
- Developing your skills at using that information
- Identifying and avoiding the toughest players
- Carefully selecting your bluffing and doubling-up targets
- Ruthlessly criticizing your own mistakes

If you are not willing to make that choice, if you try to play NL without having the natural gifts or working hard, you will almost certainly be disappointed. Conversely, if you work hard on all of the tasks, you can outperform people who have more natural talent, but aren't willing to work hard.

Thomas A. Edison, the world's greatest inventor, once said something that applies to poker: "Genius is one percent inspiration and ninety-nine percent perspiration." Since you don't have great intuition, you have to outwork the people who do have it.

Apply active-learning principles *now* by taking a mini-quiz about what you have just read. Turn to Appendix E and answer those questions about this chapter.

Which Games Should You Choose?

Game selection is always important, but when you lack NL experience, it is absolutely critical. If you pick your games well, you can quickly become a winner. If you choose poorly, you will almost certainly become a loser. In fact, selecting the right game can have more impact on your bottom line than any other skill.

Roy Cooke wrote: "Your success at poker depends, not on how well you play, but on how well you play in relation to your opponents. . . . This presents a significant problem. . . . Almost all players put themselves closer to the front of the pack than they deserve to be."[1] His words reinforce the importance of basing your game selection on objective self-analysis. If you kid yourself about your abilities, you are going to choose the wrong games and suffer the consequences.

Game Selection Is More Important in NL Than in Limit

There are several reasons. First, NL rewards and punishes abilities differences much more than limit. If you are stronger than your opponents, you will win faster; if you are weaker, you will lose faster. In limit a bad play will cost you a few bets or a pot, but in NL it can cost you your stack.

Second, as an earlier chapter argued, NL requires more knowledge, skills, and abilities than limit. Third, inaccurately assessing yourself and your opposition is particularly common when you first switch to

1. Roy Cooke, "A Great Game?" *Card Player,* May 10, 2002.

NL. You may not recognize your weaknesses and your opponents' strengths. For example, many new NL players greatly overemphasize selecting good starting hands and look down at people who play weak cards. But under certain conditions you should play weaker hands in NL than limit.

Fourth, NL demands certain psychological traits, and if you are new to NL you may not know whether you have them. For example, until you have faced many all-in bets, you cannot know how you will react. Perhaps you will remain cool and analytical, perhaps not. Certain types of games can create more pressure than you can handle.

What Should You Look For?

Assume that you do not know any of the players, the blinds are $1 and $2, and the buy-in is exactly $100. To pick good NL games you must consider all the limit game factors, plus the stack sizes. You must also think differently about the pattern of action.

Stack Sizes

In limit, stack sizes don't matter much, and you may want large stacks because people are probably gambling, and you can win more money. But in capped NL games, large stacks have a very different meaning. Let's say that you can choose between two games:

1. A brand new one: Everyone has exactly $100.
2. One that has been going on for hours: The average stack is $400, the smallest is $200, and the largest is over $1,000.

Although the second game seems to have more potential, avoid it because some—perhaps even most—of the players are winners. Remember, they could not have bought those chips; they had to win them. Some of them may have rebought, but they still had to win a lot of chips to build those stacks.

They are probably stronger players, and winning usually makes people play better. They become more confident, decisive, and aggressive. Also, because they have larger stacks than yours, they can run over you. You probably don't have enough experience, judgment, and emotional control to challenge tough players with large stacks.

The first game's players are probably strangers to each other as well as to you. After playing together, the second game's people know how the others play. You have to study nine players, while they can concentrate on learning about you.

The Pattern of Action

The action is always important, but you must think about it differently in NL, especially when you lack experience. Let's say that no seats are open. All the tables have roughly the same stack sizes: an average of about $200, with the smallest under $30 and the largest over $500. You see three very different patterns:

1. A "limp-fest." Most pots are not raised pre-flop, and about six people see most flops. Post-flop bets are small, raises are infrequent and small, and many hands go to a showdown, often with more than two players. There is hardly any bluffing and there are no huge bluffs.

2. Wildly aggressive. Most pots are raised, and the first raise averages over $20. Reraises occur quite often, frequently for entire stacks, making monster pots.

3. Tight-aggressive. Most pots are "raise and take it," with an average first raise to $7. Most hands don't get to the flop, and if there is one, usually only two or three players see it. Few hands go to showdown.

Table three is definitely not right for you:

There are lots of reasons not to play, and hardly any reasons for playing. You are probably going to lose, and you may lose much more than you can afford. If you win, you won't win much. The game can be so stressful and demanding that you can't relax. If you do not play your very best, you have no chance at all, and, even then, you may easily lose. So, why bother?[2]

When I wrote those words in *The Psychology of Poker*, I was describing tight-aggressive limit games, but they certainly apply to NL. Most pros and other good players are tight-aggressive, and you want to avoid tough players. You can't win much money, and you won't have much fun.

Table two may seem attractive, but it is much too dangerous. Even if you crush wild games when playing limit, avoid them until you become comfortable with NL's huge swings and intense stresses. An excellent NL player disagrees. He thinks you can beat wild games quite easily: just wait for premium hands and push them hard. That strategy would work for him, but, as a new NL player, you probably can't apply it. For example, what do you do with your unimproved aces when a Maniac raises after the flop? Fold automatically? Push all-in? You don't have enough experience to decide.

Wild games can create more stress than you can handle. Loose-aggressive players are always hard to read, and for reasons discussed earlier, you may be unable to tell whether they are good players or bad ones. You don't have the experience or judgment to decide how to play many hands. You may become weak-tight because you are scared or play too loosely and aggressively because your greed and competitive urges become aroused. You may even shift back and forth from playing too timidly to playing too aggressively. And the occasional losses of your stack can severely upset you. You can't play poker well unless you are calm and controlled, and you probably can't be that way in a wild NL game.

Until you have more experience, don't try for huge wins. The games that can produce big wins will often cause huge losses. Strive

---

2. Alan Schoonmaker, *The Psychology of Poker*, 262.

for frequent, small wins until you become competent and comfortable.

The limp-fest is the place to be. People who limp frequently are loose-passive, and they don't know much about NL. Loose-passive players are the easiest to beat in all forms of poker, and they are especially easy in NL. They will rarely make large bets, and when they do you can easily fold. And when you have a winner, they will often pay you off.

Always Consider Your Own Emotional Reactions

Poker experts generally ignore their own emotions, but they affect everything you do. Experts focus on how you should play, not on the emotional and other factors that make you (and most other people) react irrationally.

Any kind of game can cause emotional reactions. You may become so bored in tight-aggressive games that you play too many hands. The limp-fest players will repeatedly frustrate you by beating your good hands with trash. But wild games arouse the strongest feelings, a volatile combination of greed, excitement, fear, and machismo. Their risks and opportunities can cause two diametrically opposed reactions: playing scared and playing sheriff.

Playing scared is always destructive, but it is deadly in NL. You may check when you should bet, call when you should raise, and make small bets and raises when you should make large ones. You will not get full value from your good hands, and giving away cheap or free cards will cost you many pots. You will also get bluffed repeatedly.

Playing sheriff is the macho overreaction, and it is extremely destructive. Countless stacks have been lost by people who overplayed their hands just to prove—to themselves or other people—"You can't run over *me!*"

NL is a very stressful game, and because you haven't faced some of its stresses, you may not know how you will react to them. For example, until you have to risk a large stack, you don't know what you will do. Wild games add to the stress: by forcing you to make difficult decisions, they will repeatedly test your emotional reactions. Don't face those tests until you are ready for them.

Final Remarks

If you select the wrong games, you may become so frustrated that you will give up on NL before learning whether it is right for you. Conversely, if you select the right ones, you may start winning almost immediately, and you will certainly feel more comfortable and get better results.

Apply active-learning principles *now* by taking a mini-quiz about what you have just read. Turn to Appendix E and answer those questions about this chapter.

Where Should You Sit?

Many players don't even think about where they should sit, but Ray Zee, a great player and writer,[1] said that picking the wrong seat was one of the ten top reasons for losing. A bad choice will give you poor position.

Choosing the right seat in NL is also much more difficult than in limit. In limit you must consider only the other players' skills and styles. In NL these qualities have a greater effect on you, and you must also take into account everyone's stack sizes.

Position Is More Important in NL Than in Limit

Position is always important, but in NL it is a *much* bigger asset when you've got it, and a *much* bigger liability when you haven't. I asked Bob Ciaffone, a noted authority on both limit and NL, "How much more important is position in NL than in limit?" He hesitated to get the right word, then said, "It's *miles* more important."

My discussion group was polled about the relative importance of various skills in limit and NL. "Understanding and using position" ranked fourth for several reasons:

1. In NL check-raising occurs much less frequently, which increases the value of position. In limit you often check-raise

1. He is the author of *High-Low Split Poker for Advanced Players* and coauthor of *Seven Card Stud for Advanced Players,* both published by Two Plus Two. His positions here are from "Top Ten Reasons You Lose," twoplustwo.com's *Internet Magazine,* May 2006.

to create unfavorable pot odds for your opponents. In NL you can create whatever odds you like without risking free cards.

2. Traps are much more important in NL, and they are much easier to set and avoid with position.

3. Your NL results depend primarily on a few large pots, and you want more information before making decisions that can double up or bust you.

Your Opponents' Skills and Styles

A few general principles apply to both limit and NL but are more important in NL:

1. Because skilled players are dangerous, you want them to your right so they will act before you. Because they can hurt you more in NL, you *really* want position on them.

2. Because the weaker players can't hurt you too much, you want them to your left so they will act after you.

3. To avoid surprises, you want the predictable players to your left, and the unpredictable ones to your right. Because surprises in NL can cost you your stack, having position on the unpredictable players becomes more important. Although predictability is related to skill, it is also related to style.

The Psychology of Poker was written when nearly everybody played limit poker, and it does not discuss NL. The chapter on each style contained a section titled "Where Should You Sit?" Because Mason Malmuth and David Sklansky edited the text, I believe it accurately described position principles for limit games. I will summarize some points and say how NL should change your decision.

Loose-Aggressive Players

Most discussions of position and styles focus primarily on loose-aggressive players (LAP) because they have so much impact on your results and emotions. Your position relative to LAP, especially the most extreme ones (Maniacs), is even more important in NL than in limit.

In limit sit to their immediate left so they will act before you do. Generally, you want to be to the left of loose players, whether they are aggressive or passive. You can raise and isolate them to exploit their tendency to play weak hands.

Position is especially important for LAP. You want them to raise before you act, not afterward. If you act first, you may put in one bet, then another with a hand that you would not willingly play for two bets.

However, if someone is predictably loose-aggressive, sit to his *right.* That predictability can come from:

- Being an utter Maniac who bets or raises nearly every hand
- Telegraphing when he will fold, check, bet, or raise

Because many LAP—particularly Maniacs—lack patience and self-control, they often telegraph their intentions. In fact, they will occasionally act out of turn. You can fold marginal hands and check-raise and slow-play your strong ones

In NL your decision is more complicated, because the size of the bets and raises is so important. You need to win only a few large pots, and nobody builds bigger pots than an LAP, especially a Maniac. You therefore want to be to the immediate *right* of an LAP who frequently makes very large bets and raises even if he does not always raise.

You can check or just call with big hands, hoping he will make a move, which will drive the rest of the table into you. The other players will often overplay their hands because they don't respect his bets and raises. Of course, you may slow-play but be disappointed: he may not bet or raise. But you take that risk whenever you slow-play, and he is more likely than anyone to make a large bet.

If he attacks only a few times but traps one or two others, they may be too pot-committed to fold when you make a large raise. They may have even gone all in before you can act. Your chances of winning a monster pot go way up.

If you sit to the left of a Maniac, some other players—especially the better ones—will slow-play into him, then trap you between them. You may overplay a hand because you don't respect the LAP's bets or raises but then find someone to his right coming over the top.

When you are on his immediate right, you will be last when he bluffs, and most LAPs love to bluff. If you are on his left and suspect a bluff but have someone behind you, you cannot call with a marginal hand. You would hate to snap off his bluff, but have someone overcall.

The only serious downside to sitting to his right is that you will often be raised when you want to play cheaply. If you limp with suited connectors, hoping to get multiway action, he may raise too much, knock out everyone else, and ruin the odds for you. This risk is much less important than the preceding advantages.

The bottom line is: *Sit to the left of LAPs in limit, but to their right in NL.*

Passive Players

You generally want passive people—regardless of how loose or tight they are—on your left. Then you don't have to worry much about a raise behind you.

In limit you want tight-passive players (TPPs) to your left. You can steal their blinds with very little risk, but it is much harder to steal from loose-passive players (LPP).

In NL you want TPP to your right. First, blind stealing is much less important. Second, a TPP's actions provide much more information than an LPP's, who just calls, calls, calls. If a TPP calls ahead of you, you know he has a good hand and can act cautiously. If a TPP bets or raises ahead of you, you can confidently fold everything but a powerhouse. If a TPP is behind you, and he calls your large bet or raise, you may be in trouble.

Tight-Aggressive Players

Because tight-aggressive players (TAP) are often the best players, you want to avoid them. However the way to do so varies.

In limit sit as far away from TAP as possible. If you sit to their right, they have position on you, and you certainly do not want to give the toughest players that edge. If you sit to their left, they will steal your blinds.

In NL sit to their left. Blind stealing is much less important, and it is much easier to avoid TAP when you are on their left.

Final Remarks

Deciding where to sit is more important and more complicated in NL than in limit. You should always try to get position on the most dangerous players. If the wrong players have position on you, your risks can become so high that you should leave the game. I'll return to the stay-or-go decision after discussing your position relative to the large stacks.

Apply active-learning principles *now* by taking a mini-quiz about what you have just read. Turn to Appendix E and answer those questions about this chapter.

Where Do You Want the Big Stacks?

The preceding chapter told you that you want the most dangerous players to act before you do. Now we will apply that principle to an issue that is almost irrelevant in limit, but critical in NL: stack sizes.

The Huge Stacks

You want players with huge stacks on your right for three reasons:

1. They can bust you.
2. They can double you up.
3. They probably play differently.

Most NL books do not discuss one effect of capping the buy-in. If people have huge stacks in a capped game, they are probably winning. They could have lost several buy-ins before getting hot, but they are almost certainly ahead for the last hour or two, and they are probably ahead for the night.

They are therefore good, lucky, or both—which means they are dangerous. You do not want dangerous players to your left, especially not when they have huge stacks, feel lucky, and are winning. Winners often feel and play more confidently and aggressively.

Having a huge stack adds to that confidence and aggression. They can afford to take chances because they can bust you and the others, but you can't bust them. In fact, if their stacks are much bigger than yours, you can't even hurt them very much.

They may therefore think and act like players on a rush, and the other players may respond emotionally. As I said in "Defending Against the Rush," everyone may "share a delusion—the laws of probability have been suspended—and they may all misplay their hands. The rusher pushes too hard, and the others let him run over them."

Because players with huge stacks can bust you and may be playing more aggressively, you want to sit to their left so they act before you do. Sitting there also lets you double up by isolating a huge stack with an all-in raise. Because you can't hurt him badly, he may be more willing to gamble with you. Because he can easily reraise to put the others all in, they may be afraid to call your raise.

A pro told me that these points were incorrect because, "Busting people has nothing to do with cash game play. All chips have the same value. If I have $200 and double through, I have $400 whether I got it from a huge stack or an equal one." He's right economically, but many people don't think that way.

As I noted earlier, most people *hate* losing their stack on one hand, even if the money is economically unimportant. Poker experts often assume that people think objectively and dispassionately about expected value and profits: "A dollar is a dollar is a dollar." The experts may think that way, but most people have strong, irrational feelings about money, and you want to exploit those feelings. Winners and people on a rush think, feel, and play differently from losers or people who feel unlucky.

Research supports another irrational reaction: "The pain of a loss is about twice as much as the joy of a gain."[1] Don't mistakenly assume that people treat chips as having the same value. Learn how they *feel* about their chips and then exploit irrational feelings.

The Fairly Big Stacks

People with fairly big stacks are probably winning, but you can't be sure. So ask them indirectly by saying, "You seem to be doing very

1. Barry Tanenbaum, "Understanding Poker Errors Through Prospect Theory—Part 1," with coauthor Rachel Crosen, *Card Player*, October 25, 2005.

well tonight." Of course, some people will ignore you or lie to you, but you may get valuable information. "Yeah, I'm only in one buy-in," or "No, I had to buy in five times." If someone with a fairly large stack is winning, apply the same general rules as for those with huge stacks, but a bit more moderately.

What About the Small Stacks?

You want players with small stacks on your left for two reasons:

1. They can't hurt you very much.
2. They can actually help you.

Both effects come from the size of their stacks and the way that having a small stack affects their style. They tend to play either scared or very aggressively. They either wait for premium cards or gamble to double up or go home. The fact that they have not rebought suggests that they are reluctant or unable to do so.

If they are playing scared, you can often steal small pots. They will not risk going broke without excellent cards. The megapots do not occur very often, and buying more than your share of these "For Sale" pots can be quite profitable. Because these players' stacks are small, you can buy these pots without risking many chips.

If they are playing "push and hope," you still want them on your left. Their all-in raises cannot hurt you very much, and they can re-open the betting for you and provide some very useful information. Some of them get so bored or desperate that they push with marginal or weak hands.

If they are acting emotionally, they may even telegraph their intentions. If you sense that they are going to raise, you can limp or slow-play, let them raise, and then see how the larger stacks react before committing yourself. If everyone folds, and the pot odds are right, you can call with marginal hands because you cannot lose any more chips.

Sometimes, players with the small stacks will even "buy the button" for you without forcing you to take a serious risk. If you have a good, but not great hand, you may want to make a "pot-sweetener raise," but hesitate to do it. If you reopen the betting, someone can come over the top and force you to fold. But, if a small stack is behind you, he may push all in with a small raise. You can wait to see what the others do before making a commitment. If someone to your left cold-calls the raise, or if a limper ahead of you reraises, you can fold. If only people ahead of you call, you can overcall, knowing that you will act last on later betting rounds.

Don't Hesitate to Change Seats

As conditions change, your seat should change. For example, if someone with a large stack loses it or leaves, switch seats to get position on the players with the largest stacks remaining at the table. If a Maniac sits down, or you see that a player telegraphs his intentions, change seats to exploit the situation.

Some of my friends are unwilling to change seats. They think it is too obvious that they are trying to get position. They may be right for the better players, but the weaker ones don't know what they are doing. Even if some players recognize and adjust to your move, you still get position. So, if you can get a better seat, take it.

What About Bad Seats?

If you are stuck with the huge stacks and wrong players on your left, don't panic. Ask for the first seat change. If your room does not have a seat change system, look for signs that people are ready to leave and lock up the better seats before someone else does it.

If you cannot change seats, seriously consider leaving the game. You may not want to do it, but staying in the wrong seat is just asking for trouble. In the article mentioned previously, Ray Zee wrote:

You have to move to find a spot at the table where you get the best of other players' faults. And at the same time do not suffer from a seat that lets the good players or aggressive ones pound you to death. Many times great games are not worth staying in because you cannot move position at the table.

If you cannot change seats and do not want to leave the game, adjust your style. Play more conservatively, but do not become weaktight. If you find that you are so uncomfortable that you are playing badly, swallow your pride and *get out of the game!*

The Ideal Seat

You will rarely get it, but you should always look for a seat with an utter Maniac to your immediate left, and the largest stacks to your immediate right. Because the Maniac will raise so often, you will not be able to play many hands, but you will win a few monster pots, and that's what NL is all about.

Apply active-learning principles *now* by taking a mini-quiz about what you have just read. Turn to Appendix E and answer those questions about this chapter.

Making the Transition

The preceding chapters discussed several issues to consider when deciding whether to switch to NL. If you decide that you have the potential to succeed at NL, plan a transition strategy. Learning new skills is just one step in that process, and it is not the toughest or most important one. The critical task is *changing your mind-set,* the way you think and feel about poker.

Changing it can be extremely arduous. You are not a computer. You cannot just click on a program and suddenly change everything you do. In fact, for the first few months of playing NL, you will often react like a limit player.

The introduction to this part of the book said that you should ask yourself three questions:

1. Do I have or can I develop the right skills?
2. Do I have the right mental abilities?
3. Do I have or can I develop the right psychological traits?

Let's assume that you have answered yes, to at least questions two and three. You can win at NL if you lack a skill or two, but you do not have much chance without the right traits and mental abilities.

Let's also assume that you are a winning limit player. If you cannot beat limit games, you probably cannot beat NL, because it is a much more demanding game. However, winning at limit does not guarantee success at NL. Some of my friends did very well at limit but tried and could not make the switch.

Despite their skills and discipline, they could not change their mind-set enough to play winning NL. I can certainly understand their problem because I made many serious mistakes by reacting like a limit player.

The poker literature often reminds me of my management consulting days. Experts tell readers what they should do and naively assume that they will follow their advice. Many consultants made the same assumption. They wrote brilliant analyses of the flaws in the current organization and drew a new organization chart. Then they left without telling management how to change the procedures, attitudes, and behavior patterns that the new organization demanded. The result was predictable: Many reorganizations were abysmal failures. People kept thinking and acting in the same old ways.

Don't make the same mistake. Don't expect to become a good NL player just because you think you know how to play NL. Make a plan for changing your mind-set. Let's look at some things you should do in the first few months.

Don't Expect Too Much

It is critical that you don't place your expectations too high. If you expect quick improvements, you will almost certainly be disappointed. You may even become so discouraged that you give up on NL. Beware of two types of unrealistic expectations:

1. *Immediate, dramatic changes in your mind-set:* Altering it is almost always a slow, painful process.

2. *Immediate, large profits:* Even though some terrible players give away their chips, don't expect to make a lot of money immediately.

In fact, your win rate will probably go *down*. Let's say you have been winning $20 per hour playing a mixture of $10–$20 and $15–$30. Accept that you will probably win less at first, and you may even be a short-term loser. Regard that lost income as tuition or an investment in a new business. You have to spend money to make money.

Play *Only* NL Cash Games

Virtually every winning limit player (including me) played both limit and NL at first, but it was a huge mistake. We also made another mistake: we played in NL tournaments, even though they require a different strategy from that for cash games. Don't repeat our mistakes. Play *only* NL cash games until you gain some mastery and confidence.

Playing varied games will almost certainly slow down your progress. The demands are so different that each game interferes with the others. You will think like a limit or tournament player while playing another game.

For example, if someone makes a standard raise, everyone folds, and you're on the button with pocket threes, you'll probably fold because it's the right play in a limit game. But, if you both have enough chips, you should call. If you flop a set, you can bust him. If you don't, you won't lose much.

Let's say that you call and flop that set. If you think like a tournament player, you may overprotect it by betting too much immediately. You don't want to risk being knocked out of the tournament if he makes a better hand. Since you will flop a set less than once every five hours, you should often take the risk of trying for his stack.

Trying to play both limit and NL or both cash games and tournaments is like trying to learn Spanish while continuing to speak English. You will think in English and translate into Spanish, and you will do it badly. Many language schools use "total immersion." Because you speak only Spanish, you quickly shift to thinking in Spanish. By immersing yourself in NL cash games, you will shift your mind-set much more quickly.

People play both limit and NL partly or entirely to minimize their lost profits during the transition period. Some need the cash flow to pay bills, while others just don't want to see their winnings decline. The best way to reduce these feelings is to budget an amount you can afford for the transition and regard that money as an investment in your future. If you can't afford—either financially or psychologically—to have your win rate drop temporarily, don't switch to NL.

Play in Small Games

You may want to play in larger games because you can win more money, and they are more stimulating and challenging. You may also be embarrassed to play in small games, especially if you enjoy the status of playing in fairly large limit ones. But you should avoid bigger games at first.

The players in small games are weaker, so you'll win more often. You won't win much, but so what? If you have budgeted for a period of reduced profits, you won't need to win much or anything. Besides, you can't be sure that you'll win, no matter how well you play limit hold'em.

Jim Brier had beaten limit games up to $100–$200. When he first switched to NL, he played in $50 buy-in games. He made this suggestion to our discussion group:

> Set up little targets for yourself such as I will play one hundred hours of no limit at the lowest levels I can find and see if I can at least break even. If so, I may re-evaluate and play another hundred hours. If I can't break even, I will either drop no limit and go back to limit, or I will remain at the lowest level of no limit until I am a proven winner.

Many players refuse to play small games. They may need the kick of playing for higher stakes, or they may worry, "What will my friends think if they see me here?" That's a silly reaction, but a very human one. If Jim Brier, with his reputation as a player and writer, was not ashamed to play in tiny games, why should you feel embarrassed?

Remember, your primary goal should not be to maximize your immediate profits, and it certainly should not be to impress your friends. Instead, lay a solid foundation for the future.

Concentrate on developing your skills and confidence; nothing develops confidence more than winning. In addition, if the stakes are low, you will be more willing to experiment with new and extremely uncomfortable strategies such as playing weak hands in late position and making large semi-bluffs with good draws.

The lower the stakes, the less fear you will have of losing your stack, and that fear can be crippling. Many good limit players play scared in NL, and the better players can easily run over them.

If the stakes are too high, you will become uncomfortable, and that discomfort can cause you to do what you have always done: think and act like a limit player. You will wait for premium hands, avoid draws without pot odds, overprotect your big hands instead of trying for your opponents' stacks, and so on.

Avoid Wild Games

Even though I made this recommendation earlier, I feel obliged to repeat it. Those games are seductive, but dangerous. You cannot play poker well unless you are calm and controlled, and it is extremely hard to remain that way in wild games, especially when you are new to NL.

In addition to arousing such strong feelings that you don't play well, you will have occasional large losses even when you play perfectly. These losses can make you quit NL without giving it a chance. Don't play in wild games until you are very comfortable and confident about NL.

Play *Only* Short Stacks

Many games have a minimum and a maximum buy-in such as $50–$100 or $100–$300. Buy the minimum, and if you build your stack to over one hundred big blinds, cash in, move to another table, or do whatever else will let you continue to play a short stack.

You will probably dislike this advice because you may have several reasons for wanting to play with a large stack:

1. Big stacks are intimidating, and you naturally want to be the intimidator, not the victim. This principle applies to tournaments, but not cash games. You won't be so afraid of losing a small stack because you can easily buy more chips.

2. It's so boring to play the ultratight, small-stack strategy that you may "cheat" by playing too many hands.

3. If you build up your stack, you won't want to quit or change tables, especially if you would have to go on a waiting list. You came to play, and it looks like tonight can be a big night.

4. You may want to play "real no limit," not some watered-down, simplified version of it. You may yearn to emulate those people you see on TV with daring bluffs, brilliant folds, and heroic calls that snap off huge bluffs.

Someday you may be able to play that way, but you are not ready *yet*. Forgive the cliché, but it's true: You have to walk before you can run. If you try to run too soon or too fast, you will fall on your face. Short-stack NL is walking rather than running, and there are several reasons for playing it:

1. Short-stack NL "is surprisingly simple, significantly more so than limit hold'em. . . . You will need only a simple strategy to win."[1]

1. Ed Miller, *Getting Started in Hold'em*, 118. Much of this material about short-stack NL is derived from the next few pages of that book.

2. You should avoid big losses to prevent becoming discouraged. You are certainly going to make some mistakes, and the smaller your stack, the less they will cost you.

3. You need to book some wins—even if they are small—to build your confidence and comfort with NL's stresses. The short-stack strategy is so simple and effective that "a robot playing a short stack can beat even relatively tough no limit games."[2]

4. In short-stack NL starting hands are very important. This priority is consistent with the emphasis in limit. In deep-stack NL your first two cards are much less important, and it takes considerable time to change the way you think about starting hands.

5. When you have a small stack, the players with deep stacks will make negative EV plays against you because they will focus on the other large stacks. Let's say that you have only fifteen big blinds. There is a standard raise, a call, and then you push all in with pocket aces. If two players have huge stacks, they may call with pocket eights or suited connectors. If they make a big hand, they have a chance to bust the other guy. They are not getting remotely the odds needed to call your bet, but they don't care much about you, and you don't care about the side pot.

6. "After you are all in, your opponents will keep betting, sometimes forcing people to fold. Whenever someone folds . . . you gain, and in this case you gain without having to risk anything further."[3]

2. David Sklansky, and Ed Miller, *No Limit Hold'em: Theory and Practice* (Henderson, NV: Two Plus Two, 2006), 204.

3. Ibid., 200–201.

7. Fear of losing your stack is a major problem for new NL players, but you will be less afraid of losing a small one than a big one. The first time you lose your stack, it's devastating. The second time doesn't hurt quite as much as the first. The tenth hurts much less than the second. The fiftieth should be just another, "Oh well."

Set a Schedule for Moving Up

Although you should start with short stacks in small games, you don't want to remain at that level. If you have to stay there, why bother to learn NL? But move up in a slow, controlled way.

Some players don't wait to prove they can win, and their reasons for moving up can be extremely silly. For example, they may just be bored. Or they may insist that they play too well to beat small games because the players are too weak. Of course, countless people—including some terrible players—have said the same thing about small limit games, and this rationalization is no more valid for small NL games. If you cannot beat small games, you will probably lose even more in larger ones.

Even if you can beat the small games, you should not move up too quickly. Far too many people have beaten small games and prematurely decided, "I'm too good to play here. I'm going to take a shot at the big game." They often take huge losses.

Study the Poker Literature

As I said earlier, the NL literature has not been nearly as helpful to me as the books and articles about limit. There are at least four reasons for this problem:

1. It is much easier to learn how to play limit from printed material, because the principles are simpler and more formu-

laic. NL is more an intuitive art, and it is very hard to learn an art from books.

2. There are not as many good books on NL, partly because most people played only limit until quite recently.

3. Most experts have not played or written about the small, capped NL games, which are the only ones you should play at first.

4. All of the books deal only with knowledge and skills. None of them seriously discuss the ways to assess and develop your psychological traits and mental abilities.

Despite its weakness, you should still study the literature. First, it is the fastest way to learn poker theory. Second, there are a few works that can help you, and more will certainly be published soon.

Start with the articles at cardplayer.com by Barry Tanenbaum and Jim Brier, because they directly contrast limit and NL. This contrast will help you to see the specific changes needed in your mind-set. Barry's series began on April 4, 2006, and Jim's began on July 15, 2006.

Angel Largay has been a big winner in the $2–$5 blinds games, and his new book, *No-Limit Texas Hold'em: A Complete Course,* focuses on the smaller games.[4] Matt Flynn, Sunny Mehta, and Ed Miller wrote *Professional No Limit Hold'em.*[5] David Sklansky and Ed Miller wrote. *No Limit Hold'em: Theory and Practice.*[6] It is the most comprehensive book I have read on NL, but it focuses primarily on deep-stack games. Read it for the general principles, but don't try to master the math or to apply deep-stack strategies until you are ready for them.

4. Published by ECW Press, Toronto, Ontario, Canada, 2006.

5. Published by Two Plus Two, Henderson, NV, 2007.

6. Published by Two Plus Two, Henderson, NV, 2006.

All the *Harrington on Hold'em*[7] books are outstanding, but they focus on tournaments. A book on cash games should appear in 2008. Tom McEvoy and Brad Daughtery's *No-Limit Texas Hold'em: The New Player's Guide to Winning Poker's Biggest Game*[8] is a good text for beginners. Many other books were in the publishing pipeline when I wrote this book,[9] and you should certainly consider them.

Discuss NL Regularly

Although books and articles can develop your theoretical knowledge, you have to go much further than passive study. You will develop your skills and mind-set much more quickly by discussing the books and articles you read, the hands you play, the games you choose, and many other subjects. You particularly need to discuss psychological issues such as your strengths, weaknesses, fears, confusion, boredom, and other feelings. For these discussions you have four options:

1. Poker discussion groups
2. Internet forums
3. A coach
4. A poker buddy

I have discussed all of them in this book, and I urge you to reread those pages.

In addition to all their other benefits, all four alternatives will give you a detached, objective look at the way you think and play. Because you are naturally biased about yourself, you need that objectivity.

7. Two Plus Two has published three volumes, and I believe more are planned.

8. Published by Cardoza, New York, 2004.

9. Kensington will publish three NL books in 2007: *Killer Poker No Limit!* and *Killer Shorthanded No-Limit Hold'em* by John Vorhaus, and *No-Limit Hold'em Hand by Hand* by Neil Myers.

Continually Monitor Yourself

As I noted earlier, most poker players don't monitor themselves as frequently and thoroughly as they should. Careful self-monitoring is always important, but it is particularly critical when you are playing a new game. Because you are unsure of how you should play your cards, you will focus primarily on making the technically right play, not on your own mental and emotional state.

Self-monitoring is more important in NL than in limit, because your mistakes can be so costly. If you don't recognize that you are thinking and playing poorly, you can easily lose a lot of money, perhaps your entire bankroll.

Self-monitoring is also more difficult when you first start playing NL. In addition to the usual questions about your play and state of mind, you should repeatedly ask yourself: *Am I thinking like a limit or a NL player?*

Be as specific as possible. Try to understand exactly *how* you are thinking or acting like a limit or NL player. For each of the following questions, the correct answer is different in a limit or NL game. Ask yourself: Am I giving the proper weight to

- Stack sizes?
- Position?
- Pot odds versus implied odds?
- Manipulating the pot size?
- Pre-flop hand selection versus my chances to win a huge pot?
- Protecting my investment in the pot versus taking a risk to bust someone?
- Playing cards versus playing people?

Afterthought

Even though the NL games offer many advantages, many successful limit players have been disappointed and discouraged by their early results. They expected too much and failed to consider the huge psychological obstacles to switching to NL.

They continued to think and act like limit players and then wondered why they did so poorly. Some of them complain bitterly about the "idiots" who busted their big pairs with trash hands. Others are just baffled. How can good players like themselves do so poorly? What's wrong with NL?

Of course, there is nothing wrong with NL. They just don't understand that it requires a fundamentally different mind-set, and they haven't changed their own quickly enough.

You should learn from their frustration. If you have the necessary talents and drives, and you can change your perspective, NL can be ideal for you. It's the hottest game, the one that can give you the largest edge, most glamour, and biggest opportunities. There has never been such an incredible party, and there will probably never be another one like it. A horde of weak players are eager to give away their money at the game they see on TV, but don't begin to understand.

To take advantage of this unprecedented opportunity you will have to rethink your entire approach to poker, break out of your comfort zone, and take an extremely hard look at yourself. It may be uncomfortable, but it can be *very* profitable.

Apply active-learning principles *now* by taking a mini-quiz about what you have just read. Turn to Appendix E and answer those questions about this chapter.

PART FOUR

Developing Yourself

Introduction

Poker writers always stress "the long term." They insist that you should emphasize expected value (EV), not immediate results. If it's higher EV to fold than to call, don't worry if the next card would have won a monster pot. You made the right decision, and if you repeat it one hundred times, you'll be well ahead.

Although they focus on the long term when discussing how to play hands, many poker writers have a short-term and narrow focus. They concentrate on how to play hands, not on your long-term personal development. They also ignore or minimize every motive except the desire to make money.

Of course, EV and profits are important, but you play poker for many reasons, including some that *reduce* your EV such as the desires to relax, socialize, and test yourself against tougher players.[1] These chapters focus on your longer-term development, and they consider all your motives. They discuss three extremely important questions:

1. Should you move up?
2. How can you plan your poker improvement?
3. Should you quit your day job?

Various experts have written about the first and third questions, but they have overemphasized the financial gains and risks. This reaction is natural because we all know people who did well at one level,

---

1. Other motives are discussed in Appendix A: "Why Do You Play Poker?" Read it and complete the questionnaire before making any major decision about poker.

moved up, and went broke. Some have done it many times; they just can't accept that they aren't good enough to beat larger games.

We also know how hard it is to make a good living as a pro. We all have friends who have tried and failed. So we tell readers the unpleasant truth: most pros—including some you have seen on television—don't have much money, and some of them are broke and in debt.

Only a few of us have written about the other negative aspects of being a pro: the life is stressful, it's lonely, you can easily burn out, and so on.

Despite all our warnings, thousands of people are going to move up to games they can't beat, and/or quit their day jobs and ruin their lives. Poker *looks* so easy and glamorous. You can make lots of money, play when you feel like it, be independent, maybe even get on television.

People make these mistakes because they don't plan. Poker players are usually opportunists, not planners. If they see a good game, they say, "Deal me in." If they build up their bankroll, they go looking for bigger games. If they enjoy playing poker more than their day job, they say, "I quit," without carefully considering the wider and longer-term implications.

The net result is that many poker players—even great ones—have little sense of where their lives are going, and they often don't like where they end up. In any large poker room you will see people who once had a lot of money but now live pathetic lives.

They once played in big games and won thousands of dollars. Now they barely survive by playing in tiny games. They live in crummy motels or crash on their friends' couches. They owe everyone. They are isolated and lonely. If you doubt me, just watch the DVD "Poker Bustouts"[2] or read Nolan Dalla's "So You Wanna Be a Tournament Pro? Fuhgetaboutit!"[3]

When I recommended that DVD, I encountered massive denial:

2. You can buy the DVD at pokerbustouts.com.

3. See www.pokerpages.com/articles/archives/dalla27.htm.

"You don't know what you're talking about"; "They weren't good players"; "Today's situation is different because of rakeback, television, and . . ." The fact that some of the bustouts once had bankrolls of more than $500,000 was ignored. The fact that Johnny Moss and Stu Ungar, the greatest players of their eras, ended up broke was irrelevant. They insisted, "It can't happen to *me.*"

Nonsense! You are not as talented as Johnny and Stu, nor are you immune from the weaknesses and temptations that caused them and many other excellent players to ruin their lives. Nor do you care only about making money.

I do *not* insist that you never move up or turn pro. All I recommend is that you think carefully about these decisions before making them, because they can have a much greater impact on your life than anything you do at the poker table. These chapters will help you to understand why you play poker and what you want out of life. Then they will help you to plan your self-development.

Should You Move Up?

Most winners ask themselves: should I move up? They wonder whether they will have more fun and make more money in bigger games. The answer is that old standby: "It depends." The right answer for you may not be the right one for someone else.

Moving up violates the "select soft games" principle because larger games are usually tougher. You should violate that principle only for very good reasons, and many people move up for the wrong ones. Base your decision on

- Your motives
- Your abilities
- Your bankroll

Unless they are all favorable, don't move. Unfortunately, many people deceive themselves about all three.

Your Motives

Motivation comes first because you should always understand *why* you want to do something before doing it. Instead of analyzing their motives, many people just yield to their impulses; then they wonder why things go wrong so often. Take a careful look at both the type and level of your motives.

Types of Motives

There are five primary reasons for moving up:

1. Profit
2. Stimulation
3. Status
4. Testing yourself
5. Developing your game

These motives often pull in different directions. For example, you may make more money playing for lower stakes but enjoy the status of a higher-stakes player. Countless players who could succeed at one level struggle to break even at higher ones.

In addition, satisfying these motives may frustrate some others. Larger games are more stressful, and they are often less social. Instead of a relaxed, "let's have fun" atmosphere, they may be much too serious for you. Moving up may satisfy some motives but reduce your overall satisfaction. The critical point is to consider *all* your motives. Otherwise, you can make foolish decisions.

PROFIT. If you can win the same number of bets per hour, your profits will obviously increase, but you probably cannot do it. Because the games get tougher, you could easily shift from a winner to a break-even or losing player.

You should also decide what the added profit *means* to you. If poker is your primary or secondary job, profit is economically important. If you are a recreational player, and the gains and losses are just a way to keep score, you may be wiser to stay put. You are getting the pleasure of winning regularly, and you may feel less satisfied by winning more money, but fewer big bets per hour (BBPH). For example, you may feel much better winning $9 per hour playing $3–$6 (1.5 BBPH) than winning $10 per hour in a $10–20 game (0.5 BBPH). Your swings would be much larger but produce only one extra dollar per hour.

Many people don't need the money but want to feel they are winning enough to satisfy an ego drive. One Wednesday Poker Discussion Group (WPDG) member wanted to move from the smaller games she beat to $15–$30, at which she had lost consistently. In a personal e-mail she said, "The theoretical win per hour in the larger game is attractive to me, because I don't want to work for 8 or 10 or 16 bucks an hour. My time is . . . simply more valuable than that, and I can make tremendously more by trading or consulting, etc."

Because she can make "tremendously more" by working, profit's importance is clearly psychological, not economic. If she needs the money, she should obviously work instead of playing poker. She confuses work and recreation. Bill Gates plays small games, and his time is worth immeasurably more than hers.

In fact, most recreation costs money. Golf, travel, and skiing are expensive, and boating is a bottomless pit. If you enjoy poker, don't need the money, and win a few dollars, you are way ahead of people who spend serious money having fun.

STIMULATION. As games get bigger, the money becomes more interesting, and the players get better and more exciting. If you are bored for the right reasons (e.g., because it is too easy to win), perhaps you should move up. If you are bored for the wrong reasons (e.g., because you crave more action, even though you lose), you should stay where you are—or even move *down*.

Of course, you may enjoy your current game but still want more kick. You can beat most small games just by being tight and aggressive. Because larger games are usually tighter and more aggressive, you cannot win on style alone; you have to be deceptive, imaginative, and analytic, which can make the games much more stimulating.

STATUS. High-stakes players have higher status than low-stakes ones, and some people need that status. If they used to play $100–$200, they may feel as embarrassed in the $25–$50 game as the $4–$8 player feels playing $2–$4.

They may say there are no seats available, or they don't like the players' looks, or somebody there irritates them, but they let everyone know they don't belong in "this little game." Some of them criticize the other players, compare them to their old crowd, and never let them forget they were higher-stakes players.

TESTING YOURSELF. We want to move up for the same reasons that tennis players challenge people above them on the club's ladder. If we don't test ourselves, we will never know how good we are, not just at poker, but at anything.

In the same e-mail mentioned earlier a WPDG member wrote: "I do like the 'challenge' of playing the higher limits and do in fact want to 'prove' (to myself) that I can beat the game at a level which is 'worthwhile.'" Her attitude is fine because she has already proved her worth in much more important competitions, but lots of people seek challenges for unhealthy reasons.

If too much of your identity and self-esteem depends on your poker-playing ability, you've got problems. First, the inevitable losing streaks can devastate you. Second, how will you feel when you fail? And you must ultimately fail. We all have limits, and they may be much lower than you would like. Countless players beat little games but get wiped out in larger ones. Even if you can move up again and again, only a handful of players can beat the biggest games, and there is only one World Series Champion each year.

When you reach your limit, you may feel like a failure. It's illogical, but it happens everywhere. Many super-successful people in business, sports, and politics, and other competitive arenas feel like "second raters" because someone is above them. For example, some Wall Street people are miserable because they made "only" $5,000,000 last year. In many hierarchies one of the unhappiest people is the one in second place; nearly everyone is below him, but he can't get the top job. If you doubt it, just read about former vice presidents of the United States. Many complained bitterly, and John Nance Garner said the job "wasn't worth a bucket of warm spit."

Don't let your feelings about yourself become too dependent on poker (or anything else). Some $2–$4 players are great human beings, and some high-stakes players are bums.

DEVELOPING YOUR GAME. If it's too easy to beat your current game, you won't reach your potential. If you can win enough playing your B-game, you won't play your A-game or work to improve it. You need better competition to force you to improve yourself. If developing your game is very important to you, you probably should move up, even if it temporarily reduces your profits. Do it *only* if developing your game is more important than your immediate profits.

Levels of Motives

Even if moving up would satisfy most of your motives, it could be a mistake. If you are too motivated, your satisfaction and results will probably suffer. The higher risks, tougher players, challenge to your self-esteem, and other factors can hurt your game (and more important things such as your self-esteem).

Research clearly proves that moderately high motivation produces the best performance. If you don't care, you will perform badly. Many high-stakes players are careless in smaller games; Stu Ungar even said he couldn't beat a $5–$10 game.

If the stakes get too high, performance will deteriorate, because you will not be detached. Instead of regarding bets as "just chips," you may think, "Oh, my God, this pot is more valuable than my car!"

Let's look at a theoretical illustration: People have to walk thirty feet on a six-inch-wide plank. If you lay it on the ground, some people will carelessly fall off. If you raise it three feet, most people will get to the end. If you raise it one hundred feet, most people will be too scared to take a single step. The task will have remained constant, but the performance will have varied enormously.

I am not recommending that you stay at your current level, just that you know what you are trying to accomplish. If the gains exceed the costs and risks, go for it. If not, stay where you are and enjoy it.

Your Abilities

Ask yourself: "How talented am I?" *YWPE* contained several chapters on "Evaluating Ourselves and the Opposition" that argued that you are probably *much* less talented than you think. Since you can't trust your self-assessment, use three measurements:

1. Proof that you have won consistently
2. The ability to observe, understand, and avoid your opponents' mistakes
3. A coach's objective assessment

Proof That You Have Won Consistently

Without solid proof of success for hundreds of hours, you are probably not ready to move up. The *minimum* seems to be about 1 BBPH at $10–$20 or lower, and somewhat less at $15–$30 or above. "Proof" means careful, complete records. Without them you may "forget" some losses, exaggerate some wins, and underestimate the number of hours played.

Some losers say they will move up *because* they play too well to win at their current level! They whine about the "idiots" who are too stupid to fold, suck out on them, make such stupid bets that they can't put them on a hand, and so on. They are going to move up to a game where their superior skill will pay off.

Nonsense! If you cannot beat your current game, you will lose more money in a larger one (unless your style fits your new opponents very well). No matter what stakes you play, you will encounter "idiots," suffer bad beats, and get confused by people who don't think the way you do. But the weak players are net losers. Your problem is that you are kidding yourself. If you cannot beat weak players, you have very little chance of beating better ones.

However, even if you have won consistently, "The Peter Principle" can defeat you. The book with that title stated that employees get promoted by performing well until they reach "the level of their incompetence." Because they don't have the talents needed at their new level, they stay there, performing poorly. Their poor performance prevents further promotions, and their pride and organizational inertia prevent demotion. For example, many good sales reps become bad sales managers because managing is different from selling.

The same thing happens in poker. Countless players have moved up until they have reached a level they can't beat and then have stayed there. Because they are too proud to admit they can't beat the larger game, they don't move back down. So they shift from being winners to losers. Their egotism destroys them.

The Ability to Observe, Understand, and Avoid Your Opponents' Mistakes

In "Moving Up"[1] Mason Malmuth wrote: "You should be able to observe numerous errors in the play of some of your opponents . . . and understand exactly why they are mistakes." You should also know why you don't make those mistakes and have a reason for all your actions. If you can't understand why you are winning, it may be just luck or your opponents' weakness. Don't move up until you understand your own and other people's play well enough to adjust to a tougher game's increased demands.

A Coach's Objective Assessment

Even if you pass the first two tests of your abilities, you may not have the talent to beat larger games. Beating your current game, spotting lots of mistakes, and understanding why you are winning do not mean you can move up successfully. Larger games require different skills, and *you can't know what they are because you've never had the experience.*

You can beat small games just by being tight and aggressive. You can see, understand, and avoid the most common mistakes that small-

1. *Poker Essays, Vol. II,* (Henderson, NV: Two Plus Two Publishing, 1996), 38–42.

games players make: playing too many hands, chasing, and not being aggressive enough. But larger games require more deception, aggression, card-reading skill, and other talents that you may not have.[2] Ask a coach to assess your readiness to move up and suggest changes in your play.

Obviously, your coach must have beaten those games. He should also be willing to observe and discuss your play. If he wants a fee, pay it with pleasure. It could be a great investment.

If he says you've got the basic talent but recommends strategic changes, take his advice. If he says, "You're not ready," don't get mad. He is more objective than you are, and he knows much more than you do about bigger games. Instead, thank him, because he has saved you a lot of money and grief.

Your Bankroll

Discussions on Internet forums and Mason Malmuth's essays indicate that you need a much larger bankroll than most people believe. Of course, you need much less if you just want to "take a shot" occasionally at larger games. Many posters have said they went broke because they moved up without a large enough bankroll. Many business experts have made a similar point: the number one reason new businesses fail is undercapitalization, but countless businesspeople and poker players insist they can prosper with *much* less capital than the experts recommend.

If they are lucky, they survive, but far too many go broke or are forced to move back down. People move up with short bankrolls for at least four reasons:

1. They don't play as well as they think they do. The more poorly they play, the lower their win rate and their co-

2. An excellent analysis of the differing skills required for larger games is Barry Tanenbaum's "Where Does One Big Bet Per Hour Come From?" www.pokerplayer.com/articles/archives/tanenbaum04.htm.

efficient of variation (the win rate divided by the standard deviation), meaning they need *much* more capital to move up.

2. They are unable or unwilling to keep records and compute their win rate and standard deviation. Statking and CPA make these calculations automatically, so you should use one of them.

3. They kid themselves that other people may need a large bankroll, but they don't. They essentially say, "I'm so talented that I can make it with a lot less."

4. They overestimate their "psychological bankroll," the amount they can lose without getting so upset that their play deteriorates. They may have enough cash to survive the financial swings, but they can't handle the mood swings. They may even go on tilt and blow everything.

If any of these points apply to you, *don't move up.* However, you may consider "taking a shot." You can play occasionally in larger games but continue to spend most of your time in your regular ones.

Planning and Making Your Move

Enough warnings! Let's say that you've decided to move up. The final question is: *How should you do it?* Don't just walk over to the bigger game; make a careful plan.

In *Your Worst Poker Enemy*, "How Should You Prepare Logically?" stated that intuitive people can just trust their instincts, but most of us should prepare carefully. This principle applies to every poker decision, including moving up. A friend with excellent skills and intuition told me he preferred to make spontaneous moves, waiting until he felt good and saw a good game, then "taking a shot."

That approach works for him, but it wouldn't work for me or others who share my logical, conservative approach. Because larger games are tougher and riskier, we should prepare more thoroughly, not just for how we will play our cards, but for many other important decisions. Here are some tips.

Don't play "scared." You may think you can handle higher stakes, but you can't be sure until you play for them. If you find that you're playing scared, move back down *immediately*.

You can't play well without a detached attitude toward your chips. They are a different color, but you must still see them as "just chips." If you're afraid, you'll play weakly, and your opponents will sense it and run over you. Fear is so important and common that many of my recommendations are designed to reduce it, but only you can tell whether you can handle it. Unfortunately, your own machismo or pride may cause you to deny reality.

Move up when you are running well and playing your A-game. We all have times that we see more clearly and act more decisively. We snap off bluffs, make great raises, and bet marginal hands for value. When you're getting good cards and playing them well, make your move. In addition to playing well, you're feeling more confident, and you'll be less afraid of losing "their" money. However, don't confuse luck or feeling lucky with great play; the fact that you're winning does not necessarily mean you're playing well.

Decide exactly how you will play differently. You need additional skills to move up successfully. Even if you have the potential, you may not have developed these skills because you could succeed without them. Now you need a more complete game, and you should make explicit plans to develop it. Ask yourself and your coach: How should my style be changed? How can I be more deceptive? What steps will improve my card reading? What other skills do I need?

Get back to the books. Study both the books you thought you had mastered and some more advanced texts. Look for the advanced techniques you'll need in the tougher games.

Move slowly and cautiously. Because you will not know whether you can handle a game until you try it, experiment in a carefully controlled way. Spend weeks or months playing at both your current and the higher level. When the games are good and you're playing well, move up. When the conditions are unfavorable, move back down.

Don't risk your entire bankroll. Set aside an amount you can afford to risk, and plan to buy exactly that many chips. If you lose that amount, don't buy any more. From a purely expected-value perspective, it may be foolish to walk away from a game you think you can beat, but I am a psychologist, not a mathematician. I'm absolutely convinced that most people kid themselves about their abilities, including their ability to handle losses.

You may believe you're playing so well that you can beat this game, that only bad luck has caused your losses, that you can buy more chips and get even, that if you lose one more rack you 'll quit. Perhaps you can, but I doubt it. More important, the risks are too high.

If you're right, you'll get back some or all of the money you've lost. If you're wrong, you'll buy a rack, then another, then more until you're broke. Once your losses pass a certain point, you may be unable to stop buying and losing more chips. It has happened thousands of times.

Pick your games very carefully. Since the games are generally tougher, be *much* more selective than usual. Pick the softest possible games, and be ready to run if you've misjudged them, or they get tougher. Weekend games are usually softer, because there are more tourists (or other infrequent players). Late-night games are usually softer because some players are tired, have been drinking, or are trying to get even.

You want weak players, but not wild ones. Unless the players are total idiots, avoid wild games. The combination of higher stakes and wild action can easily make you play scared or otherwise harm your play. Your A-game may be good enough to win, but if you can't play it, you can get badly hurt.

For example, a friend consistently beat the $20–$40 games in Las Vegas; he went to L.A., jumped into an apparently "juicy" $30–$60 game, and got slaughtered. He told me ruefully, "Moving up and going to L.A. was a 'double whammy.' A $30–$60 game in L.A. is like a $40–$80 Las Vegas game."

Profile the players. Profiling is always a good idea, but it becomes more important as you move up. Because the players get better, you have to work harder at reading them. As many experts put it, you have to play not just your cards, but your people.

Start by making mental or written notes about the regulars, the ones you will encounter repeatedly. Because the number of players gets smaller as you move up, it is easier to keep track of them. Record each regular's basic style such as tight-passive or loose-aggressive, plus how he plays key hands in various positions such as ace-king, large and small pairs, and suited connectors. How does he play draws and made hands after the flop?

Monitor your progress. You must continually guard against the natural tendency to kid yourself. For example, if you're losing, you can easily believe that you've just been unlucky. Perhaps you were, but the game may be too tough for you, or you may be playing poorly.

Good records are particularly important when you move up. Without them you can easily deceive yourself about your results and talent. In addition to numerical records, you should take detailed notes about your own play. Reread and apply the principles in this book's chapter "Taking Notes" and in "How Should You Review Logically?" in *YWPE*.

Take frequent walks to review your notes. Write down questionable hands and discuss them and your entire session with your coach or poker buddy.

Be ready to move down. If you find that you can't beat the larger games, don't let your pride destroy your self-confidence or your bankroll. Accept that you're not ready to move up, move back down to your old level, and work on your game. If you want to try again, the bigger games will always be there.

When you find your level, relax and enjoy it. Sooner or later you will hit your limit, the biggest game you can handle. Don't let your pride, machismo, or greed force you to keep trying to move up. Stay there, and enjoy yourself. It is far better to win consistently at $4–$8, $15–$30, or whatever than it is to struggle at $50–$100 or higher.

Apply active-learning principles *now* by taking a mini-quiz about what you have just read. Turn to Appendix E and answer those questions about this chapter.

The Coaches' Dilemma

Many of my friends are coaches. They teach poker strategy, while I deal only with psychology. Even though we offer different kinds of advice, we all have the same problem: *We tell our clients what to do, but they often don't do it.*

All Advisors Have This Problem

You may not think of doctors, lawyers, accountants, and psychologists as coaches, but all advisors are essentially coaches. We have no authority to give orders, and we are often frustrated by our clients' foolishness. We may even say, "Why do you pay me but ignore my advice?" Some clients completely disregard it. Others second-guess us, taking only the advice they feel like following.

For example, a doctor sees that a patient is close to a heart attack and sternly says, "Follow this rigid diet, exercise regularly, stop smoking, and take these medications three times a day." But the patient cheats on his diet, does hardly any exercise, smokes when he wishes, and often "forgets" to take his medications, especially if they have unpleasant side effects, even trivial ones.

The Central Problem Is Feedback

Psychological research has shown that immediate rewards and punishments have much greater effects on our actions than long-term consequences. Unfortunately, ignoring a coach's advice may be immediately rewarded or have no immediate effects. That's why in the previous example the patient ignored his doctor's advice.

The immediate feedback was neutral or positive. Nothing seemed to happen. Or he enjoyed eating certain prohibited foods and avoided the unpleasant effects of exercise and medication. The immediate feedback had more influence on him than the longer-term consequences, which are obviously terrible: his chances of having a heart attack become much larger.

The same principles apply to poker coaches. Luck has such huge short-term effects that you will frequently be *rewarded* for ignoring your coach's advice. You may cold-call three bets with nine-seven off-suit, flop the nut straight, and win a monster pot. Or your coach may tell you to go home because you are on tilt, but you go on a huge rush, recover all your losses, and win two more racks. You will probably remember those lucky wins long after you have forgotten all the money you lost by ignoring your coach's advice.

Coaches Need Balance

We must avoid two extremes:

1. If we go too far toward the ideal strategy, it may not be implemented well or at all.
2. If we go too far toward the client's preferences, the strategy will be ineffective.

Bad doctors just tell patients what they should do and essentially say, "If you don't follow my advice, don't blame me for what happens." Good ones negotiate compromises between the ideal treatment and what the patient wants to do. For example, instead of insisting that a patient jog three miles a day, a doctor and patient may agree that he will walk one mile. Instead of prescribing the ideal drug with unpleasant side effects, the doctor may prescribe a less effective drug without them. Good doctors know that *an inferior, but implemented treatment plan is much better than a perfect, but ignored plan.*

A coach may believe that jack-ten suited is the weakest hand to play under the gun, while the client wants to play seven-eight offsuit. They may compromise that he will play nothing worse than nine-eight suited. That compromise may not be ideal strategically, but it may be loose enough to keep the client from "cheating."

The Poker Coach's Special Problems

We often must be more flexible than traditional professionals, because we have less credibility and implementing our recommendations requires more understanding. Poker players may accept a doctor's advice almost on faith, but they often believe that they know how they should play. They wouldn't prescribe their own drugs, but they may decide which parts of a coach's advice are "right" or "wrong." In addition, they don't have to understand why they should take a certain drug, but they must understand why they should make most poker decisions.

Doctors are notoriously bad patients because they think they know how to treat themselves, and poker players often do whatever they like to develop themselves. For example, they may read numerous books and take a little from each one, usually the advice that fits their natural desires. They essentially insist on developing their own system, even though they don't have enough knowledge or judgment to do it well.

The Three Critical Factors

Regardless of his specialty, a coach's primary task is not to recommend the ideal plan. It is to develop one that will work for *you*. It will balance three factors:

1. What *should* you do?
2. What are you *able* to understand and do?
3. What are you *willing* to do?

The first question is usually easy to answer. Any competent coach can quickly identify your mistakes and tell you how to correct them. Answering the other questions can be very difficult.

For poker strategy coaches, the second question is usually more important. We all know that the best strategy depends on the situation. There are so many factors to consider and you must act so quickly that a strategy coach has to understand and adjust to your information-processing capacity.

If a coach just tells you, "Here is what *I* would do," fire him. He isn't doing his job, because you don't have his talents or experience. He has to tell you what *you* should do, considering all your strengths and weaknesses.

Experts often consider far more information than you can process effectively. Therefore, your strategy coach must help you to do the following:

- Assess how many factors *you* can consider without becoming confused and indecisive.
- Determine which factors are most important for *you* (and their importance depends on your abilities and style).
- Evaluate these factors quickly and accurately.
- Act decisively on that evaluation.

My task is much simpler conceptually because you don't need a Ph.D. to see most psychological flaws. Harry can't control his anger. Barbara overestimates her skill. Joe has an overwhelming craving for action. Tom belittles his opponents. Susan doesn't accept responsibility for her results. Joan has a pathological need to get even for the night. Bill can't handle bad beats.

My problem isn't making an accurate diagnosis; it's getting clients to accept it and do something about it. Many people won't admit psychological weaknesses, or they minimize their negative effects. A few even regard some weaknesses as *strengths*. For example, they may insist that overestimating their skill is a sign of confidence and decisiveness: "You have to believe in yourself." So they play in games that are too tough for them and lose regularly.

Why Should You Care?

You may think the issues we've discussed are irrelevant. You aren't a coach, nor do you have one. But if you want to develop your own game your dilemma is quite severe. A good coach has a much broader and deeper understanding of theory than you do, and he is also more detached and objective than you can be about yourself. Self-deception is so powerful that even experienced coaches may be blind to our own shortcomings. We may make the same mistakes we criticize in others.

Traditional professionals have the same problem, and we are taught to separate our personal and professional lives. Most doctors would not perform serious surgery on a relative. Attorneys have a wonderful saying: "The lawyer who represents himself has a fool for a client." If good lawyers get in trouble, they immediately retain an attorney. They know they can't be objective about their own legal problems.

Try to look at yourself in the detached way that a coach would. Ask yourself

- Exactly what am I doing right and wrong?
- What are my intellectual strengths and weaknesses?
- What are my psychological strengths and weaknesses?

If you can't do it by yourself, get help from a professional coach, poker buddy, discussion group, or Internet forum. Then work out a development plan that:

- Fits your unique pattern of strengths and weaknesses
- Is close enough to your preferences to be implemented effectively

Many self-development plans are *much* too ambitious, whether they relate to poker, health, or anything else. For example, how many times have you made ambitious plans for dieting and exercise that never got implemented? So make a plan that is ambitious enough to move you in the right direction, but modest enough to be carried out.

Apply active-learning principles *now* by taking a mini-quiz about what you have just read. Turn to Appendix E and answer those questions about this chapter.

Your Poker Improvement Plan: Part I. General Principles

If you don't have a Poker Improvement Plan (PIP), you will probably waste money, time, and effort. These chapters discuss only improving your poker. Full-time professionals should also have financial plans. Executives and professionals take planning very seriously, and they often study books or take courses. Yet, as Barry Greenstein stated in *Ace on the River,* "Most players don't have a long-term plan to improve their playing ability."[1] Why? Let's look at the reasons:

1. *Poker is a very* now *game.* When it is your turn to act, you must make a quick decision. You naturally focus on how you will play this hand or how much you are winning and losing tonight, not on how to develop yourself. Planning for two, five, or more years from now seems almost irrelevant.

2. *Planning takes time and effort, and the benefits are neither clear nor immediate.* Do you remember that patient who ignored his doctor's advice because he didn't see any immediate effects of skipping his medications and so on? The same principle applies to planning. If you don't do it, your results won't change quickly. But planning will slowly improve both your progress and your feelings about yourself.

3. *Planning and the self-critical analysis it requires can be unpleasant.* You may not like to plan or look hard at yourself. But you can't win without doing many unpleasant things

1. Barry Greenstein, *Ace on the River* (Fort Collins, CO: Last Knight, 2005), 88.

such as folding weak hands, avoiding certain games, and suppressing your emotions. Planning is just one of those unpleasant, but necessary, activities.

4. *You can't predict the future, and unexpected events often defeat plans.* You may think this unpredictability reduces the value of plans, but the opposite is true. The less you can predict the future, the more you need to plan. The written PIP is less valuable than the process of writing it. Carefully setting goals, analyzing yourself and your situation, and writing a PIP will prepare you to react effectively to unexpected events.

Overview of the Planning Process

The process is easy to describe, but quite difficult to perform. The four steps have a circular relationship to each other. When you take a later step, you will often realize that you made a mistake on an earlier one. You may have to go back and modify various steps again and again until they all fit together. For example, when you assess your assets and liabilities, you may realize that your goals should be revised. Or you may recognize that you need to work on skills that you had not considered. The steps are as follows:

1. Set good goals.
2. Objectively evaluate your assets and liabilities.
3. Write a PIP for reaching your goals.
4. Monitor your progress and revise your PIP.

Steps 1 and 2 can be taken in either order. You can start with where you want to go (your goals) or where you are now (your assets and liabilities). Let's start with your goals but accept that they depend on your assets and liabilities. As you clarify your assets and liabilities, you may change your goals.

Step No. 1: Set good goals. If you don't know where you want to go, you probably won't like wherever you end up. Despite that fact, many players either don't set goals or set ones with little planning value. Clearly defined, realistic goals provide both a sense of direction and the motivation to move toward them. Let's look at some poor-quality goals:

- *To become an expert:* This is too fuzzy. "Expert" is poorly defined, and you don't know how far you have to go to become one.

- *To become as good a player as I can possibly be:* This is worse because you can't measure your progress toward such a vague goal.

- *To win The World Series of Poker Championship:* This is completely unrealistic for nearly everyone, a fantasy that hinders intelligent planning.

Goals should include a target date to help you measure your progress. Let's say you're beating the $6–$12 game for $12, 1 BBPH. A good goal would be to beat the $10–$20 game for $20, 1 BBPH, in one year. That goal is ambitious, but attainable (with a lot of hard work). The target date lets you measure your progress.

Step No. 2: Objectively evaluate your assets and liabilities. All of poker is based on comparisons. Hands have only relative value; a flush is good only if nobody has a better hand. Your results depend on how you compare to the competition. If you're better, you're a favorite. If they're better, you're an underdog.

Instead of making only a general comparison, think of specific qualities. If you have more of a favorable quality (such as knowledge or discipline), you have an asset. A liability is exactly the opposite: less of a good quality or more of a bad one (such as a tendency to tilt).

Your assets and liabilities change as you move upward. You may read cards better than the $6–$12 players, but more poorly than the $10–$20 players. Your card-reading skill is an asset while playing $6–$12, but it becomes a *liability* when you move up. Because most people don't compare themselves on specific qualities, they don't recognize that shift.

Step No. 3: Write a PIP for reaching your goals. Some people confuse goals and plans. A goal is what you want to accomplish, and a plan is the steps you will take to reach it. Let's use a trip to clarify the difference. Your *goal* is to drive from Las Vegas to Denver by 5:00 P.M. tomorrow. Your *plan* is to leave at 5:00 P.M., drive north on I-15 and east on I-70. You will book a hotel room in Richfield, sleep there, and drive again at 9:00 A.M.

This plan has a subgoal: sleeping in Richfield. Your PIP should also have them, such as beating the $10–$20 game for $15, 3/4 BBPH, in six months.

Once you have established your goals, determine which knowledge, skills, and other assets you need to reach them. Write plans to acquire them, such as reading certain books and taking lessons. Be specific and include target dates such as "Read *The Theory of Poker* by December 31." If you vaguely decided to read a book someday, you may never read it.

Step No. 4: Monitor your progress and revise your PIP. Don't set your goals and plans in concrete. Keep track of your progress and revise them if necessary. Ruthlessly evaluate yourself, and ask friends or professionals to comment on your progress. If you're moving faster than expected, you can set more ambitious goals. Conversely, you may realize that you're not ready to beat that $10–$20 game and decide to move back down to $6–$12, to spend more time working on your skills, or to hire a coach.

"That's Too Much Work"

After reading all my planning essays, a good friend said that most people won't work that hard. I agree, so let's do the sort of compromise I recommended in "The Coach's Dilemma."

That system was adapted from my book *Executive Career Strategy*. It was translated into French, German, and Spanish, and thousands of Mobil Oil employees took a program based on it. The system clearly works well, but it does require a lot of work. If you don't want to work that hard, select only a few types of knowledge, skill, and so forth that:

- Are personally important to you
- You have a realistic chance of improving
- You are willing to work on

You could even choose just one such as card reading. Make a PIP with all four steps just for it. After seeing how the plan improves your card-reading, results, and feelings about yourself, you may decide to work on more subjects.

Final Remarks

Planning helps you to decide where you are going and how you will get there. A PIP will improve your results and give a sense of direction. I hope that I have convinced you to take planning seriously. In the next chapter, we will work through all four steps.

Apply active-learning principles *now* by taking a mini-quiz about what you have just read. Turn to Appendix E and answer those questions about this chapter.

Your Poker Improvement Plan: Part II. Setting Your Goals

Although poker is extremely results oriented, not all your goals should be in dollars. Set goals for developing the qualities you need to win those dollars, such as improving your knowledge and skills. Without a poker improvement plan for those qualities, you probably won't get those results.

The *Smart* Formula

Many planners recommend the *SMART* formula for goals: <u>S</u>pecific, <u>M</u>easurable, <u>A</u>chievable, <u>R</u>elevant, and <u>T</u>ime based. Unfortunately, many goals can't fit all these criteria, but try to get as close as possible.

Specific

"To become a better player" and "to win more money" are too vague. Instead, set specific goals for your results and a few of the factors that will help you achieve them. The following goals are fairly specific, but they have other problems, which I'll discuss later:

- *Results:* Increase my win rate by 20 percent in my current game.
- *Knowledge:* Master Doyle Brunson's "No Limit Hold'em" chapter in *Super System 2*.
- *Skill:* Improve my card reading.
- *Mental abilities:* Develop my multiple-level thinking (what does he think I think he has?).

- *Psychological traits:* Increase my impulse control and emotional control so that I will stop making stupid mistakes.
- *Personal situation:* Change to a job that will give me more time to play and study poker.

Note that there was only one goal for each category. You may want to work on more than one skill, for example, but don't try to fix everything at once. If you set improvement goals for too much knowledge or other improvements, your actions will lack focus. You may also make so little progress that you will become disheartened. Set goals for the things that you need most. Or work on only one subject to see how this process works.

Measurable

If a goal isn't measurable, you probably can't tell whether you've achieved it or how much further you have to go. You need to feel that you're making progress to stay focused and motivated. Some of these goals are not measurable, and none can be measured precisely.

Let's take "Increase my win rate by 20 percent in my current game." That goal seems measurable because it includes a number. You may think that good records will tell you whether you have achieved it.

Wrong! Because luck has such huge effects, it is not as measurable as it appears. You could play very well but be unlucky, or play badly and be lucky. Despite this problem, results goals are the most measurable. Because you can't improve your results without developing your knowledge, skills, and so on, they indirectly measure the progress toward your other goals.

It is very difficult to set measurable goals for knowledge and other goals. How do you know that you have "mastered" Doyle's chapter? And knowledge is easier to measure than multiple-level thinking or impulse control.

Despite these problems, try to set goals that allow you to see approximately how much progress you have made. You can't say exactly how much your skills and so forth have improved, but you should see whether you have made no, small, or substantial progress.

Achievable

Goals should be challenging enough to bring out your best, but not so ambitious that you cannot realistically hope to attain them. Achieving a challenging goal increases your confidence and motivates you to keep working. If goals are too modest, they will not motivate you. If they are too ambitious, you may get discouraged and give up.

Take that goal about increasing impulse and emotional control. Of course, you want to stop making stupid mistakes, but the word *stop* is unrealistic. You (and everyone else) will *always* make some stupid, emotionally based mistakes. But you can realistically hope to make them less often and less destructively. So estimate how often you now make them, and plan to reduce their frequency and impact.

If you now make one every night, a reasonable goal would be to make one every other night. If you now go on tilt once a month and lose $1,000, set a goal to go on tilt only once every three months and lose only $500.

You may think, "I can't afford to lose that $500," but it is a lot more affordable than the $3,000 you are losing now. If your goal is to never go on tilt, you will almost certainly fail to reach it. Then you may say, "The hell with it. I've already failed, and it doesn't matter what I do."

All goals should be realistic. Alas, many players fantasize, and this tendency has been greatly reinforced by the highly publicized success of Chris Moneymaker and some other instant celebrities. Winning a million dollars, making a televised final table, and becoming a top player are theoretically possible, but your chances are so slim that they are fantasies. Yet several people—including some mediocre players—have told me that they have such goals.

Unless you have *extraordinary* talent and commitment, you have no chance at all to become a top player. Poker may look simple on television, but the top players are as different from you and me as the top athletes.

Relevant

Your goals should fit your current situation, reinforce each other, and move you in the right direction. Unfortunately, many people set goals and make plans that conflict with each other. They try to develop knowledge, skills, and so on that are almost irrelevant to where they want to go.

Let's say that you intend to remain a recreational player but would like to increase your win-rate. If you play mostly no-fold'em hold'em, don't make "becoming deceptive" a goal. In those games deceptiveness is almost useless. Instead, work on value betting, because it can greatly improve your bottom line.

If you want to improve your results as a grind-it-out semi-pro, learn how to select soft games and spend most of your time in them.

If you want to become a top player, you should sometimes go in the opposite direction: occasionally pick tough games, even if you lose money in them. You need that experience to develop the necessary skills.

When goals are written, you can easily see that various ones don't fit together. Unfortunately, most people never write their goals, so their goals often work against each other.

Time Based

Without target dates you cannot measure your progress. A good goal would be: "To cash three times in my casino's next twelve monthly tournaments with at least one final table." You can easily see whether you are on schedule. If six months have passed, and you have not cashed once, you have a problem. Conversely, if you have cashed in three of the first six tournaments and made one final table, you may want a higher goal for the rest of the year.

Now that we understand the SMART formula, let's apply it to two types of goals: your ultimate objective and your annual goals.

Your Ultimate Objective

Your most important planning decision is setting your ultimate objective, yet few players do it. After setting it, you can think intelligently about how to get there. You will probably see that you are doing several things that conflict with your ultimate objective, and that you are neglecting some essential steps. The actions that help you toward one objective may interfere with your progress toward a different one. Although there are others, we will consider only four ultimate objectives:

1. To enjoy playing without caring much about improving your results
2. To continue as a recreational player but improve your results
3. To become or continue as a grind-it-out pro or semi-pro but with better results
4. To become a top player

The first objective is reasonable for purely recreational players. If you want it, you have no reason to plan. You need more planning to move toward objective no. 3 than toward no. 2, and you probably need *lots* of it to become a top player.

Everything you do should contribute to reaching your ultimate objective. If an action will move you in the right direction, do it. If it will take you in another direction or hinder your progress, avoid it. That obvious point is often ignored. People take many actions that directly conflict with their ultimate objective.

For example, some people claim they want to turn pro but take actions that virtually guarantee that they cannot do it:

- They refuse to study the literature, take lessons, or make any other serious investment in developing themselves.

- They play only in small games against weak players. You cannot make a living in small games, and the skills and habits you develop there do not prepare you for the larger games you must beat to earn a living.

- They deplete their bankroll by spending too much money. With a short bankroll you cannot afford to turn pro.[1]

If someone said that his ultimate objective was to turn pro but acted this way, I would doubt his commitment, and you cannot succeed as a pro without intense commitment. This example illustrates the circular relationship between setting goals and other actions. If you are not willing and able to do everything it takes to reach your ultimate objective, revise it.

Your Personal Qualities

To reach your ultimate objective you need to become a certain kind of player and person. Try very hard to determine the personal qualities needed and then plan to develop them.

Because these qualities depend on your objective, I can't say which ones you need. Read some noted authorities' opinions on the characteristics of winning players.[2] To get a fairly complete list, I have borrowed from all the authorities. These characteristics can be divided into at least five categories:

1. Knowledge
2. Skills

1. You may have to play in small games to build a bankroll. If so, live very modestly so that you can move to larger games to develop the skills you'll need as a full-time pro.

2. Go to barrytanenbaum.com, Roy Cooke's *Real Poker* and his columns at cardplayer.com, twoplustwo.com (for Mason Malmuth's and David Sklansky's work), loukrieger.com, and barrygreenstein.com. The best source is Barry Greenstein's *Ace on the River*

3. Mental abilities
4. Psychological traits
5. Situational factors

Nearly all poker writers focus on knowledge and skills and pay much less attention to the others, even though they can have huge effects. Their opinions sometimes overlap or conflict. For example, different writers have called the ability to adjust to changing conditions a skill, a trait, and a mental ability.

So many qualities can affect your results that nobody can work on all of them. These lists are like the food in a cafeteria: take the ones you want.

Knowledge is the amount of poker information that you understand. It has two dimensions: breadth (the number of subjects you understand) and depth (how well you understand them). You need several types of knowledge, including poker theory, strategy, statistical principles, game theory, probabilities, and psychology (of yourself and other people).

You can measure some types of poker knowledge by taking various quizzes. You can indirectly measure poker knowledge by discussing theory, strategy, and so forth. You will often realize that other people understand these subjects better than you do, and the discussion process will broaden and deepen your understanding.

Skills are the ability to apply knowledge well. Some people can ace an exam on poker theory but can't apply their knowledge while playing. You need many skills, and their importance changes as you move upward. You can beat many small games just by selecting your starting hands well and not chasing without pot odds.

As you move upward, you need other skills: raising, check-raising, bluffing, stealing blinds, defending your blinds, semi-bluffing, snapping off bluffs, inducing calls and bluffs, avoiding traps, isolating weak players, manipulating pot size, betting for value, deceiving opponents, reading tells, reading cards from betting patterns, adjusting to different types of players and games, shifting gears, slow-playing, betting and raising the right amount in limit and NL, buying a free card, projecting the right image, manipulating opponents into making mistakes, playing shorthanded, using position, and selecting good games.

Although this list is long, it is far from complete. You may want to add others. But don't overdo it. You probably can't evaluate yourself on all these skills, and you certainly can't improve all of them quickly.

Mental abilities are absolutely essential, and some writers ignore the fact that many readers don't have their abilities. They make recommendations that can be implemented *only* by gifted people. Unfortunately, because your mental abilities were created by your genes and a lifetime of experiences, you can't improve them much. I discussed this problem in "The Essential Mental Abilities."

If you don't have an expert's gifts, accept and work within your limitations. For example, if you don't have great intuition, don't rely on your first impressions. If you can't do complicated math while playing, keep it simple. If you have a poor short-term memory, play hold 'em or Omaha instead of stud. If you can't stay focused for more than a few hours, play short sessions of cash games and avoid multi-table tournaments.

No tests predict poker success the way that IQ tests predict academic grades, and IQ scores may be almost irrelevant to poker. They measure language, math, and other academic abilities that may be unimportant at the poker table. They also compare you to the general population, but winning poker players are much smarter than the average person (regardless of their IQ). You have to measure mental abilities indirectly, by seeing how well you can read other people, compute odds, remember how hands were played, and so forth.

You need to possess general intelligence, analytic capacity, math proficiency, psychological sensitivity, long-term memory, short-term memory, multiple-level thinking, attentiveness to detail, deductive and inductive logic, alertness, concentration, mental speed, the ability to see the big picture, handle many variables, think under pressure, and learn from mistakes, and that poorly defined ability called "feel." And there are certainly other abilities.

Because you can't change them much, set goals you can attain with your current mental abilities or with *slight* improvements in a few of them.

Psychological traits are not as clearly defined as knowledge and skills, nor can you significantly change many of them. I discussed this problem in "The Critical Psychological Traits." Their effects are much greater than you may believe. If you work only on your knowledge and skills, you will probably be disappointed. *Most players do not get the results their knowledge and skills should produce because they lack important mental abilities and psychological traits.*

For example, if you aren't honest with yourself, you'll play against players who are better than you. If you lack discipline, you won't use your skills well. If you can't control your emotions, you'll yield to destructive impulses.

Barry Greenstein's *Ace on the River* contains a list of personal traits of winning players.[3] I've included all of them, but I put a few in the "mental abilities" category. In ascending importance he listed: sense of humor, prideful, generous, outgoing, insensitive, optimistic, independent, manipulative, greedy, persistent, self-centered, trustworthy, aggressive, competitive, survivors, empathic, fearless, motivated, in control of their emotions, honest with themselves, and psychologically tough.

Some other important traits (which he may have stated in different words) are patience, discipline, deceptiveness, the ability to accept responsibility for results, accept losses, admit mistakes quickly, depersonalize conflicts, and adjust to changes, as well as stamina, pressure tolerance, a detached attitude toward chips, frustration tolerance, a ruthless killer instinct, self-confidence, decisiveness, and a strong work ethic.

Some traits are "two-edged swords." They help you to become a winning player, but too much of them can be harmful. Fearlessness

3. Barry Greenstein, *Ace on the River*, 56–70.

helps you to attack aggressively, but if you are too fearless, you will take foolish chances. Intense competitiveness creates an edge, but some "supercompetitors" cannot accept their limitations or handle bad beats and losing streaks.

Since childhood you have been repeatedly urged to make huge changes in your motivation, courage, patience, and so on, but you probably cannot do it. You should therefore follow the same rule as for mental abilities. Set goals you can achieve with the traits you have or with *slight* improvements in a few of them.

Most psychological traits and mental abilities can be measured only by comparing yourself to other people. These comparisons are tainted by your own biases, especially your desire to preserve your self-image. The next chapter will provide a procedure for making those comparisons.

Situational factors can be critically important. For example, if you work long hours, have heavy family responsibilities, or are committed to another hobby, you do not have much time to develop your game.

Some important situational factors are your bankroll, living expenses, discretionary income, free time, family's and friends' attitudes toward poker, whether you are married or single, other family needs, availability of live games in your area, and the quality of your computer and Internet connection. Some situational factors are easy to evaluate and change: you can buy a better computer or move to an area with more games. Others are very hard to evaluate or improve, such as your family's needs or attitudes.

Your Annual Goals

Your ultimate objective provides the overall direction for your plans, but it is too far in the future to guide your day-to-day decisions. Annual goals will help you to move in the right direction and to measure your progress.

The Goal-Setting Questionnaire

That's enough "theory." It's time to start writing. Because you may want to change answers, use a pencil or, even better, a computer. Ask yourself whether you have the commitment and time to do whatever it takes to reach a goal. If not, set a goal you can attain by the actions you will take.

Your Ultimate Objective
Because everything should be consistent with your ultimate objective, think very carefully before answering the following questions:

What is your ultimate objective?

Why have you set it?

How committed are you to it?

What kind of person and player do you have to become to achieve it?

Your Annual Goals
Each year set goals for your results and the qualities that will help you to achieve them. Your results goals are, of course, the most important, but you probably won't attain them without improving your personal characteristics.

Your results: Unless you steadily improve your results, you probably won't reach your ultimate objective. Because you can't improve your results without developing your knowledge, skills, and so on they indirectly measure your progress toward your other goals:

What results should you try to get in the next year?

Why have you chosen these results?

How will they help you to progress toward your ultimate objective?

Your knowledge: Without the right kinds of knowledge, you probably won't improve your results.

What new knowledge will you need?

Why did you select this knowledge?

Your skills: Without the right skills, you have almost no chance of improving your results.

Which skills should you improve?

Why did you select them?

Your mental abilities: You can develop some mental abilities. Be brutally realistic. Select the one or two that (1) you need to reach your results goals and (2) you can actually develop.

Which abilities should you improve?

Why did you select them?

Your psychological traits: Because they are hard to develop, be brutally realistic. Pick traits that (1) you need to reach your results goals and (2) you can actually develop.

Which psychological traits should you improve?

Why did you select them?

Your situation: Some situational factors are easy to change, and others are almost impossible. Pick a few that (1) you need to change to reach your results goals and (2) you can actually change.

Which situational factors should you change?

Why have you chosen to change them?

Final Questions

How close do your answers come to satisfying the SMART formula for goals (Specific, Measurable, Achievable, Relevant, and Time based)?

How can you make your goals more specific, measurable, and so on?

How can improve the way your goals fit together so that you are moving toward your ultimate objective?

Get a Second Opinion

Ask someone you trust to answer the goal-setting questions about you. Then compare and discuss your answers. You may be shocked, but you will clarify your goals and lay a better foundation for planning your poker career.

Apply active-learning principles *now* by taking a mini-quiz about what you have just read. Turn to Appendix E and answer those questions about this chapter.

Your Poker Improvement Plan: Part III. Evaluating Your Assets and Liabilities

After setting your goals, evaluate the assets that will help you to reach them and the liabilities that will hold you back. Assess how much you have of each quality by comparing yourself to your competition. As you move upward, the competition becomes tougher, shifting some qualities from assets to liabilities.

You may be more knowledgeable, skillful, and disciplined than your current competition, but weaker than the players you must beat to reach your ultimate objective. Make separate comparisons for various levels of competition.

Many people dislike this comparative process. They essentially say, "I am good at bluffing, reading cards, et cetera, and I don't want to compare myself to other people."

These comparisons are also quite difficult. You do not know how smart, skilled, knowledgeable, and so forth other people are, and it is very hard to find out, particularly for games you have never played. But, regardless of how difficult and unpleasant the task is, if you want to improve your results, you must compare yourself to others. *The central fact of cardroom poker is that nearly everybody loses. And the primary reason for losing is playing against better players.* It really is that simple.

The most important decision you make is your choice of games, and you cannot make it intelligently without comparing yourself to the competition. In addition to your overall prowess, compare yourself on many specific dimensions. Even if several opponents are equally skilled, you will do better against certain kinds of players.

The more accurately you compare yourself to others, the better decisions you will make. This unpleasant, difficult process will also help you to go beyond crude generalizations such as "I'm a good player" or "I'm better than Harry, but not as good as Barbara." When you see *where* you are stronger or weaker, you can plan your development.

I wish that there were accurate tests and that the comparison process took less time and effort, but we have to work with what we've got. If you're losing, these comparisons will suggest ways to become a winner. If you're winning, they can help you to win more and to move up. This procedure is far from perfect, but it's better than anything I've seen.

Your Poker Balance Sheet

Your poker balance sheet (PBS) divides all the qualities we have discussed into three groups: assets, liabilities, and don't know/don't care. Don't know/don't care will be the largest group, because you have so little information about many qualities.

Because your assets and liabilities change for each game and level, you would ideally prepare a separate PBS for each one. Let's learn the procedure by applying it to just one group. When you fully understand the method, you can easily apply it to others. Follow a few simple rules:

1. *Don't guess!* If you are unsure of how to rate yourself, don't call a characteristic an asset or a liability. Temporarily rate it as "don't know." If it's unimportant, ignore it. If it's important, get the information you need to rate it.

2. *Use a computer.* You can then edit your ratings as you get more information. You may originally regard something as an asset, but after getting more information, you may realize that it's actually a liability. Let's say you understand theory

better than the $10–$20 players. You may think it's an asset in the $15–$30 game but then realize that those players know more than you do. "Theoretical Knowledge" would be an asset in one game, but a liability in the other.

3. *Start by comparing yourself to the players you know best.* You can't accurately compare yourself to strangers. Later you may use the same procedure for every group you play or want to play against, but start by preparing the easiest PBS. Describe your competition briefly such as "the Las Vegas regular $10–$20 players."

4. *Lay your PBS out like this:*
Comparison Group: _____

	Assets	Liabilities
Knowledge		
Skills		
Personal traits		
Mental abilities		
Situational factors		

5. *Compare yourself to that group on every item that you believe is important in the lists of knowledge, skills, and so on.* The first time you make a PBS, select only one to three items from each category and ignore the rest. Use the following rating scale:

- 1 = Much worse
- 2 = Worse
- 3 = Equal or don't know
- 4 = Better
- 5 = Much better

6. *Put the qualities rated 4 and 5 into the assets column, and the ones rated 1 and 2 into the liabilities column.* Ignore the ones rated 3 or get the information you need to rate them.

7. *Emphasize the qualities rated 1 or 5.* Because they are your biggest assets and liabilities, italicize them and put them at the top of the assets or liabilities column for each category (such as knowledge).

8. *If you want to do a thorough job, review the important qualities that you could not rate.* Get the information you need to make those comparisons. Don't bother to take this step the first time you make a PBS.

9. *Get a second opinion.* Ask your coach or poker buddy to comment. Tell this person you want the truth, not some tactful soft soap. Doctors have much better tests and are more objective than you are, but they frequently get second opinions.

Understanding and Using Your PBS

You can skim over or even ignore this section unless you have tried to compare yourself on many dimensions. If you have done all that work, this section will help you to understand and use your data.

Count the number of "3" ratings. If you tried but can't rate yourself on many important qualities (such as card-reading skill, emotional control, or theoretical knowledge), you haven't been comparing yourself to the competition. You'd better start doing so because these comparisons determine your results.

Get comparison data in many ways. Participate in Internet forums and discussion groups. You will learn more about whatever you discuss while gaining information about your strengths and weaknesses.

Do the quizzes in various books and ask others how well they did on those quizzes. Compare your card reading to that of other players by saying, for example, "I put him on a big ace. What did you think?" Make learning about yourself a top priority.

Explain the inconsistencies. There should be a consistent pattern between the number of assets and liabilities and your results.

If you have more assets than liabilities, you should be winning. If you are losing, these are the two most probable causes:

1. You have overestimated your assets and/or underestimated your liabilities. Both errors are *extremely* common. Ask someone to tell you the truth. If he says that you have made these errors, stop kidding yourself, move to an easier game, and/or work harder on developing yourself.

2. Some of your liabilities may be very powerful. For example, if you go on tilt easily or love to gamble and to challenge superior players, your other assets and liabilities don't matter much. Unless you control those liabilities, you will continue to lose.

If you have more liabilities than assets, you should be losing significantly. Because the house takes so much out of the game, you must be better than the competition just to break even. If you are winning, these are the two most probable causes:

1. You are too self-critical. It is much rarer than the opposite tendency, but it does happen. Ask yourself and others whether you underestimate yourself.

2. Some of your assets may be very powerful. For example, if you read cards superbly, you can win despite liabilities such as limited theoretical knowledge or math skills.

If your assets and liabilities are about equal, you should be losing slightly (because of the rake). If your results are different, the preceding patterns probably suggest the causes.

Understand the implications of the consistencies. If your results are consistent with your assets and liabilities, analyze the causes and their implications.

If your assets greatly exceed your liabilities and you are winning a lot of bets per hour, you are probably playing below your level. You are not getting the full benefit of your talents. Of course, that conclusion depends on your motives. Perhaps maximizing your profits is not as important as enjoying the game and winning frequently. Or you may not have the bankroll to move up. If you have the bankroll and want to make more money, you should seriously consider moving up.

If your liabilities greatly exceed your assets and you are losing a lot, you are probably playing above your level. Answer two questions:

1. Why are you doing it? If you are deliberately paying tuition to develop your game and you can afford the losses, it *may* be reasonable to stay where you are. But examine your motives carefully. You may want to play in the larger games for the thrill or the status. Of course, if you can afford to pay for those pleasures, you can continue to do so, but at least be honest about your motives.

2. Can you afford it? If not, you may be a pathological gambler. Your own analysis says that you are playing in games you cannot beat and losing money you cannot afford. Your analysis strongly suggests that you cannot control self-destructive impulses. Consult a professional or go to Gamblers Anonymous[1] before you ruin your life.

---

1. You can get useful information at www.gamblersanonymous.org.

Use the PBS to direct your self-development. The PBS should indicate the assets to exploit and the weaknesses to correct or plan around. I know an excellent player who realized that he was studying the wrong subjects. He was well above his competition on every type of knowledge except game theory. He had been buying books on subjects he knew well, but he hadn't studied game theory. Once the picture became clear, he knew what to study.

Others have told me that the PBS helped them to see why their results were disappointing. One realized he was not as intensely competitive as the better players at his level and decided to avoid some of them. Another saw that he had to work hard on his card reading. These are the sorts of insights you can gain.

Because they don't systematically compare themselves to the competition, many people focus on the wrong areas. For example, some players know theory well but lose because they gamble too much. So what do they do? They buy more books and study more theory. Don't follow in their footsteps: work on your weaknesses, not on what you enjoy doing.

Apply active-learning principles *now* by taking a mini-quiz about what you have just read. Turn to Appendix E and answer those questions about this chapter.

Your Poker Improvement Plan: Part IV. Making Your Plans

The steps described in the previous chapter should have clarified where you want to go and the factors that will help or hinder your progress. Now take four more steps:

1. *Review your ultimate objective.* The PBS may have indicated that your original objective is unattainable. Remember, you can't change yourself very much. If you can't reasonably expect to develop the qualities needed to reach your ultimate objective, replace it with one that's more achievable.

2. *Review your annual goals.* Many people try to move too quickly. Their impatience prevents them from developing the qualities needed to reach their ultimate objective. Set a schedule that's challenging enough to motivate you, but not so demanding that you can't meet it.

3. *Decide* how *you will reach both your ultimate objective and your annual goals.* Clearly specify the steps you will take to develop the qualities and situation you need.

4. *Repeat steps 1 and 2.* The act of writing down how you will achieve your goals may make you realize that some of them are unattainable. If so, set more realistic ones.

Let's focus on step 3, *how* to achieve your goals. We'll start here by discussing the general way that Barry Tanenbaum planned his career.

Then, in the following section, we'll discuss a detailed plan for achieving your goals.

Barry is now a successful $30–$60 pro, coach, and *Card Player* columnist, but it took him several years to reach that level. He decided long ago to spend a great deal of time studying and discussing poker. He read most of the good poker books, and he discussed theory and strategy very frequently. He decided to move up only after hundreds of hours of winning play at many levels: $2–$4, $3–$6, $6–$12, $10–$20, $15–$30, and $20–$40.

He was occasionally tempted to skip a step, but he didn't do it. A few times he moved up, lost, and moved back down. Then he analyzed what he had done wrong, rebuilt his bankroll, and moved up again. As his current success shows, his patience and careful planning have paid off.

You may not have either the patience or the realism to move so slowly and carefully, but I urge you to take all the steps. Barry has a lot of natural ability, but he still moved slowly. If you try to move too quickly, you will probably fail.

Decide *How* You Will Reach All Your Goals

You need more than patience and realism to reach your goals. You must carefully plan the steps needed to acquire all the necessary knowledge, skills, and other qualities. Apply three general principles:

1. Commit enough resources to developing yourself.
2. Make self-development part of your routine.
3. Apply the appropriate active-learning principles.

Principle No.1: Commit enough resources to developing yourself. You can't develop yourself fully without committing serious money and time. Buy books and DVDs, and if you're very ambitious, hire a coach or work closely with a poker buddy. Then get full value for your money by spending a lot of time:

- Studying and discussing poker
- Getting practice and feedback on your skills
- Working on your personal weaknesses

Most players are more willing to work on skills and knowledge than on their personal weaknesses. It's a reasonable choice. If you don't know how to play, you can't win. However, if you have good knowledge and skills but are dissatisfied with your results, you should work on the personal weaknesses that are causing your problems.

You should occasionally sacrifice some expected value (EV) by playing against tough players. Playing only in soft games will increase your immediate win rate but prevent you from reaching your full potential. If your goals are ambitious, you should occasionally play in games that are so tough that you will lose money. That notion sounds like heresy, but Matt Lessinger stated it in his very first *Card Player* column: "I have played in games in which my EV was very clearly negative. . . . [They] were learning experiences, and thus well worth the sacrifice. I was willing to pay my 'tuition' in order to get schooled."[1]

Principle No. 2: Make self-development part of your routine. Time is an extremely limited resource. There are only twenty-four hours in a day, and most of them are committed to other activities. Developing yourself may be left for "when I have time for it," which often means that it doesn't get done at all.

Commit yourself to spending enough time each week on *all* the developmental activities: studying the literature, discussing hands and strategy, and working on your personal weaknesses. Unless you commit to all of them, you will neglect some of them, especially the ones you dislike. The more you dislike a developmental activity, the more you need it. For example, who needs exercise more, the naturally active person or the couch potato?

Many professions demand continuing education courses. You can't

1. Matt Lessinger, "Less Is Back for More," *Card Player,* June 6, 2003.

keep your license as a physician, attorney, or psychologist without them. The authorities know that many people won't develop themselves without coercion.

Poker doesn't have any formal requirements, but you get tested every night, and you pay dearly for your mistakes. Because poker is continually changing and some opponents are working hard, your alternatives are brutally simple: you must either develop yourself or fall behind them. Two steps can help:

1. Schedule your development activities.
2. Include experiments in your plans.

1. *Schedule your development activities.* The more specific you are about spending time on an activity the more likely you are to do it. You can commit yourself to:

- Spending specific times: "I will participate on twoplus-two.com's forums from 8 to 10 P.M. every Tuesday" or "I will meet with my poker discussion group every Monday evening."
- Spending a certain amount of time: "I will spend four hours per week reading poker books and participating in forums at cardplayer.com."

You need a control system to make sure that you stick to your plans. Make a note every time you miss a commitment. If you miss a Tuesday night session on the forums, be sure to go there on Wednesday.

You will get the most value from your developmental activities if you do them when you are sharp, motivated, and able to give them your full attention. If your favorite games are on the weekends or you get sleepy in the afternoons, don't plan to study or discuss strategy at those times. If you are a morning person, study theory when you first get up.

2. *Include experiments in your plans.* You, I, and everyone else are used to doing things a certain way, and unless you experiment regularly you will probably stay in your comfortable rut. Frequent experiments will help you to break out of that rut and learn something new.

Some experiments will fail, but you can learn a lot from them. If you try a loose-aggressive style, you may take a serious loss but gain insight into how loose-aggressive players think.

Some experiments will succeed. You may find that a loose-aggressive style doesn't work in one game but is extremely successful in another one. You may learn when and how to switch gears.

You can experiment by trying various styles, by playing in larger or different types of games, by changing table positions (such as from the left to the right of Maniacs), and in many other ways. These are the important points:

- Do it regularly.
- Decide exactly what changes you will make.
- Know why you are making these changes.
- Analyze your experiences to maximize your learning.

Principle No. 3: Apply the appropriate active-learning principles. "Learning Efficiently" stated that active learning is much more efficient than passive learning. "Reading and Adjusting to Players" described an active-learning system for developing those skills. Several other chapters suggested ways to develop various knowledge, skills, and traits. For example, the techniques for acquiring knowledge are quite different from those for developing skills. Use only the appropriate learning techniques for each quality.

Knowledge: List the books and articles you will read, the people you will consult, and the Internet forums you will visit. When will you do these things? State the order in which you will do them, because some kinds of knowledge cannot be acquired until after you know other things. For example, you need a good understanding of bluffing before you can apply game theory to bluffing.

How much time and money will you spend on developing various kinds of knowledge? Base that investment on the value of the knowledge. Spend your time and money where you will get the best return on your investment.

Skills: Because you cannot develop skills without practice and feedback, plan ways to get them. Ask and answer the same questions about time and value that you answered for knowledge.

Put your skill-development plans into a logical order. Some skills require learning more fundamental ones first. For example, before working on semi-bluffing, memorize the odds of making various draws and be able to

- Count the pot automatically.
- Count your outs quickly.
- Assess your opponents' styles to make accurate estimates of the probability of being called.

Mental abilities: Remember, most mental abilities can't be changed much, and many can't be changed at all. Exactly what will you do to develop each one? Why do you believe it will work? Will you get enough value from this work to justify the investment?

Psychological traits: Clearly state how you will develop the ones you believe you need. Remember, most traits can't be changed much, and a few can't be changed at all.

Situational factors: Clearly state how you will change the factors you think should be modified. Make sure your plans are realistic.

The Final Questions

After you have written your plans, ask yourself the critical question: *Will I really do everything I have planned?*

"The Coach's Dilemma" said to set goals and make plans that are "ambitious enough to move you in the right direction, but modest enough to be carried out." If you won't do all the things you have written down, cross out the ones you won't do.

Then ask yourself the next question: *Can I reach my goals by doing only the things I will do?* If not, revise your goals downward. Be brutally honest about where you are going and how you will get there. Set achievable goals and make realistic plans. Work on what you can improve, and find ways to compensate for the qualities you can't or won't change. It's immeasurably better to set goals that you can reach by actions you'll take than to set unrealistic goals or to make plans you won't implement.

Apply active-learning principles *now* by taking a mini-quiz about what you have just read. Turn to Appendix E and answer those questions about this chapter.

Your Poker Improvement Plan: Part V. Monitoring Your Progress

Most self-development plans fail. There is no research on poker players' plans, but there have been thousands of studies on other self-improvement programs such as dieting, exercising, quitting smoking, and learning Spanish. This research clearly proves that most people don't achieve their goals. The plans may be excellent, but people don't implement them well.

You have probably had similar failures. You started enthusiastically. You told yourself, *"This* time will be different." You stuck with the program until your poker improved, or you lost so many pounds, got into shape, and so on. But after a month or a year, you ended up right back where you had started. The same will probably happen to any plans you make unless you monitor your progress; get help in sticking to your plans; and, if necessary, revise them.

There is no research about poker, so let's examine a study from *The Journal of the American Medical Association* that compared four dieting programs: Atkins, Ormish, Weight Watchers, and Zone. The researchers described Atkins and Ormish as "more extreme" and Weight Watchers and Zone as "more moderate." About 50 percent of participants on the Atkins and Ormish diets were able to stick with those plans, but about 65 percent of participants on the Weight Watchers and Zone diets stuck to those plans.

These percentages are much higher than those that other studies of these programs found. One reason may be that people knew they would be "tested." When people don't have anyone monitoring their progress, they are much more likely to quit. The lesson for you is quite clear: if you monitor your progress, you are more likely to implement your plans.

The differences between the moderate and extreme diets caused the researchers to conclude: "The bottom line was that it wasn't so much the type of diet followed that led to successful weight loss, but the ability of participants to stick with the program for the entire year's time."[1] This conclusion agrees with the central point of "The Coach's Dilemma": *"An inferior, but implemented treatment plan is much better than a perfect, but ignored plan."*

That chapter was concerned with making plans that you would implement. Now let's focus on what you must do after making your plans to increase your chances of completing them. Let's use Weight Watchers as a model. It has been more successful than most programs for several reasons:

1. Participants closely monitor their results by weighing themselves at weekly meetings.
2. Participants closely monitor what they eat.
3. Participants can choose from a wide variety of foods.
4. Participants belong to a group that gives them support and advice.

The weekly meetings are critically important. Knowing that they will record their weight and food consumption puts pressure on them to stick to their plans. Put similar pressure on yourself, but monitor your progress less frequently, perhaps once a month. That period is short enough to exert steady pressure, but long enough to reduce luck's effects.

Closely Monitor Your Results

Poker is a bottom-line game, and your results *seem* easy to measure. If you win significantly more money than usual, you are probably playing better. However, because luck has such extreme

1. www.ars.usda.gov/is/AR/archive/maro6/dieto306.htm.

short-term effects, you cannot be sure. Of course, the longer the period, the more confidence you can have in the results.

Despite this problem, you should compare your results to your plans. Nothing will affect you more than your profits or losses. If they differ greatly from your plans, ask yourself why. Have you been lucky or unlucky? Have you been careless, inattentive, playing too loosely or tightly, too passively or aggressively?

Unfortunately, for the reasons discussed earlier, it is even harder to measure how much you have improved your knowledge, skills, and so forth. You can easily focus on the few times that you did something well but ignore your mistakes (or vice versa). Despite measurement problems, you should get as much information as you can from many different sources to monitor your progress.

Closely Monitor What You Have Done

If you have written a good PIP, it's easy to compare your actions to it. You can see how much time, energy and money you have invested. If you planned to buy and read a certain book, or to spend eight hours a month discussing strategy on forums, or to have two sessions with a coach, you can easily see whether you have stuck to your plan. Your records should answer questions like these:

- What books have I read?
- How much time have I spent discussing poker on Internet forums, in discussion groups, and in one-on-one sessions with poker buddies or a coach?
- How often have I done various exercises such as predicting what people will do and comparing their actions to my predictions?

Your answers will often tell you why your results have been disappointing. You probably spent much less time developing yourself than you had planned. It's the equivalent of the dieter's comparing his food consumption to his plans. If he ate more than he intended, he knows why he didn't lose much weight.

Revise Your Plans

In Weight Watchers, if this food doesn't work for you, you can try that one. The same principle applies to your PIP. If it isn't working, try another way to develop your knowledge or skill.

For example, suppose you bought a book, read three chapters, and were disappointed. You could force yourself to read the rest of it, but you should probably just read a different book. Or suppose you spent the eight hours you planned on a certain forum but felt that you didn't learn that much. Next month you could plan to spend four hours on a different forum and four hours working with a poker buddy. Or suppose you need to improve your card-reading skill, but the system I recommended in "Reading and Adjusting to Players" doesn't work for you. You could hire a coach or ask a poker buddy to help you.

In other words, make plans and try hard to implement them, but, if necessary, make new ones that you are more willing and able to do.

Get Help from Other People

Weight Watchers uses groups well. Because they meet regularly with others who are struggling to lose weight, people don't feel so isolated and helpless. When they feel frustrated or don't know what to do, they can talk to the others to get support and advice.

I have repeatedly recommended Internet forums, discussion groups, and coaching relationships with professionals or poker buddies. Professional coaches can provide better advice, but discussion groups and poker buddies will probably be more supportive. They probably share some of your confusion and frustration, and that common bond can be extremely helpful, especially when things go badly.

Final Remarks

Some people think that poker is unique, that the principles that worked well in business, the military, schools, and other places are ir-relevant. I emphatically disagree. Barry Greenstein, one of the world's greatest players, said that most poker players don't plan their long-term development.

They don't do it for many reasons, including the fact that nobody has told them why or how to do it. This planning system was adapted from ones used in business, career strategy, and dieting programs. It works in those places, and it will work for you.

You can start small by working on only a few qualities, but take all four steps. Then, when you see how this system improves both your results and feelings about yourself, you can work on more knowledge, skill, and so forth.

Do it!

Apply active-learning principles *now* by taking a mini-quiz about what you have just read. Turn to Appendix E and answer those questions about this chapter.

Should You Quit Your Day Job? Part I[1]

About seven years ago I wrote an appendix to *The Psychology of Poker*, "Don't Quit Your Day Job" (DQYDJ). Since writing it, the poker world has been turned upside down:

- Online poker is everywhere, and some people are making lots of money at it. Of course, far more people are losing than winning.

- Tournaments—including televised ones—occur so often that nobody can play in all the big ones. Until recently only the top tournament players made a living, but now far more people are doing it. Best of all, for the top players some tournaments are free rolls, meaning that they risk nothing but can win huge prizes.

- Top poker players and writers now have large incomes from books, DVDs, seminars, speeches, Web hosting, and even product endorsements.

- Some good, but not great players are also getting significant incomes from these sources.

- The number of new players has exploded.

1. "Should You Quit Your Day Job?" Parts 1 & 2 were published in an online magazine before Congress passed the Unlawful Internet Gambling Enforcement Act of 2006. It went to Lyle Stuart, my book publisher, a few days after Congress passed it. Several months have passed but nobody really knows what effects the Act will have. I have *not* discussed them.

- Games in B&M rooms are so soft that even mediocre players are winning, and good ones are making more money than they ever expected.[2]

Because of these changes, many people—including some extremely young players—have turned pro or are seriously thinking about it. Today's opportunities are so much better that it would be foolish to insist flatly, "Don't quit your day job." However, it would be even more foolish to quit without fully understanding the pros and cons of becoming a full-time pro.

My current position can be summarized succinctly: Don't quit your day job unless you

- Play *very* well.
- Fully understand what you will gain and lose.
- Are willing to take *very* large risks.
- Can handle the emotional roller coaster.
- Are willing and able to make some huge changes in your attitudes and lifestyle.

The first point should be unnecessary, but some mediocre players have turned pro, and many more of them are considering it. They had never won much until recently but have won more over the past year or two. They may not realize that the *only* reason for their success is that the games were so soft, and that they will get tougher fairly soon.

They may know that they aren't that good but think, "If I play full-time, I'll get a lot better." Nonsense! If you haven't won enough to live on for at least one year or 100,000 online hands (preferably much longer), don't even think of turning pro.

This chapter discusses the points I made in DQYDJ and other peo-

---

2. Online games have gotten *much* tougher since the new law reduced the influx of new players. B&M games continue to be very soft because the supply of new players continues to grow (partly because they can't play online).

ple's counterarguments. Part II discusses the steps you should take as a full-time pro.

You Probably Won't Make It

I wrote in DQYDJ: "Unless you are an excellent player with a big bankroll and extreme discipline, you haven't got a chance." This point aroused the strongest feelings. Some people were enraged by my "negativism," while others made reasonable criticisms. One critic wrote in an online forum: "I don't think he's considering the drastic impact of being able to play 8+ tables online and also get rakeback for all those tables."

He's right. When I wrote DQYDJ, hardly anyone was playing multiple tables, and I believe that rakeback did not exist. Very few people play eight-plus tables, but many people are playing two to four. With all these hands against weak players, plus rakeback and other "bonuses," you do not need to be an excellent player to make a living *today*. However, any career decision should consider the long term, and tomorrow's games will almost certainly be much tougher,[3] and many pro wannabes will go broke.

Even if you are an *excellent* player, the odds are against you. Shortly before the poker explosion, my discussion group asked two famous professionals, "What are an *excellent* middle-limit player's chances of making it as a full-time pro?" One said fifty to one, and the other suggested two hundred to one.

Because conditions are so favorable now, those odds are less—for the short term—but they're still very high, perhaps twenty, thirty, or forty to one. By any rational definition of the word *probably*, those two professionals and I still believe that you probably won't make it.

3. Several chapters of *YWPE* explain why the games will be tougher. The 2006 Anti-internet gambling law accelerated the Darwinian pressures. The weak players disappeared much earlier, not because they went broke, but just because they ran out of cash in their accounts. They could not deposit additional funds because their Neteller accounts were frozen, and other payment options were closed.

You wouldn't bet your life savings against those odds. Why bet your entire life?

There's Little Money and No Future

I wrote in DQYDJ:

> Professionals have great nights or weeks, but their annual incomes and hourly 'wages' are not at all exciting. David Sklansky, Mason Malmuth, and David Hayano found that an excellent professional can average 1 to 1.5 big bets an hour in middle-sized games, much less at larger limits. . . .

That $20 or more per hour is a nice bit of change for just having fun, but it is much less than you can make at most highly skilled jobs. If you are smart and disciplined enough to be an *excellent* player, you can probably make more money doing something else. . . .

The best players in your card room make much less than a mediocre doctor, lawyer, or executive. . . . Hardly any full-timers can afford to retire.

A critic in another online forum wrote: "This book was written in 2000, so I think poker was really starting to spread its wings in society. Again, I'm not sure he's taking online into consideration, but the future of online poker or rakeback, I think, is something to seriously consider."

Again, I agree. It is unquestionably easier to make an okay living now. David Sklansky wrote: "Making well over $50,000 per year playing $3–$6 hold 'em is now no big deal."[4] However, $50,000 is not that much money; most highly skilled jobs pay much more.

Of course, a few players are making much more exciting incomes. The top players' winnings were literally inconceivable just a few years ago, and these players now get all sorts of risk-free money. For the immediate future the very best players can make a lot of money.

---

4. Ed Miller, David Sklansky, and Mason Malmuth, *Small Stakes Hold'em* (Henderson, NV: Two Plus Two, 1996), 2.

But they make and keep *much* less money than you may believe. After covering the tournament circuit for over a decade, Nolan Dalla wrote:

> One of the most troubling aspects of the tournament circuit is seeing how many players are constantly broke. I'm not talking about bad poker players or novices. I'm talking about names and faces everyone would recognize. . . .
>
> The obvious question that needs to be asked is—*can you make a living as a tournament pro?* I have my doubts. Except for a rare few players who possess exceptional talent and have the bankrolls sufficient enough to play in the biggest events . . . most people don't stand a chance of earning a living on the circuit.[5]

In addition, our incredible party will not continue indefinitely. When poker goes out of fashion—as it *certainly* will[6]—the tournaments and cash games will get tougher, and the nonplaying income will shrink. More important, turning pro has a "burning your boats" element to it. If you bust out or burn out, you may not have a feasible Plan B.

That's what I meant about the risks being very large. Some wannabes think, "I'll play for a few years, win some easy money, have a lot of fun, and then, if I go broke or don't like the lifestyle, I'll do something else." Let me quote again from DQYDJ:

> Hayano's research[7] found that none of the full-timers was over 43 years old. At just the age that people become well-established in

5. "So You Wanna' Be a Tournament Pro? Fuhgetaboutit!" www.pokerpages.com/ articles/archives/dalla27.htm.

6. Countless people have insisted that the poker boom will continue indefinitely. They obviously have no sense of history. There have been thousands of booms over the centuries, and *every one* of them ended.

7. David Hayano, *Poker Faces: The Life and Work of Professional Poker Players* (Berkeley: The University of California Press, 1982). His book is very dated, but anyone considering turning pro should definitely read it.

most careers, they had to start a new one. . . . Just look around your card room. You'll see former high-stakes players hustling the tiny games or working at menial jobs to get another stake.

Although pros are winning much more money than ever before, that pattern hasn't changed much. Most pros either are young or have an income from nonpoker sources. I'm glad that Ed Miller and others are suggesting that pros plan financially, and that some pros are buying houses and health insurance and contributing to tax-sheltered retirement programs. Unfortunately, they are a tiny minority. The typical pro does hardly any long-term financial planning.

Again, the situation is better than it has ever been. Because of TV, playing poker is much less disreputable than it once was. But prospective employers still want credentials and experience. If all your resume says is that you played poker successfully, hardly anyone will give you a good job.

It's Extremely Unhealthy

I wrote in DQYDJ: "The lifestyle is almost a 'prescription' for a heart attack and other nasty problems. Nearly every full-timer spends far too many hours on back-destroying chairs, in smoky rooms, with hardly any exercise, and a steady diet of unhealthy food."

In 2000, nearly every room allowed smoking, but many now prohibit it. Some rooms have slightly better chairs, but most of them are terrible for long sessions. Some online pros have solved this problem with orthopedic chairs.

Some players have stated that their lifestyle is unhealthy whether they play online or in live games. Victor, an online pro, said in an online forum that he was making a great deal of money, but "It is so easy to become a worthless, unhealthy shut-in. All my friends envy me, but I often wish I could find a routine that contributes to my health and lessens my listlessness." x2ski wrote: "I sit in front of a computer screen playing poker all day and only take breaks to walk upstairs out of my basement to have a smoke." Elysium said: "It is unhealthy to be sitting around in a dirty, filthy cardroom all day."

A few people pointed out that the pro's lifestyle is not intrinsically unhealthy. USGrant stated: "In comparison to many jobs today, I'm not sure what's unique about online poker that would induce an unhealthy lifestyle." I agree, and Part II will say more about this subject.

It's a Dreary Life

I wrote in DQYDJ:

It's not just the finances that are dreary; it's the entire life . . .

They play poker, eat (often right at the table), sleep, and then play poker again. They may play for more than 24 hours, and 16 hours is quite common. If any boss insisted you work such hours, eating lousy food, sitting in an uncomfortable chair, in a smoke-filled room, with no financial security or benefits, you would go on strike against the "unfair working conditions."

Alvarez's book, *The Biggest Game in Town,* was about the top players: A few of them have nice homes, fancy cars, and other expensive toys, but even the big winners live pathetic lives.

A critic wrote in an online forum: "Again, I think all of these [issues] relate to someone just playing live." In general, I agree with him. Playing online does not automatically lead to a dreary lifestyle. In fact, because their hourly win rate is so high, some online pros work relatively few hours, exercise, have other hobbies, relate to people, and live quite pleasant lives.

Unfortunately, I think only a tiny percentage of online pros live that way. I don't have any systematic data, but in *Your Worst Poker Enemy* I discussed some complaints about depressions and other effects of a dreary lifestyle in the chapter titled "Don't Take Poker Too Seriously."[8]

8. See *Your Worst Poker Enemy,* 305–315.

You must also consider one other factor: multi-tabling may not be tolerable year after year. Virtually all the online players who are making big incomes are multi-tabling. Because it has been possible for only a few years, there are no data on its long-term physical and psychological effects. Many former B&M pros quit after ten or twenty years, complaining about "burnout." Playing one game in a cardroom must be less tiring and stressful than playing several of them online.

Multi-tabling resembles working on an assembly line, but because you can lose a lot of money if you make mistakes or get unlucky, it is probably more stressful. The extensive research on working on assembly lines indicates that many workers *hate* it. If you do it for more than a few years, you will probably "burn out." Do you want to spend the rest of your life imitating a robot?

But It's a Great "Second Job"

In DQYDJ I wrote:

> Lots of people supplement their incomes by playing poker. They play in all size games and can be almost any age. . . . Part-timers can be dealers, barbers, lawyers, waiters, or whatever. They play well, but not well enough to make it as full-timers, or they want more security or a more balanced life. They have regular jobs and may even be committed to their careers. They play when they feel like it, in whatever games they like, and can spend their winnings however they wish. Sounds good to me.

Hardly anyone has disagreed with the idea that poker is a great second job, and many successful full-time pros recognize that another job would provide several extremely important advantages:

• You get health insurance, retirement plans, and other benefits to reduce the danger of ending up broke.

- You avoid holes in your resume so you can get a good job if you go broke or burn out.

- You will be less vulnerable to financial and emotional swings.

- You can play larger games because you don't have to worry so much about your bankroll.

- Your hourly win rate will be higher because you can be much more selective about your games. If you have to cover your rent, you will sometimes be forced to play in unattractive games.

- Having a steady job essentially gives you another "out." Many pros have said, "When you bluff, have an out." And the same thing holds true for just about everything. The diversification principle says, "Don't put all your eggs in one basket." If your financial and psychological well-being is too dependent on your ability to win at poker and to keep committed to it, you are in danger.

Final Remarks

My flat imperative "Don't quit your day job" doesn't fit today's realities. Because the situation has changed so dramatically, turning pro has become a much more desirable and realistic option. However, I think that many, perhaps most, wannabes will not do remotely as well as they expect—not financially or in any other way.

And anyone who wants to become a full-time pro should plan more carefully than most wannabes seem willing to do. If you just decide to "take a shot," you can easily do irrevocable damage to your entire life. You need to do more than just make sure you have enough money.

Apply active-learning principles *now* by taking a mini-quiz about what you have just read. Turn to Appendix E and answer those questions about this chapter.

Should You Quit Your Day Job?
Part II

Part I created considerable controversy. Threads on twoplus-two.com's forums contained more than 125 posts, and they were read by more than 6,000 people. Some people agreed with me, but far more disagreed and criticized me for being too negative.

After writing that article, I viewed a DVD, *Poker Bustouts*. It tells the stories of several pros—including ones with very good track records—who are now broke. Before deciding to turn pro, go to poker-bustouts.com to learn more about this side of poker. I mentioned this DVD on a forum, but some people insisted it was irrelevant, because the busted pros were all B&M players. They ignored the people who said on this forum that they had made a great deal of money online but were broke, depressed, and disillusioned.

A few posters even stated that it's easy to make it as a full-time pro. Nobody with any objectivity and knowledge of the poker world would agree with that ridiculous position. Of course, online poker is different, but many of the problems of being a full-time pro are very similar, and it's wishful thinking to believe that it's easy to succeed just because you're playing online. This chapter is addressed *only* to people who

- Are seriously considering becoming full-time pros.
- Accept that it's a difficult life.
- Have the five qualifications listed in Part I.
- Want to increase the probability that they will succeed.

To improve your chances to succeed, you should take the following steps:

1. Keep Tight Control Over Your Finances

Read Ed Miller's articles at notedpokerauthority.com on going pro. Some people have objected that his position is too conservative, but a cautious approach dramatically increases your chances of surviving. If you are not careful about your finances, you will probably end up busted no matter how much money you make. It has happened to thousands of very good players.

Unfortunately, many pros are financially irresponsible. Some live beyond their means. Others have leaks such as craps or sports betting. Others arrogantly think: "I don't have to be conservative because I'm so talented." They will almost certainly go broke.

Too many talented players have failed because they did not manage their finances well. The two most obvious examples are Johnny Moss and Stu Ungar. They were the greatest players of their eras, but Johnny lived his final years on the Binion's charity, and Stu died broke and in debt in a crummy motel room. Becoming a full-time pro is essentially the same as starting a new business, and the most common causes for new-business failures are undercapitalization and poor financial control.

In addition to starting with enough capital, you must tightly manage your finances *forever*. Countless pros have made a pile of money and then blown it. Some of the famous names you see on TV are broke. For example, after winning over $1,000,000 in the 2005 WSOP championship, Mike Matusow was asked what he would do with all that money. He said he would pay off *some* of his debts (because he could not pay all of them). To succeed as a pro you *must* have the same sorts of financial controls as any other business. If you spend too much, gamble too heavily, or move up too quickly, you will probably go broke.

2. Accept Responsibility for Your Results

Accept that nobody twisted your arm to make you quit your job, that you're taking a risk, and that the odds are against you. Poker is a ruthless meritocracy, and only the best can thrive as full-time pros.

If you go bust or don't like the lifestyle, don't blame bad luck, bad players, or anyone but yourself. Shrug your shoulders, say, "Oh, well," and decide what you will do with the rest of your life.

3. Don't Burn Any Bridges

Don't tell off your boss, give up any licenses, walk out on any debts, drop out of college, tell everyone you're becoming a full-time pro, or do anything that will make it harder to return to the "straight world."

There are two types of barriers to returning. The first is objective. If you tell off your boss or give up your license, it will be much harder to get a straight job. The second, psychological barriers, can be almost as destructive. For example, you may be tempted to brag, "I'm not like you suckers. I'm giving up the nine-to-five world because I can make a fortune playing poker." If you go broke or just don't like the life, you may be too embarrassed to admit that you made a mistake. *Keep your options open.*

4. Don't Take Poker Too Seriously

I ended *YWPE* with this subject, but now I'm concerned only with current and prospective full-time pros. Some of them are *much* too serious. They overreact to the inevitable swings, becoming depressed when losing, feeling invulnerable when winning. They don't talk at the table except to tell others to hurry up or to criticize their play or habits. They play *only* to win money. They hurt themselves both financially and psychologically:

- The weaker players don't want to play with them.
- The better players may try harder to beat them.
- They are more likely to become lonely and depressed.

Many writers have made the first two points, but hardly any experts have written about loneliness and depression. I believe they are serious problems for pros. Our game is intrinsically lonely because we try to take each other's money. If you don't lighten up, that "everyone is my enemy" mentality can have a devastating effect on your relationships and moods.

5. Get Involved with Support Groups

I believe that many pros fail because they can't cope with the emotional side of their life. Forums contain hundreds of posts about being depressed, misunderstood, and lonely. Forums are an excellent source of information and advice, but they don't provide much help with loneliness, depression, and frustration

Nearly all of us need to meet regularly with people we know and trust, including other players. I belong to the Wednesday Poker Discussion Group (WPDG) and its spin-offs. These groups improve our play but also provide psychological support.

When we get angry, lonely, or depressed, we need to be with people who understand and care about us. We get together all the time, not just at meetings. We have coffee or a meal, or play poker together, or go to the movies. Sometimes, we don't even talk about poker. We just enjoy each other's company. You can get the same support by joining or starting a discussion group.

You should also relate to nonplayers. It doesn't matter whether you meet them at church, the Kiwanis Club, or the golf course—spend time with people who have common interests besides poker.

6. Don't *Always* Try to Maximize Your Win Rate

That statement may sound heretical, but I think it's essential. Even if poker is your full-time profession, don't forget that it's a *game,* and it should be played—at least partly—for pleasure. Sometimes you should play just for fun or education.

If you *always* try to maximize your win rate, you will become bored and boring. You will be grinding out "wages," living the sort of life you were trying to escape by becoming a full-time pro. One day will seem just like another, and you may wonder, "Where did my life go?"

Focusing too intently on your win rate will also increase your vulnerability to emotional swings:

- When the inevitable bad beats and losing streaks occur, you will not have much defense against them.
- You will be more isolated. People don't want to be around someone who thinks only of making money.

Because they recognize the dangers of becoming too profit oriented, some successful pros take various negative expected-value actions:

- A few occasionally play crazily in low-stakes games and small, multiple rebuy tournaments. They may rebuy twenty times to blow off steam and satisfy their gambling urges. Then, when the big money is on the line, they can play more sensibly.

- WPDGers often get together to play poker. Because there are no really bad players, nobody has much of an edge, and the group as a whole must lose money to the house, but it's fun.

- BARGE[1] and its spin-offs may have the world's toughest low-stakes games and tournaments. Some top pros and other

---

1. BARGE stands for Big August Recreational Gambling Excursion. There are many similar organizations. You can get more information at barge.org.

great players are BARGERS. How often can you play for low stakes against top pros? Some pros don't even record their results because they "aren't working."

- You should play occasionally against tough competition just to improve your game.

7. Maintain a Healthy Lifestyle

A pro's lifestyle is not *intrinsically* unhealthy. The freedom and flexibility offer opportunities to live any way you like. One online pro wrote in a forum: "I'm playing at home, in a big leather chair, no smoke, any healthy food I want, and the opportunity to take plenty of breaks for exercise." Alas, many people don't take full advantage of the opportunities to live healthily. They join gyms, start diets, and so on but don't stick to them. Don't talk about it—*do it!*

8. Have a Passion for the Game

Barry Tanenbaum once e-mailed me: "Long-term successful poker play requires a real love for the game. It must not be just a living, but a passion." If poker is just a way to make money, the negative side of being a full-time pro can ruin you. The swings, frustrations, and loneliness can make you into one of the bitter, whiny people we meet all the time. That's no way to live.

But, if you have a passion for the game, you'll cope with the negatives because you're doing something you love. So take a hard look at why you play poker. If you don't love it, don't quit your day job. If you love playing and you have all the other qualifications, it may be the right career for you.

Apply active-learning principles *now* by taking a mini-quiz about what you have just read. Turn to Appendix E and answer those questions about this chapter.

Afterthought

This book and *Your Worst Poker Enemy* end with the same general recommendation: *Don't let poker take over your life.* Enjoy it, work on your skills, compete intensely, but don't let it become an obsession.

Many players live on a roller coaster. When they win, they feel great. When they lose, they become so depressed and angry that they work poorly, neglect other responsibilities, and harm their personal relationships. In a few extreme cases, players even ruin their physical or mental health.

Poker is a great game, the best I've ever played, but that's all it is. I love playing, talking, and writing about it, and I value my relationships with other players. But it's not my whole life, and it shouldn't be yours.

Poker is great recreation that arouses our competitive instincts, presents intellectual and emotional challenges, lets us socialize with varied people, and develops valuable coping skills. Unlike baseball, football, and other physically grueling sports you can play at any age. Most recreation costs money, sometimes a lot of it, but you can play poker cheaply or profitably. If you have enough talent and commitment, you can even make a good living at it.

The critical issue is balance. If you do not take poker seriously enough, you will lose to the people who do. If you take it too seriously, you will probably have the same financial, emotional, and social problems that so many others—including some *great* players—have had.

You should also balance short- and long-term actions. If you overemphasize maximizing your immediate profits, you will neglect some actions (such as studying and playing against better competition) you should take to reach your full potential.

I began *Your Worst Poker Enemy* with a quotation from Stu Ungar, the greatest player of all time. It seems fitting to end with it: "At the table, your worst enemy is yourself."[1] Stu was extraordinarily unbalanced. Nobody has ever had so much talent, and hardly anyone has all of his terrible weaknesses, but thousands of serious players have the same general pattern. They are just less extreme.

Stu and they get so caught up in the immediate kick of playing well and "living large" that they do not think much about where they are going and how they will get there. Stu's tragedy should be a warning to all of us.

Keep poker where it belongs. Take it seriously enough to get the results you want, but don't let it destroy the more important parts of your life. The same point could be made about almost anything, such as sex, food, work, and politics. Wise people have always sought to balance their lives.

So look hard at yourself and decide where you want to go with poker. Study the literature, discuss the theory and your play with other people, and do whatever else it takes to get where you want to go. But don't deny reality or let poker take over your life. If you do so, you can become your worst poker enemy.

Conversely, if you accept and enjoy poker for what it is, are honest with yourself, work intelligently on your skills and attitudes, and remember that it is only a game, you will become your best poker friend.

1. Quoted by Nolan Dala and Peter Allison, *One of a Kind: The Rise and Fall of Stuey "The Kid" Ungar, the World's Greatest Poker Player* (New York: Atria Books, 2005), 282.

Appendix A:
Why Do You Play Poker?[1]

If you asked people why they play poker, many would reply, "To make money," but they would be kidding themselves. First, most players lose, and any loser who claims to be trying to make money is obviously denying reality. Second, we do hardly anything for just one reason. For example, most of us don't work just to make money; we also want other satisfactions such as making a contribution, being respected, enjoying our jobs, and meeting people. If we *work* for more reasons than money, why would anyone claim that we *play a game just* for money?

Because poker is a macho game with a macho culture. Machismo is so important that some people who don't really care about winning pretend they play to win.

Humans are competitive creatures, and we compete about almost everything: poker, golf, cars, houses, social positions, whatever. We play games because we are so competitive, and lots of us take them very seriously—even if no money is at stake.

Because the money we win or lose measures our success at poker, we naturally overemphasize it. Lots of golfers play for money, but you will never hear one say, "I play just to make money." They play for fun, and winning money is part of the pleasure.

The myth that people play just or mostly for money is reinforced by many poker books. If their authors don't win, they don't eat. Because winning is so important to them, they commit the Egoistic Fallacy by assuming that their readers have the same priorities.

---

1. This material was taken from pages 32–38 of my book *The Psychology of Poker*. Because I have combined quotations and paraphrases, I omit quotation marks.

Nonsense! Many people want to win lots of pots, even if it means they lose money. Why else would they make so many loose plays? They know their looseness is very expensive, but the kick of winning many pots is more important to them than the money.

For most of us poker is a *game,* not a business. We play games for all kinds of reasons, but mostly for pleasure. The dollars won and lost are essentially the same as strokes in golf—just the way to keep score.

It is competing, winning for its own sake, cutting strokes off their handicap that drives many people, not the money. In addition, *everybody*—even the most profit-oriented professional—has completely unrelated motives, such as the desire for excitement, machismo challenges, socializing, and just having a pleasant time.

You cannot understand your own or any other player's motives until you realize that the *insistence that most people play to win is just flat wrong.* We are not willing to do everything it takes to win the most possible money. We would have to treat poker like a job, and it is not a job to us. *It is a game,* and we should never forget that fact.

So stop kidding yourself about why you play poker. Ignore what other people say you should want and discover why you really play by completing the following little questionnaire. The procedure is quite simple: just divide your total motivation (100 percent) into as many pieces as you think are correct. For example, if your only motive is to make money and you treat poker as just a job, assign 100 percentage points to "Make money."

If your primary motive is to make money but you also enjoy socializing and meeting people, like to test yourself against competitive challenges, get a little kick from taking a risk, and want to pass time, you might rate "Make money" 40 percent; "Socialize, meet people" 20 percent; "Test self against competitive challenges" 20 percent; "Get excitement of risk" 10 percent; and "Pass time" 10 percent.

If you really don't care about making money, if the chips are just score-keeping tokens, you might assign all your points to other categories.

If you have motives other than the ones listed, write them in the blank spaces and assign numbers to them.

Use a pencil so you can make changes, and make sure your numbers add to exactly 100 percent.

My Motives for Playing

Make money _____ %

Socialize, meet people _____ %

Relax _____ %

Get excitement of risk _____ %

Test self against competitive challenges _____ %

Sense of accomplishment from winning _____ %

Pass time _____ %

Other (specify)

_____ _____ %

_____ _____ %

_____ _____ %

Total (must be 100%) _____ %

Whenever you have to make an important decision such as whether you should move up or quit your day job, refer to this questionnaire. Consider the effects of your decision on *all* your motives.

Appendix B:
Don't Waste Your Time in Lectures

Many years ago, when I was still a professor, I wrote: "There is only one intelligent response to lectures: *Don't go.*"[1]

Some of my colleagues were horrified, and some poker experts will feel the same way. They make good money lecturing, but the evidence proves unequivocally that lectures are a ridiculous waste of time.

The word *lecture* is derived from the Latin verb *legere*, which means "to read." Before the printing press was invented, books were too expensive for most people to purchase, and teachers stood in front of groups reading books aloud while the students wrote down what they said. When the printing press was invented more than five centuries ago, lectures became obsolete.

Because the educational establishment is extraordinarily incompetent, lectures are still the primary teaching method. Teachers like them because they are essentially no-brainers. The teachers can stand there reading their notes (which may not have been updated for years), and the students have to listen or pretend to do so. It is much easier to lecture than it is to design the sort of active-learning exercises I described earlier.

Because they have been conditioned by a lifetime of listening to lectures, some people are more comfortable listening to lectures than reading. And they would much rather listen passively than do those stressful active-learning tasks. Active learning *is work*, and most people don't really want to work, especially not about a game.

1. Alan Schoonmaker, *A Student's Survival Manual,* page 220. Most of the material covered here is from various parts of that book. If you won't avoid lectures, read pages 220–223 to learn how to make them more useful.

Lectures Are Extraordinarily Inefficient

If two groups are exposed to the identical lecture but one listens to it while the other reads a transcription of it, most people in the reading group will learn much more. The reasons are obvious:

- You can read much more rapidly than anyone can talk. You can read the transcription again and again in the time it takes to listen to it once.
- You comprehend written material much better than spoken.
- If you get confused, you can go back and look at what was written earlier.
- People learn at different rates. The lecturer will go too fast for some people and too slow for others.
- You can underline and make marginal notes.
- When you try to take notes about what the lecturer just said, you will often miss what he is saying now.
- Most important, instead of frantically scribbling notes, you can concentrate on what the lecturer *means*.

Because the academic world is more than five hundred years behind technology, so are most poker teachers. What else could they be? Because they have listened to lectures all their lives and have never studied learning research, they naturally repeat their teachers' mistakes.

Most poker classes are lectures; so are most DVDs and videotapes. A few DVDs and videos use technology more intelligently, and I urge you to buy and use them. But don't waste your time or money on lectures whether they are live or taped. Instead, get more value for your time and money by buying and reading the lecturer's books. If he hasn't written a book, read one by somebody else.

If you want entertainment, buy a DVD. If you want to learn, buy and study the book. Your time is too precious to waste passively listening to a lecture.

Appendix C:
If You Have Psychological Problems

Because I am a psychologist, some people have told me that they were seeing professionals for problems with their families, with work, or for serious clinical problems such as anxiety, depression, and drug or alcohol abuse. A few people have even asked me for advice that I am not qualified to give. Because I am not a clinician, I asked Dr. Daniel Kessler, a clinical psychologist, to help me with this appendix.

We came to the conclusion that if you have significant psychological problems you should *not* play poker for serious stakes unless these problems are well controlled.

We are *certain* that you should not play without discussing this issue with a mental health professional. Don't ask an outsider, even an apparently qualified one such as myself, for advice on such an important subject. Your mental health professional knows you a lot better than I do and has the training needed to help you.

Gambling can threaten your mental stability, and you should not take that risk without your mental health professional's agreement. The emotional roller coaster of winning and losing can aggravate your psychological problems. If you are in remission, these emotional swings increase the probability of a relapse.

Some medications can interfere with clear thinking, and they may reduce your ability to make good decisions. You may be tempted to skip taking them to improve your play, but doing so is very foolish. You would essentially be self-medicating, and you are not qualified to make that decision. Make sure you discuss everything with your mental health professional before changing your medications. Changing them may be much more dangerous to your mental health (and to your bankroll) than taking them while playing.

If your problem is related to substance abuse or addiction, you probably should never play poker for more than trivial stakes (and perhaps not even then). Gambling has large effects on the brain, and these effects, primarily the stimulation of dopamine, are very similar to those caused by drug abuse. This stimulation increases your risk of relapse or of substituting gambling addiction for your substance addiction.

Relapses on drugs and alcohol can be triggered by *both* the depression that comes from losses and the joy of a big win. Because both of these feelings can cause relapses, you should probably avoid gambling, even if you have been in remission for years.

The bottom line is that if you have serious problems you should discuss them thoroughly with a qualified mental health professional before playing poker. If you don't feel comfortable doing so, you probably shouldn't play at all. Your mental health is much too important to risk.

Appendix D:
Biased Data Samples

If you draw conclusions about your play (or about anything else) from a biased sample of data, you will make huge mistakes. Unfortunately, nearly every poker player relies on biased samples. We naturally remember the hands and other information that support our beliefs and ignore or forget contradictory data:

- If we think we have great intuition, we will remember the few great calls we made to snap off bluffs but forget the times we were *sure* someone was bluffing but he had the nuts.

- If we think someone plays badly, we will remember his mistakes but ignore, forget, or misinterpret his good plays.

- If we think we are unlucky, we will remember our bad beats but forget our good beats (the times that we were the lucky idiot who caught the miracle card to win a huge pot).

Some people think that a large sample is automatically a good one, but size is much less important than the way a sample is selected. A small, well-selected sample is immeasurably better than a large, but poorly selected one.

For example, a friend insisted that another player was very good, but extremely unlucky. His only evidence was over a hundred online hand histories that the player had sent him. They both believed that the sheer size of this sample *proved* that he was unlucky. How could he have so many unlucky hands but lose only a few dollars if he wasn't terribly unlucky? His opponents had made this runner-runner flush and that set, and he had lost again and again with pocket aces, TPTK, sets, and so on.

My friend was quite offended when I told him that the data were utterly useless because the player had selected the hands. When you select your own hands to report, you can prove anything you want to prove. The sheer number of hands presented is absolutely irrelevant. Unless they are taken using random sampling techniques, they are worthless.

One of the most extreme examples of the dangers of biased samples occurred during the 1936 presidential election campaign. *The Literary Digest* used the largest sample ever taken in a political poll, many times larger than the ones used today. It predicted that Alf Landon would win the 1936 presidential election, but he took a terrible beating.

The huge sample was worthless because of a systematic sampling error: it used lists of telephone owners, magazine subscribers, and car owners. These people liked Landon. But it was the middle of the depression, and most people could not afford telephones, magazines, and cars. The poorer people greatly preferred FDR.[1]

The same sort of bias caused—deliberately or unconsciously—my friend's player to select hands that supported his belief that he played well, but was unlucky. I am certain he did not remember all the times that his aces or TPTK held up, or all the flush draws he made, or all the times *he* was the lucky guy who caught a two-outer to win a monster pot.

Systematic biasing is such a serious problem that it is absolutely forbidden by law in drug testing. If you do not use carefully matched samples and double-blind research methods, the Food and Drug Administration will not approve your drug, and you cannot sell it. Or just look at television ads for diets and investment schemes. They report, for example, "Jane lost sixty pounds in three months" or "John

---

1. The pollsters made some other methodological mistakes that I won't discuss.

made $5,000 in two weeks." But if you look at the bottom of your TV screen, you will see a notice required by federal law stating that these results are not typical. Why? Because the evidence is overwhelming that the people who report huge weight losses or huge profits from trading options are not remotely typical. Most diets fail, and most amateur options traders lose heavily. In fact, some of the people who have been featured in those ads ultimately regained the pounds they had lost or ended up going broke.

Yet gullible fools buy those worthless diets and options trading courses because those case histories *sound* so convincing. They are real people who lost real pounds and made real money.

Don't be so naïve. Don't let your desire to believe something make you accept worthless evidence. Don't trust yourself to be impartial because *nobody* is impartial. Consciously or unconsciously you (and everyone else) will select or remember data that support what you expect or want to believe.

Perhaps the greatest strength of Poker Tracker and Poker-Spy is that they record *all* your hands. When you analyze your play, make sure you don't select the ones that support your biases. Look at the complete picture.

Appendix E: Mini-Quiz

After reading each chapter in this book or any other text, or after having any experience that has an impact on you, take this mini-quiz. It will help you to understand the reading material or experience. More important, it will help you to understand and develop yourself.

Think about the reading or experience for a few moments, and then write your answers to the questions. If possible, use a computer and keep all your mini-quizzes in one computer folder. You can then write long answers and revise them if you think of something else.

From time to time review your answers and, if appropriate, revise them.

Name of reading or brief description of the experience: _____

1. What did you like about this reading or experience?

2. What did you dislike about it?

3. How does this reading or experience relate to others?

4. What did this reading, experience, or your reactions to it teach you about yourself?

5. How can you use what you have learned?

6. Compare your answers on this mini-quiz to your answers on the others. What does this comparison tell you about yourself?

If you have used a computer, you can send your quiz answers to me as an e-mail attachment. My address is alannschoonmaker@hot-mail.com. I will comment on your answers and use your data for research purposes. I will not violate your privacy.

Appendix F: Recommended Coaches

Choosing a coach is an individual decision. The right coach for you could be wrong for me. Each coach works his own way and has his own strengths and weaknesses. A critically important element is "chemistry." If you feel more comfortable with a particular coach, you will probably get better results.

I know all these coaches well, and I have confidence in their ability and integrity. I will *not* tell you which one is best for you, because, like almost everything else in poker, "It depends."

To avoid the appearance of ranking them, their names are in alphabetical order. I urge you to go to their websites, read how they work, contact them by e-mail, and talk to them on the telephone. You should contact at least two, preferably more.

Do *not* feel embarrassed about contacting several of them. It is an important decision, and you want to make the right choice.

Name	Website	E-mail
Tommy Angelo	tommyangelo.com	tomium@aol.com
Bob Ciaffone	pokercoach.us	thecoach@chartermi.net
Matt Lessinger	mattlessinger.com	mlessinger@hotmail.com
Tom McEvoy		Tom McEvoy@cox.net
Jan Siroky	sirokypoker.com	jsa@pcisys.net
David Sklansky		dsklansky@aol.com

Name	Website	E-mail
Al Spath	pokerinstructors.com	alspath@alspath.com
Barry Tanenbaum	barrytanenbaum.com	pokerbear@cox.net

Appendix G:
Recommended Readings

The texts listed here are organized first by skill level and then alphabetically within each level. Concentrate on the books that match your level. It is okay to read a book below your level, because we all need to study the basics occasionally. Do *not* read books above your level, for three reasons:

1. You need to *master* the simpler concepts to understand the advanced ones.
2. Studying advanced concepts can actually confuse you and make you indecisive.
3. You may try plays you do not understand and mess them up.

As I have stated repeatedly, most people overestimate their knowledge and skill. Try to resist this tendency. It is far better to master basic concepts than to gain a superficial knowledge of more advanced ones. If you are not sure that you are ready for advanced strategies, stick to the more basic books.

Incidentally, I believe that it is better to master one system than to take bits and pieces from several books. Every well-crafted book presents an integrated system. The actions fit together to reinforce each other. If you try to develop your own unique strategy, it will probably not hold together well. I therefore urge you to *study* just one or two books rather than superficially read many of them.

For Beginners and Near Beginners

Until you can break even at low-limit games, don't read *anything* more advanced. You need to master the basics.

Caro, Mike. *Fundamental Secrets of Poker.* Las Vegas NV: Mad Genius Info, 1991. A short, easy-to-read book with lots of ideas on strategy and psychology. Don't read it until after you have read at least one of the more basic books.

Jones, Lee. *Winning Low Limit Hold'em.* A solid book for near beginners. Read it after you have read *Getting Started in Hold'em* or *Quick and Easy Texas Hold'em.*

Malmuth, Mason, and Lynn Loomis. *Fundamentals of Poker,* 3rd ed. Henderson, NV: Two Plus Two, 2000. This book is very basic.

Miller, Ed. *Getting Started in Hold'em.* Henderson, NV: Two Plus Two, 2005. This book is only for people who want to *begin* playing hold'em. His chapter on no-limit hold'em is the best I've seen for beginning players or ones making the transition from limit to no limit.

Myers, Neil. *Quick and Easy Texas Hold'em.* New York: Lyle Stuart, 2005. It's a basic guide for beginners.

Oliver, Gary. *Low Limit 7-Card Stud, Casino Strategy.* Phoenix: Poker Tips, 1991. It proposes a very simple strategy only for beginners.

Percy, George. *Seven Card Stud: The Waiting Game.* Self-published, 1979. Since the most common and destructive mistake is being too loose, his "play very tightly" advice is well worth taking, especially for beginners.

For Players Who Can Beat Low-Limit Games

Do *not* read these books until you are at least breaking even. You need to master the fundamentals first. Once you are good enough to break even or beat low-limit games, you will be ready for some more advanced material.

Caro, Mike. *The Body Language of Poker: Mike Caro's Book of Tells.* Hollywood: Gambling Times, 1984. Distributed by Carol Publishing, Secaucus, NJ. This book has appeared with many different titles and publishers. Buy whatever one you can find; they all have nearly identical (and excellent) content. It can help anyone from this level upward.

Carson, Gary. *The Complete Book of Hold 'em Poker.* New York; Lyle Stuart, 2001. It's for advanced beginners and intermediate players. His strategy is somewhat different from the conventional wisdom, but some people have had good results with it.

Ciaffone, Bob. *Improve Your Poker.* Saginaw, MI: self-published, 1997. A solid book that covers basic concepts that apply to stud, hold'em, Omaha, and other games.

Matt Flynn, Sunny Mehta, and Ed Miller, *Professional No-Limit Hold'em: Volume I,* Henderson, NV: Two Plus Two, 2007. Because it was published slightly after my book was submitted, I know very little about this book. However, I have so much confidence in the publisher and authors that I am sure it will be excellent.

Krieger, Lou. *Hold'em Excellence,* 2nd ed. Pittsburgh: Conjelco, 2000. A well-organized, well-written, fairly basic book.

———, and Sheree Bykoffsky. *Secrets the Pros Won't Tell You About Winning Hold'em.* New York: Lyle Stuart, 2006. A compendium of a large number of tips that are not covered in many books.

Largay, Angel. *No-Limit Texas Hold'em: A Complete Course.* Toronto, Ontario: ECW Press, 2006. By far the best book on capped buy-in no-limit games.

Lessinger, Matt. *The Book of Bluffs.* New York: Warner Books, 2005. Some of this material may be too advanced for you, but you *must* learn when and how to bluff to continue your progress. Return to it again and again.

Miller, Ed, David Sklansky, and Mason Malmuth. *Small Stakes Hold'em: Winning Big Through Expert Play.* Henderson, NV: Two Plus Two, 2005. This book takes up where *Getting Started in Hold'em* leaves off. Its goal is to take you from being a small winner to someone who can *crush* small-stakes and other loose games. I highly recommend it.

Othmer, Konstantin, with Ekkehard Othmer. *Elements of Seven Card Stud.* Cupertino, CA: Strategy One, 1992. It is extremely well organized and provides more solid evidence than you will find in most books. However, some parts of it are hard to read.

Schoonmaker, Alan, Ph.D. *The Psychology of Poker.* Henderson, NV: Two Plus Two, 2000. It provides a simple system for categorizing players and games, then adjusting your strategy. It also discusses some of the factors (such as your motives) that prevent you from playing well.

————. *Your Worst Poker Enemy.* New York, Lyle Stuart, 2007. It lays the foundation for *Your Best Poker Friend* and discusses some problems not discussed here.

Sklansky, David. *Hold'em Poker.* Las Vegas: Two Plus Two, 1976, 1989. The first serious book on hold'em. Read it after you have read *Getting Started in Hold'em.*

————. *The Theory of Poker.* Henderson, NV: Two Plus Two, 2005. My own and many other players' favorite book. It is only for serious players. You may want to read it when you first reach this level and then study it more thoroughly when you become an advanced player. Instead of focusing on one game, Sklansky discusses theoretical issues that apply to all games. His chapter titled "Fundamental Theorem of Poker" contains the most original and useful material I have ever read about poker.

For Advanced Players

Brunson, Doyle (with many collaborators). *Super System: A Course in Power Poker,* 2nd ed. Las Vegas; B&G, 1994. It's often been called "The Bible of Poker." It's a good book, but not remotely the best. Brunson and his collaborators are champions, and they offer advice about all of the major games. The book is a little dated, but very worthwhile. However, people without great intuition could get into serious trouble trying to imitate Brunson's style in no-limit hold'em.

————. *Super System II: A Course in Power Poker.* With contributions by Crandell Addington et al. New York; Cardoza, 2005. It's a new edition of *Super System,* and some of the material has been dramatically changed. It also covers new games such as triple-draw lowball. The chapter on no-limit hold'em should have been updated, because the game has changed enormously.

Ciaffone, Bob, and Jim Brier. *Middle Limit Hold'em Poker.* Saginaw, MI: self-published, 2001. A well-organized and thorough book that clearly distinguishes between the strategies needed to beat small- and middle-limit games.

Feeney, John. Ph. D. *Inside the Poker Mind*. Henderson, NV: Two Plus Two, 2000. It is a much more advanced book than my *The Psychology of Poker*. It provides concepts you need to beat larger games and tougher players.

Greenstein, Barry. *Ace on the River*. Last Knight, 2005. It provides a unique picture of the world of poker. As a psychologist, I was especially interested in Greenstein's description of the "Personal Traits of Winning Poker Players." I believe he is the only great player to provide such a long list of them.

Harrington, Dan, and Bill Roberti. *Harrington on Hold'em: Expert strategy for No-Limit Tournaments*. Volumes I, II, and III. Henderson, NV: Two Plus Two, 2004 and 2005. Additional volumes will appear over the next few years. Dan Harrington was a decade's most successful player in the World Series of Poker championship. These books will help you to understand how expert tournament players think. They are not as valuable for cash game players. A book on cash games will appear in 2007 or 2008.

Hayano, David. *Poker Faces: The Life and Work of Professional Poker Players*. Berkeley, CA: University of California Press, 1982. The most thorough and scholarly book on this subject, but it is very dated. Anyone considering turning professional should definitely read it.

Malmuth, Mason. *Poker Essays*. Henderson, NV: Two Plus Two, 1991, and many other publishing dates. Also to be recommended from the same publisher are *Poker Essays, Volumes II and III* and *Gambling Theory and other Topics*. They all contain some of Malmuth's best columns on a wide variety of subjects. On many of these subjects, he offers the best advice you can get.

McKenna, James A., Ph.D. *Beyond Tells: Power Poker Psychology*. New York: Lyle Stuart, 2005. Even though his books compete with my books, I recommend them. They provide a different way of looking at poker psychology.

———. *Beyond Bluffs: Master the Mysteries of Poker*. New York: Lyle Stuart, 2006.

———. *Beyond Traps: The Anatomy of Poker Success*. New York, Lyle Stuart, 2007.

Sklansky, David, and Mason Malmuth. *Hold'em Poker for Advanced Players: 21st Century Edition*. Henderson, NV: Two Plus Two, 1999. It is the most advanced book on limit hold'em. It includes extended discussions of general strategy and playing in loose and shorthanded games.

Sklansky, David, and Ed Miller. *No Limit Hold'em: Theory and Practice.* Henderson, NV: Two Plus Two, 2006. It provides excellent advice on deep-stack no-limit games and a simple strategy for planning short stacks.

Sklansky, David, Mason Malmuth, and Ray Zee. *Seven-Card Stud for Advanced Players: 21st Century Edition.* Henderson, NV: Two Plus Two, 1999. The most advanced book on seven-card stud with the same strengths as their other advanced texts.

Taylor, Ian, and Matthew Hilger. *The Poker Mindset.* Suwanee, GA: Dimat Enterprises, 2007. This book also competes with mine, and I recommend it for the same reason as Dr. McKenna's books.

Zee, Ray. *High-Low Split Poker for Advanced Players: Seven-Card Stud and Omaha Eight-or-Better.* Henderson, NV: Two Plus Two, 1992, 1994. I don't play either game, but my friends tell me it is the best book on them.

———, and Fromm. David, with Alan N. Schoonmaker, Ph.D. *World Class High-Stakes and Shorthanded Limit Hold'em.* It's the first book to analyze thoroughly the skills and attitudes needed to beat games of $100–$200 and up. It's for people who now play or want to "graduate" to this level.

Index

About the Author

Alan Schoonmaker has a unique combination of academic credentials, business experience, and poker expertise. After earning a Ph.D. in industrial psychology from The University of California at Berkeley, he joined the faculties at UCLA and Carnegie-Mellon University. He then became a research fellow at Belgium's Catholic University of Louvain.

Alan was the manager of management development at Merrill Lynch before starting Schoonmaker and Associates, an international consulting company. He personally taught or consulted in twenty-nine countries on all six continents for clients such as GE, GM, IBM, Mobil, Rank Xerox, Bankers Trust, Wells Fargo, Manufacturers Hanover, Chemical Bank, Chase Manhattan, Ryan Homes, Sun Life of Canada, and more than two dozen others. His personal clients' annual sales exceed $1 trillion.

Alan has written or coauthored three research monographs and has published four books on industrial psychology (*Anxiety and the Executive, Executive Career Strategy, Selling: The Psychological Approach,* and *Negotiate to Win*), one book on coping with college (*A Student's Survival Manual*), and *The Psychology of Poker*. His books have been translated into French, German, Spanish, Swedish, Japanese, and Indonesian.

Alan has published more than one hundred articles in poker and business periodicals such as *Card Player, Poker Digest,* twoplustwo.com's *Internet Magazine,* Andy Glazer's *Wednesday Night Poker, The California Management Review,* and *Expansion.* He has written and/or played the leading role in four video series. Two were parts of multimedia training programs on industrial psychology. At one time, his

Selling: The Psychological Approach was the world's best-selling computer-based program for businesspeople.

Alan has served as an expert witness about poker psychology in both an administrative hearing and a lawsuit. He plays online poker as a member of RoyalVegasPoker.com's team of experts. He has been interviewed several times on radio and television about both poker and industrial psychology.

He is the host on "Poker Psychology" at Holdemradio.com

Alan receives many requests for coaching. Most of them are referred to friends, because he is not an expert on poker strategy. He accepts a small number of clients who need coaching *only* on poker psychological issues such as controlling impulses, coping with losing streaks, going on tilt, and planning your poker career.

He welcomes readers' questions and comments at alannschoonmaker@hotmail.com. His website is being constructed, and it will be at www.alanschoonmaker.com. or poker-psychology.net.